# Churches
# respond to
# BEM

# Churches respond to BEM

Official responses
to the
"Baptism, Eucharist
and Ministry" text
Vol. IV

**Edited by Max Thurian**

Faith and Order Paper 137
World Council of Churches, Geneva

The text of the Ecumenical Patriarchate was translated by Gennadios Limouris, and that on the Evangelical Church in Hesse and Nassau by Kristi Decke. The WCC Language Service translated the following: Evangelical Lutheran Church in Oldenburg, Evangelical Church of the Augsburg Confession in the Socialist Republic of Romania, and Waldensian Evangelical Church of the River Plate.

Cover design: Michael Dominguez

ISBN 2-8254-0896-4

Typeset by Macmillan India Ltd, Bangalore 25
Printed in Switzerland

# CONTENTS

# PREFACE

Our documentation series *Churches Respond to BEM* is growing, but the end is now in sight! Two more volumes will come out by spring 1988, thus making available all the official responses to "Baptism, Eucharist and Ministry", the convergence document adopted by the Faith and Order Commission of the World Council of Churches at its meeting in Lima, Peru, in 1982. Even though the official responses are only one expression of a much broader process of discussion in the churches, they are of special importance. For they are an indication of where the churches stand with regard to ecumenical convergence on the still dividing issues of baptism, eucharist and ministry. They are also an indication of the ways in which the churches are moving forward in renewal, mutual enrichment and ecumenical commitment in common obedience to God's call and mission for the sake of God's world.

This fourth volume, like the first three, has been compiled by my colleague Frère Max Thurian. I am grateful for his work as well as for the collaboration of our colleagues in the WCC Publications Office (who are certainly looking forward to the completion of this series!). Special financial contributions from the Evangelical Church in Württemberg (FRG), the Lutheran Church in America and the United Methodist Church (USA) have enabled us to cover part of the production costs of the fourth and the fifth volumes. We are extremely grateful for these expressions of support.

Geneva, Easter 1987          Günther Gassmann, Director
                             WCC Secretariat on Faith and Order

---

• These responses have not been edited: we publish them here in the form in which they were received.

*Introduction*

# THE LIMA PROCESS CONTINUES

GÜNTHER GASSMANN

**1. Response and evaluation**

Why is Faith and Order still talking about the "Baptism, Eucharist and Ministry" (BEM) document, adopted by the Commission in Lima, Peru, in 1982? Is there nothing new in Faith and Order? Are not the churches facing more urgent problems today?

That BEM has now been discussed for more than five years is itself an indication of its great ecumenical significance. Ecumenical texts, however fascinating and creative they may be, remain useless if they are not taken up by the churches in order to serve their renewal, unity and witness. But when they are taken up, as in the case of BEM, this process of discussion and "reception" takes time. The BEM document has not pushed aside other issues with which the churches are confronted in their societies and in the world at large. But it has helped them to focus attention on some of the spiritual sources without which they would not be able to face these other issues as a *Christian* community, and as a community called to render a *common* witness and service to humanity.

Thus we continue to talk about BEM, which still occupies much of the working time and attention of the Faith and Order Commission and staff. *The process is still going on.* In 1986, staff members talked about BEM during their travels (e.g. in the Pacific and in Sierra Leone). The text is reprinted in Geneva at regular intervals. An Urdu translation (Pakistan) came out in late 1986. Students of the Middle East School of Theology in Beirut, Lebanon, held a seminar on BEM in Cyprus, as did an international group of Baptist students at Rüschlikon in Switzerland. BEM has become part of courses in theological schools. Liturgical revision in churches is undertaken with special reference to BEM. Bilateral dialogues between Christian World Communions and their member churches see in BEM a certain frame of reference.

These are just a few examples of the ongoing process. BEM is obviously not the final word on the road to Christian unity. Its "fathers and mothers" did not expect it to be. Nor is the content of this document fully accepted everywhere. There are different degrees of acceptance: this was to be expected. It is a document "on the way".

By the end of February 1987, *more than 170 official responses* of the churches had been received. Never before have so many churches reacted officially to an ecumenical document. Many of these responses have been worked out with a conscious attempt to take in a wider discussion process·in their respective churches. The majority of these responses come from churches in Australia, Europe and North America. We know that the BEM document has also been studied in many churches in Africa, Asia, the Caribbean, Latin America and the Pacific. But in many cases these churches do not have the means (commissions, staff) and the "Western" methods to carry out the complicated process of preparing an official response to an ecumenical document like BEM. However, in 1987 official responses are still coming in, and especially from churches in the so-called third world. The official response of the Roman Catholic Church is also due in 1987.

*The work of summarizing and evaluating* — so far 1,500 pages of official responses have been received—began in 1986. All the responses are read carefully and their content is summarized bearing in mind 35 points. What do the responses say about, for example:
— the implicit ecclesiology of BEM;
— consequences to be drawn from BEM;
— baptism and faith;
— the meaning of the eucharist;
— ordination, etc.

The BEM Steering Group and members of the staff and of the Commission are working on these 35 points. In 1988, their summaries will be drawn up into one comprehensive report to be presented to the meeting of the Plenary Commission on Faith and Order in 1989. It will then be submitted, through the WCC Central Committee, to the churches.

*A first consultation on the responses to BEM*, attended by ecumenical officers of Christian World Communions and representatives of Faith and Order, took place in October 1986 in Venice, Italy. It provided an occasion for a discussion of major tendencies and emphases in the responses, and also made a first attempt to identify those questions from the responses which require either clarification during the work of evaluation 1986–1988 or, because of their far-reaching nature, call for further dialogue after completion of the evaluation. Participants at the consultation were convinced that most of the issues they listed can be dealt with by way of clarification.

Here are a few examples from their list of points for clarification or further dialogue:
— concerning "the faith of the church through the ages" the following issues were raised: the source of the faith, the nature of the church, and the relation between scripture and tradition;
— the sacramental character of baptism;

—the theme of the "covenant" is not sufficiently stressed, according to certain responses;
—the meaning of the affirmation that the eucharist is the central act of the church's worship;
—for some churches the words "sign", "sacrament", do not seem to be an adequate expression of the reality of God's presence and action in the eucharist;
—why is the general priesthood of the whole people of God not more present in the whole text on ministry?
—the sacramental character of ministerial ordination (in relation to the permanent character of ministerial charism);
—ministry of men and women;
—word and sacrament as an underlying fundamental question.

*A second consultation on the responses to BEM* took place in Annecy, France, in May 1987. The BEM Steering Group reviewed the ongoing work of evaluation and began the task of clarifying several of the points listed above. This work will be continued by a third consultation later this year or at the beginning of 1988.

## 2. WCC thanks churches for their active participation

*The Central Committee* of the World Council of Churches, meeting in January 1987 in Geneva, *adopted the following recommendations* of the Unit I (Faith and Witness) Committee:

The Committee was informed about the ongoing broad and significant BEM process. The Lima document is now available in over 30 languages. It has been distributed in more than 350,000 copies all over the world, and 150 official responses from churches had been received by the end of 1986. The process is continuing in many churches and it has an impact on the thinking and life of the churches and their ecumenical relations. Faith and Order is now preparing an evaluation of and report on the BEM process and the responses.

In 1982 the Central Committee welcomed the publication of "Baptism, Eucharist and Ministry" and requested the member churches "to enable the widest possible involvement of the whole people of God at all levels of church life in the spiritual process of receiving this text" and to prepare an official response to it.

Now, four and a half years later and in view of the positive, encouraging and hopeful experience of the churches' involvement in the BEM process, the Central Committee:
a) expresses its appreciation and gratitude to the member churches for their active and constructive participation in the BEM process and for their official responses to BEM;
b) encourages the member churches to continue the process of discussion and reception of the BEM document;

xii *Churches respond to BEM*

c) urges the member churches to consider seriously, as far as their ecclesiology permits, the implications of their participation in the BEM process for their own life as well as for their ecumenical relations;

d) asks all member churches which have not yet responded to the BEM document to do so as soon as possible;

e) urges the Faith and Order Commission to continue work on BEM and the responses to it with all their different emphases as a fundamental concern for the whole ecumenical movement and in view of the next Assembly, and to present to the member churches before the coming Assembly a report which offers an evaluation of the responses of the churches.

Faith and Order is very pleased about this action of the Central Committee. It is not only an expression of well-deserved appreciation. It is also an affirmation of that continuity of the ecumenical struggle without which there would be no advance in the concern for the unity of Christ's church. This action and the reality to which it refers is a great encouragement for the work of Faith and Order. We are not alone in our efforts. The churches and their members participate in them. It is our common task.

# ECUMENICAL PATRIARCHATE
# OF CONSTANTINOPLE

**Preface**

1. Having through its competent organs studied the Lima text "Baptism, Eucharist and Ministry" (BEM, 1982), the Ecumenical Patriarchate has asked the Patriarchal and Synodical Commission for Interconfessional Affairs to formulate its reflections and judgments concerning this document.

2. First, we ourselves recognize "that the BEM text, drawn up by the Commission on Faith and Order with the participation of Orthodox theologians, is an important ecumenical document of basic theological convergences, a document which expresses an experience opening up new vistas in the history of the ecumenical movement".[1]

3. That is why this document is greeted with joy as the fruit of the efforts made during recent decades by the Commission on Faith and Order of the World Council of Churches. In this connection, His Holiness the Ecumenical Patriarch Dimitrios himself declared: "Today we rejoice in realizing that since a few years a laudable return has been made by the WCC to the search for Christian unity for which it was founded. This is shown by the activity of the Commission on Faith and Order. Recently this Commission drew up a document on 'Baptism, Eucharist and Ministry', in which the Orthodox Church finds with satisfaction many elements of its teaching on those fundamental subjects. We pray that this return and the progress of the WCC towards its essential goal will be steady."[2]

4. Despite all these facts, BEM, as it stands today, can by no means express the unity and community of the faith and tradition of the One, Holy, Catholic and Apostolic Church of the Creed, the Ecumenical Councils and the Fathers with which our Orthodox Church identifies itself.

---

- 4,700,000 members, 133 bishops, 5,935 priests.
[1] Decision of the Inter-Orthodox Preparatory Commission, Chambésy, 15–23 February 1986, on Orthodoxy and the ecumenical movement, §7.
[2] Interview of His Holiness on Italian television, 3 March 1983, in *Episkepsis*, No. 291, 1 April 1983.

5. As for the nature of this present text, it constitutes a response to the competent organs of the WCC without signifying a "reception" of the contents of BEM: it is a constructive attitude to that important piece of work. Our reply does not aim at entering into the details of the text, but will be an overall appreciation of it on the basis of the doctrinal theses of our Orthodox Church.

6. From the beginning of the ecumenical movement, the Ecumenical Patriarchate repeatedly expressed its eagerness to arrive at a theological agreement which would serve as the foundation of the unity being sought between the churches, provided these find their common roots in the apostolic faith and tradition of the undivided church. It is sufficient to mention here the Patriarchate's Encyclical of 1920 "to the churches of Christ every-where"—through which it proposed to them the setting up of a "league of churches", the ultimate goal being their unity in the common Christian faith — and its message upon the 25th anniversary of the founding of the WCC (1973). This message expresses profound esteem of the work being carried out in the WCC, while making some criticism and a necessary appreciation of its position, aims and guidelines, its issues and its objectives along the common road to unity of the churches.

7. In this manner, the Ecumenical Patriarchate has participated, and still is participating actively in all the constructive initiatives, both in bilateral and multilateral dialogues, taking as its ultimate goal the union of the churches.

**Positive elements**

8. (a) Wearied by the discussions lasting for years, which have not always produced concrete results, the ecumenical movement is trying today to discover the means to overcome its internal crisis and affront a world becoming daily more secularized and affected — being itself divided — by a multitude of non-theological factors: economic, political, social, cultural, racial and so on. . .

Within this divided world Christianity, alas, also appears divided, and approaches its third millenium groaning under the weight of its divisions.

9. Within this state of division of the world and of Christianity, the Lima text, which enters into the issues of both, shines forth in an effort to instill into them a new and powerful spirit. It is the moment in which the ecumenical movement, by its work and multilateral dialogues, is trying to discover a coherent and living theology in the service of the unity of the church, whose head is Jesus Christ.

10. (b) The Ecumenical Patriarchate wishes to congratulate the Commission on Faith and Order of the WCC for its initiative in examining the fundamental issues of baptism, eucharist and ministry, which for the Orthodox Church are holy sacraments (mysteria) of the faith and life of the church.

11. (c) The fact that this document was prepared by theologians belonging to a majority of member churches of the WCC, and to the Roman Catholic Church, is an encouraging point in its favour, and goes to show that, despite the existing divisions, the churches and their theologians are capable of dialoguing and collaborating in a joint enterprise, that of church unity, even with churches that have no definite ecclesiology or doctrinal tradition.

12. Drawn up in this manner, the document has enjoyed, since it first appeared four years ago, a wide circulation, both in the churches through their supreme governing bodies (synods, praesidia, etc.) down to parish level, in the various theological faculties and institutes and in some bilateral dialogues, and also in local church councils on various levels. This is truly a positive element. As a result of this circulation, especially in the West, the text in question has already become a point of reference in ecumenical gatherings, as well as in the wider sphere of cooperation and mutual acquaintance of Christians belonging to the divided churches.

Contributing to this wide circulation was the unusual number, for an ecumenical document, of translations made. However, this does not mean that it has been as widely broadcast as could be wished.

13. In spite of its imperfections, BEM is a contribution to the return to the teaching of the ancient tradition of the undivided church, on which church union must be grounded. Our Church hopes that its influence will be extended to Christian theology in general, and will help the churches and confessions which have received the document to fully discover their ecclesiological identity.

### Negative elements

14. The Ecumenical Patriarchate can by no means accept and share the presuppositions and consequences of the Lima text in the sense of a move towards intercommunion or even eucharistic hospitality, before all the necessary conditions for communion have been fulfilled.

15. As for the term used of "reception", it should be noted that it differs from the classical Orthodox interpretation of reception, viz. by the conscience of the whole church of the decrees and decisions of the holy Councils. Moreover, the "reception" of BEM does not necessarily entail the recognition — ecclesiological or practical — of the three sacraments (mysteria) of the churches with which the Orthodox Church finds itself in dialogue, but not yet in ecclesial communion.

16. As for the term "convergences", which is characteristic of the Lima text from its subtitle onward, our Church would like to see this term clarified. What exactly does it mean? What ideas does its use convey? Does this word imply the first steps towards a more general "consensus"? Or does it merely represent a rapprochement, as great as possible, towards a common goal not fully attainable? In both cases, the use of the term is not appropriate for

characterizing a document, before it has been properly studied and analyzed by the churches.

For Orthodoxy, the truth revealed and taught by it is a continual communion, harmonized by the power of the Holy Spirit. For us everything—tradition, doctrine, canons, even history itself—succeeds one another and forms a whole.

17. One weakness of the text, it must be admitted, is the absence of a solid ecclesiological substructure to underpin and homogenize the separate elements.

The need for a common ecclesiology constitutes for our Church the starting point of every conversation or criticism concerning the Lima text and not its finishing point. One has to have a clear idea of the ecclesiology on which BEM bases itself while studying the three sacraments (mysteria) of baptism, eucharist and ministry.

For the Orthodox Church, faith is a pathway traced by teaching (doctrine) and ecclesiastical traditions leading to salvation and deification. So it is not possible to seek a "consensus" on baptism, eucharist and ministry without the existence of an agreement on the road to salvation and deification, which presupposes an agreement on ecclesiology.

The church is and remains the body of Christ. The people of God are its living expression. As such the church is a quantity surpassing time and space.

It is in the church thus described that the sacraments (mysteria) are performed canonically and validly. According to the Orthodox tradition, the church "is signified by the sacraments".[3] So the Ecumenical Patriarchate cannot overlook the fact that the three issues of the Lima text are holy sacraments (mysteria) for the Orthodox Church and that every other perspective or dimension given to these sacraments by no matter who, and naturally by the Lima text, is unacceptable.

For the Church of Constantinople, the document BEM, on account of this basic ecclesiological lack, cannot be used by its followers as a means of catechism or worship.

18. From this point of view it is right and justifiable to express satisfaction over the report of the Inter-Orthodox Symposium, Holy Cross Theological Seminary, Boston, USA (June 1985). This report, though not a common Orthodox response, nevertheless expresses certain Orthodox ideas and judgments on BEM without being binding on the participant churches. Moreover, it contains clear opinions shared in the world of Orthodoxy, in particular concerning the concrete points of BEM which need further clarification in its three sections on baptism, eucharist and ministry.[4]

---

[3] Nicholas Cabasilas, Commentary on the Divine Liturgy, *PG* 150, 452C.
[4] Section IV of the report "Some Points for Further Clarification", in *Orthodox Perspectives on Baptism, Eucharist and Ministry*, eds G. Limouris and M. Vaporis, Holy Cross Press, *Faith and Order Paper No. 128*, 1985, pp. 162–163.

**Perspectives and recommendations**

19. First, we would express the view and the hope that ecclesiology will be among the immediate priorities in the programmes of the Commission on Faith and Order during the coming years, closely linked to the three sacraments (mysteria) of baptism, eucharist and ministry. Otherwise, one may fear that BEM will lose its importance and timeliness, until it is just one among many WCC documents. It is thus desirable that the Commission on Faith and Order inaugurate a programme that is purely ecclesiological, one which will give the churches a chance to discover points in common and true "convergences" in their theology and their joint progress towards unity.

20. The Ecumenical Patriarchate is willing to participate in such a programme, provided that the "concept" and "nature" of the church will be given due attention on the basis of the healthy teaching and tradition of the undivided church of the first centuries.

21. Another opinion and view of the Ecumenical Patriarchate, in studying and analyzing the BEM document, is that the Commission on Faith and Order needs to determine the relationship in terminology between BEM and the Toronto Declaration (1950) known as "The Church, the Churches and the WCC". It is true that in the Declaration it is said that the WCC exists so that the different churches can confront their differences, and that no church is obliged to alter its ecclesiology because it is a member of the Council.[5] But it is to be feared that BEM, with its known dimension, may go beyond the theses and guarantees given by the Toronto Declaration in respect to the ecclesiological identity of each church. For if we accept that BEM is a document of merely "converging tendencies" (convergences), without clear ecclesiological presuppositions, its contrast to the Toronto Declaration automatically becomes evident.

22. As for the third point in this field of perspectives and recommendations concerning the future of BEM, one is obliged to reflect and ask how the Commission on Faith and Order proposes to meet its responsibility for evaluating the "responses" obtained from the WCC member churches. If these replies get no feedback and evaluation, all the wearisome work and acknowledged effort involved in drawing up and publicizing the BEM document throughout the Christian world will have been in vain. And a good opportunity for a more concrete theological rapprochement between the churches will perhaps have been wasted.

Consequently, it is recommended to the Commission on Faith and Order to give some responsible information to the WCC member churches on developments concerning BEM. Not to do so would be to disappoint the churches.

---

[5] Paragraph III, 3.

**Epilogue**

Church unity is, above all, certainly the will of the holy God. But nobody can ignore the fact that it is, and will be, a fruit of the collaboration with him (synergy) of the divided churches and confessions and in general of all Christians of goodwill. Certainly not abstractly, but on concrete theological and ecclesiological premises. The "kairos" has come, the "kairos" of the Lord, so that the idea of unity may become a daily service (diakonia) and mission (apostolê) of the churches towards the common rediscovery of the apostolic faith and tradition of the one, undivided church, and towards an analogous common progress in the direction of one goal, the union of the churches, as longed for and prayed for by the church's Lord Jesus Christ: "that all may be one" (John 17:21).

# MAR THOMA SYRIAN
# CHURCH OF MALABAR (INDIA)

### Introduction

Faith and Order Paper No. 111 on *Baptism, Eucharist and Ministry* is an agreed statement from the WCC and is the result of years of study and discussion. The ecumenical movement can be proud of the distance travelled towards this agreed statement. On baptism, eucharist and ministry there have been divisions within the Christian church which are perhaps as old as Christianity itself. Therefore, despite the differences that still persist, the ecumenical movement can rejoice at the convergence reached at Lima.

The Mar Thoma Church, after careful study and discussion of the paper, feels general agreement with the statements of the paper. While expressing general agreement it is necessary to respond in detail to the three sections on baptism, eucharist and ministry.

### Baptism

The meaning of baptism is explained by the document in a fivefold way: (1) participation in Christ's death and resurrection; (2) conversion, pardoning and cleansing; (3) the gift of the Spirit; (4) incorporation into the body of Christ; (5) the sign of the kingdom. The discussions under these five headings should find nearly universal approval within the churches.

The document makes it clear that baptism, whether in childhood or adulthood, is an incorporation into the body of Christ. This is to take place in the context of the community of believers. The document also upholds the link between baptism and the gift of the Spirit. Moreover the experience of baptism and the gift of the Spirit are both portrayed as needing growth and fulfilment. Of baptism it is said: "Baptism is related not only to momentary experience, but to life-long growth into Christ. Those baptized are called upon to reflect the glory of the Lord as they are transformed by the power of the Holy Spirit, into his likeness, with ever increasing splendour" (p. 4). Of

---

● 600,000 members, 7 dioceses, 820 parishes, 5 bishops, 490 priests.

the gift of the Spirit it is said: "The Holy Spirit nurtures the life of faith in their hearts until the final deliverance when they will enter into its full possession, to the praise of the glory of God" (pp. 2–3). The acknowledgment of the growth dimension in relation to baptism and the gift of the Spirit is particularly satisfying to the Mar Thoma Church since it lives amidst sectarian groups which make baptism and the gift of the Spirit almost look like static and momentary experiences. The Mar Thoma Church is also happy that the unrepeatable nature of baptism is affirmed. "Baptism is an unrepeatable act. Any practice which might be interpreted as 're-baptism' must be avoided" (p. 4).

The reference to the missionary implications of baptism in §10 (p. 4) is certainly welcome. However, we feel that this needs to be strengthened. Baptism is in fact the ordination by which every believer is incorporated to the corporate priesthood of the church. The secular witness of the community of believers is to be seen as the exercise of the priestly ministry of the church.

The Mar Thoma Church welcomes the statement: "Both the baptism of believers and the baptism of infants take place in the Church as the community of faith" (p. 4). In the absence of this understanding adult (believers) baptism would degenerate into a private affair between the believer and God. Infant baptism would also degenerate into a magical and mechanical rite effected by the priest. The emphasis on baptism as occurring within the community of believers reminds the Mar Thoma Church about the responsibility of the church towards the baptized infants. There is always the danger of treating baptism as "valid" when administered by the minister whose ordination is "valid". It is on the strength of the faith of the community and its resolve to nurture the infant in faith that the infants are initiated into baptismal grace.

The document rightly holds together baptism and the reception of the Holy Spirit (p. 6) and speaks in favour of children being allowed to receive communion. Although the Mar Thoma Church as yet does not allow children to receive communion, we welcome the holding together by the document of baptism, reception of the Spirit and eucharistic presence of the Spirit. At the same time we acknowledge a need to study at depth the relationship between the faith of the individual and faith of the community.

**Eucharist**

The eucharist and its meaning are dealt with extensively in the document. The meaning is explained in five different ways: (1) eucharist as thanksgiving to the Father; (2) eucharist as *anamnesis* or memorial of Christ; (3) eucharist as invocation of the Spirit; (4) eucharist as communion of the faithful; (5) eucharist as meal of the kingdom.

The above fivefold treatment of the meaning of the eucharist deserves much commendation because it links the eucharist with each person of the

Trinity and it links the believer with the past, the present and the future.

In the section on thanksgiving to the Father it is said: "It is the great thanksgiving to the Father for everything accomplished in creation, redemption and sanctification, . . . the eucharist is the benediction (*berakah*) by which the Church expresses its thankfulness for all God's benefits" (p. 10). The church's eucharist is then a comprehensive act of thanksgiving. We feel that most ecclesiastical traditions stand to benefit from this statement. In some traditions the thanksgiving is narrowed down to the earthly work of redemption brought about by the Son. Some others include the work of God in creation. However, the document incorporates work of creation and redemption as well as the continuing work of the Spirit in sanctification and new creation. The Mar Thoma Church itself stands to gain by incorporating the full implications of the declaration in the document.

In the section on the eucharist as an *anamnesis* of Christ the document affirms that ". . . Christ's mode of presence in the eucharist is unique . . . The Church confesses Christ's real, living and active presence in the eucharist" (p. 12). Thus, without specifying the mode of Christ's presence in the eucharist the document affirms the unique nature of the presence of Christ in the eucharist. In the Mar Thoma Church there are those who associate a real and inexplicable presence of the risen Christ with the elements and on the other hand those who see the elements as symbolizing the real presence of the risen Christ. However, those who hold this latter position may be enriched by acknowledging that the elements are symbolic of the presence not of a remote Christ separated in space and time but of a Christ who is "real, living and active". In this connection we believe it is important to highlight the fact that the eucharist holds together the past, the present and the future. It makes present God's redemptive involvement in all history, it affirms the presence of the risen Lord through his Holy Spirit, and it looks forward to eating and drinking with the Lord in the fullness of the kingdom.

The Mar Thoma Church also welcomes the affirmation of the document about the unrepeatability of the act of God in Christ. "What it was God's will to accomplish in incarnation, life, death, resurrection and ascension of Christ, God does not repeat. These events are unique and can neither be repeated nor prolonged" (p. 11–12). But the eschatological reality which it represents needs to be "realized" in its historical contemporaneity repeatedly.

The Mar Thoma Church also welcomes the declaration of the document on the presence of the Holy Spirit on the whole eucharistic action. The whole action of the eucharist has an "epikletic" character because it depends upon the work of the Holy Spirit. This makes relating the moment of consecration with the rest of the service important. Moreover, when we remember that the presence of Christ in the eucharist is symbolic of the presence of the risen Christ in the world and in the church the work of the Holy Spirit consists in facilitating the church to receive and discern this Christ in daily life. The work of the Spirit is not to reveal Christ in the eucharist in isolation or exclusion from his presence in the world and the church but to point to his presence in these. The Holy Spirit is the Spirit of Christ indeed.

The document also proclaims the eucharist as a communion of the faithful. "All kinds of injustice, racism, separation and lack of freedom are radically challenged when we share in the body and blood of Christ" (p. 14). This reveals the tension between the contemporary reality and our hope. The church celebrates the eucharist while in the midst of injustice, racism, separation and lack of freedom, so that it may, by the power of the communion in the eucharist, overcome these. This enjoins the Indian church, including the Mar Thoma Church, to identify factors that prevent genuine communion of the faithful. For the Mar Thoma Church there is a special challenge to seek communion with those churches which are ethnically and linguistically different. Although the Mar Thoma Church is in conciliar fellowship with the Church of North India and the Church of South India which are ethnically and linguistically different, the challenge to make this a more meaningful union remains. The three churches need to put their hearts together to identify the existing barriers and devise practical steps to overcome the barriers. The Mar Thoma Church reaffirms its commitment to seek more meaningful and relevant unity.

Beyond seeking communion of the faithful the document also presents the eucharist as a foretaste of the meal of the kingdom. A meal is a sign of reconciliation. Therefore the eucharist challenges the church to share with the world the reconciliation in Christ. "As Jesus went out to publicans and sinners and had table-fellowship with them during his earthly ministry, so Christians are called in the eucharist to be in solidarity with the outcast and to become signs of the love of Christ who lived and sacrificed himself for all and now gives himself in the eucharist" (p. 15). This undoubtedly is one of the strongest statements in the document about the missionary implications of the eucharist. We feel the Indian church must work increasingly towards becoming genuinely Indian and participate in the efforts to eradicate illiteracy, ill-health, and exploitation so that these efforts become the signs of the kingdom of God in the present times. We acknowledge that the Mar Thoma Church needs to transcend its predominantly middle-class identity in order to achieve this end. Our prayer is that the power of the Spirit will challenge the Church in this direction.

## Ministry

Discussion on ministry rightly begins with the ministry of the whole people of God and not with ordained ministry. The document affirms that the basis of Christian ministry is the ministry of Jesus Christ. The Holy Spirit calls and commissions the church to share in the ministry of Jesus Christ. In the power of the Holy Spirit the church is called to "prefigure the Kingdom" and "manifest the signs of the Kingdom". The gifts of the Holy Spirit are seen by the document as the tools to manifest the signs of the kingdom, so that there may be building up of the body of Christ and strengthening of the witness of the church. By presenting this picture of the calling of the whole church and its ministry, the document places the ordained ministry in proper perspective. Discussion on ordained ministry within the framework of the ministry of the whole church to the whole world is certainly welcome. Moreover, the gifts of the Holy Spirit are rightly affirmed not as gifts made to individual Christians for self-glorification but as aids in the building up of the church and in the fulfilment of the common mission (p. 20).

One issue that has repeatedly been raised in discussions on ordained ministry is the distinction between the ministry of the ordained and the ministry of the laity. The Protestant tradition has generally held that the distinction is functional, i.e. the ordained are set apart for special functions. The Roman Catholics as well as the Orthodox have made ontological distinctions between the ordained and the laity. The document makes two affirmations in this connection. First, it says: "In order to fulfil its mission, the Church needs persons who are publicly and continually responsible for pointing to its fundamental dependence on Jesus Christ, and thereby provide, within a multiplicity of gifts, a focus of its unity" (p. 21). Secondly, ". . .the ordained ministry has no existence apart from the community. Ordained ministers can fulfil their calling only in and for the community. They cannot dispense with the recognition, the support and the encouragement of the community" (p. 22). Thus the document sees the calling of the ordained as representing the calling of the church, the whole laos of God. The church is called out of the world to point beyond itself to God that the world may believe. This of course does not mean that the church has nothing to learn from the world about God. In fact God is working out his purposes in the world and a church that is not seeking to discover that working may fail in its fundamental calling. The calling of the church is in the context of the world and the identity of the church is shaped in relation to the world. Analogously, the ordained are called apart within the church, the community of believers, so that they may point to Christ and may bring about a focusing operation within the multiplicity of gifts in the church. The ordained require a special charisma for this which they receive by the laying on of hands in the community of the faithful. Just as the identity of the church is shaped in interaction with the world, the identity of the ordained is shaped in interaction with the whole church.

Some would see the above line of thought about the nature of the ordained ministry as evading traditional questions raised earlier. However, we feel that this need not be so. The march towards unity may be helped by reframing traditional questions and not necessarily by answering traditional questions. We feel the approach towards the status of the ordained ministry outlined in the document is creative and therefore the discussion may be carried forward in this direction.

Another point which needs comment is the use of the word "priest" in relation to the ordained. The document acknowledges Jesus Christ as the unique priest and derivatively the church as a priesthood. In addition the document thinks it fit to call the ordained ministers as priests, ". . .because they fulfil a particular priestly service by strengthening and building up the royal and prophetic priesthood of the faithful through word and sacraments, through their prayers of intercession, and through their pastoral guidance of the community" (p. 23). Though the document clarifies in the commentary that the term "priest" when used with reference to the ordained minister is different in meaning from its application with reference to Jesus Christ or the church, we have reservations about the usage with reference to the ordained. This is because the New Testament uses the term with reference to the community of believers only. No individual, lay or ordained, is called a priest. The church has a priestly ministry in relation to the world and hence is a priesthood. When the ordained are called "priests" in whatever sense, it would imply that the laity are not. This violates the letter and the spirit of the New Testament which sees the whole church as exercising a priestly ministry in the world.

The section on "the ministry of men and women" is also worthy of attention. The document calls for "a deeper understanding of the comprehensiveness of ministry which reflects the interdependence of men and women" (p. 24). We wholeheartedly support this concern. The male-dominated social order which one encounters in many parts of the world is partly a reflection of technologies used by these societies which are dependent more on muscle power than brain power. The modern developments in science and technology liberate women partly because human mastery over nature is now dependent more on brain power than muscle power. Women now are able to share responsibilities which were formerly exclusively male. This change in society must be seen as an act of God. This must be reflected in increased sharing by women in the priestly ministry of the church. There is no theological barrier to such a development in the Mar Thoma Church. However, the Mar Thoma Church presently has barriers due to custom, culture and tradition in allowing women to share in the ordained ministry of the church. It is earnestly hoped that these will break down as men develop greater consciousness of the change of times and women become willing and open to new challenges that God is opening before them. At the same time we also earnestly hope that ways will be found so that ordination of women does not create new barriers on the way to mutual recognition of ministry and sacraments.

On the issue of the threefold ministry and apostolic succession the document enjoins the churches to see the succession as one of "serving, symbolizing and guarding the continuity of the apostolic faith and communion" (p. 29). The Mar Thoma Church has always had the threefold ministry. While the Church cherishes this tradition of threefold ministry, this has been a barrier to full intercommunion and unity with churches which do not share historic succession of the episcopate. The Mar Thoma Church recognizes the churchly character of non-episcopal churches but sees historical succession of episcopacy as essential to the fullness of unity and continuity of the church. At the same time we acknowledge that the issue needs fuller study. The approach outlined in the document could provide the necessary break-through.

**A word of caution**

A word of caution is necessary before we conclude this response. While the Mar Thoma Church accepts the BEM document as a satisfactory starting point for interchurch conversation, we are eager that it should not be made a confession of faith and order. If the document becomes a confession of faith there is the danger of making the church a static dogmatic category. On the contrary the church is to remain a charismatic historical movement. In fact the document itself will become stronger if this nature of the church receives greater affirmation. This is important particularly because in the third world and even in the Western countries the churches are only beginning to enter into a dialogue with non-Semitic, non-Latin, non-Greek cultures. The churches should be free to develop patterns of church life drawing upon the indigenous cultural heritage remaining in continuity and faithfulness to the authentic tradition of the church across the ages.

**Conclusion**

The Mar Thoma Church gives thanks to God for the consensus reached at Lima by the member churches of the World Council of Churches. Where the Mar Thoma Church has reservations about the agreed statement has been indicated above. We hope that the agreement itself will not become an end and that it will help the community of churches to march forward in history in communion with and as guided by the Lord.

4 October 1986                                    Mar Thoma Sabha Council

# CHURCH OF CEYLON

The Lima report on "Baptism, Eucharist and Ministry" was considered by the clergy of the two dioceses [Colombo and Kurunagala] meeting separately; it was also considered by the clergy and laity meeting in area (rural decanal) conferences, as well as in a series of studies organized by the Ecumenical Institute.

This response is being made after a residential conference of the clergy of the two dioceses.

It was noted with thanksgiving to God that the Lima report was the work of many church traditions meeting together, and yet in spite of this they had achieved a remarkable degree of agreement on the basic issues of baptism, eucharist and ministry. And such a degree of consensus should no doubt help the church in its mission, as well as promote the unity of the church.

## Baptism

Baptism is a gift of God, and has been universally practised in the church from its earliest days. This is well attested in the letters of the New Testament, the Acts of the Apostles and the writings of the fathers. And it is administered in the name of the Father, the Son, and the Holy Spirit. That the rite of baptism gives an opportunity for the person who is baptized to make a commitment to the Lord, who in turn bestows grace upon his people through this rite, was noted with much joy, since the earlier emphasis had been more on the fact that the rite of baptism was an act of initiation into the church. We need this emphasis to help our people to be conscious of their mission in the world today.

This emphasis raises the question of infant baptism as against believer's baptism. Here it was noted that the emphasis in baptism is also on God's initiative in Christ together with a response of faith within the believing community — the church.

---

● 78,000 members, 155 parishes, 100 priests.

Thus we were conscious of the need for sound teaching on the meaning of baptism to parents and godparents, in addition to the regular use of the service of the renewal of baptismal vows as provided in our prayer books.

At the same time we affirm with the Lima report that "baptism is an unrepeatable act, and any practice which might be interpreted as a re-baptism must be avoided". Thus the service of the renewal of baptismal vows cannot be interpreted as a second baptism.

We recognize therefore that the Lima text embodies the faith of the church down the ages.

Since the normal practice in our church is infant baptism, the need for teaching to parents and godparents was accepted as a high priority.

At the same time the need to give some assurance to those baptized in infancy that they are truly incorporated into Christ by a service as renewal of baptismal vows was also recognized. Such a service was not by any means a second baptism. It was further agreed that there was need for sound teaching on the meaning of baptism on the lines set out in the Lima text.

The ongoing work of the Faith and Order Commission was to dialogue with the groups that teach that only a believer's baptism was valid, and thus prevent misunderstanding between these groups and the mainline churches. The mainline churches too must be made to think of baptism more in terms of an act of commitment and not merely in terms of a rite of initiation. Such an understanding would help to forward the mission of the church that has to proclaim the gospel among a plurality of religions.

### Eucharist

Just as baptism was the distinctive ordinance for the admission of new members into the church, so it is equally clear that the practice of breaking bread was indeed central to the continuance of the fellowship in the church. For this purpose the report says that the celebration of the eucharist "continues as the central act of the church's worship".

The varied richness of content in the eucharist which is spelt out, namely: that the eucharist is a thanksgiving to the Father; that the eucharist is an *anamnesis* or a memorial of Christ; that the eucharist is an invocation of the Spirit; that the eucharist is a communion of the faithful; that the eucharist is a meal of the kingdom; is a help to all shades of opinion within the church to accept the centrality of this sacrament in the life and mission of the church.

The two dioceses thus considered the necessity of at least limited eucharist sharing with members of other denominations in order to express this fellowship in concrete terms. However no definite programme of such sharing was considered, though it was noted that at present this is practised in the two dioceses in very many places.

It was accepted that the Lima text does embody the different shades of meaning which go to make up the faith of the church down the ages.

In view of the varied richness of content in the eucharist as set out in the Lima text, the churches should actively pursue the need for a limited eucharistic sharing among the churches, so that this sacrament would be a sacrament of unity in the church, rather than a divisive force.

The Faith and Order Commission should promote such thinking among all the churches and groups, and help to make this a sacrament of unity.

### Ministry

The report stresses the truth that God calls the whole of humanity to become God's people. It is a covenant of grace which began with the call of Abraham by God.

Thus the whole people of God are called to be involved in ministry. And it is equally clear from holy scripture that each member has his or her special function. And thus it is that there are some who are set apart for the work of ministry through the invocation of the Spirit and the laying on of hands. And these ordained ministers serve as a focal point of unity to enable the church's members to fulfill their individual roles in mission.

The dioceses noted that the threefold pattern of ministry, namely bishop, presbyter and deacon, was accepted as the pattern of the ordained ministry throughout the church. Such a recognition would help the denominations in their pilgrimage to the visible unity of the church.

The emphasis on the apostolic tradition of the whole church and the emphasis on the apostolic ministry is the cause of dissension among church traditions.

It was felt that these two emphases must be held together in our thinking and teaching. In the creed the whole church confesses the truth that the church is apostolic. This is a witness to the apostolic faith taught by the church, while at the same time apostolic succession is an expression of the  continuity of Christ's own mission in which the church participates. The orderly transmission of the ordained ministry is a powerful expression of the continuity of the church throughout history.

However difficult it may seem, it was agreed that the varying church traditions have to accept and hold together these two points of view. Only then will it be possible under God to accept each other's ministries and thus fulfill the mission of Christ entrusted to the church.

The Faith and Order Commission had to give its mind to this aspect of the ministry and provide much more basic teaching in order that the churches may be helped to accept each other's ministries and thus become one church serving the one Lord and teaching the one faith.

Bishop Andrew Kurunagala
Bishop Swithin Colombo

# EVANGELICAL CHURCH OF THE AUGSBURG CONFESSION (AUSTRIA)

1. The Lima texts present a summary of the present state of discussion between the churches. With impressive profundity they deal with questions related to baptism, holy communion and ministry. Obviously these texts have been worked out with spiritual seriousness and theological responsibility, and we take notice of them with gratitude.

2. These texts are known as a "statement of convergence", which implies less than agreement yet more than dissent. We have to ask ourselves to what extent our church, which is committed to the Reformation, can accept this statement.

The unity of the church does not have to be brought about, it is there already, though not outwardly visible it exists in the spirit through Jesus Christ, the head of the church. Unity cannot be created through any kind of organization or human structure into which individuals are incorporated. Rather, unity consists in common worship, discipleship and in confessing that "Jesus Christ, true God and true man, dies for our sins and was raised for the sake of our righteousness".

We are committed to continue in our ecumenical efforts because of the unity granted through Christ.

3. Although the statement on *baptism* presents the least difficulties there are certain questions we need to raise. It cannot be accepted that the Catholic interpretation of confirmation (*Firmung*) is put on the same level with the Protestant understanding. This is because for Catholics confirmation, although presupposing baptism, is considered as a sacrament in its own right, while for Protestants confirmation means a way of teaching the baptized.

The thesis that the writings of the New Testament, as well as the liturgy of the church, present the meaning of baptism in different images can hardly be accepted, as in this way the principle of the priority of the Bible is limited. Yet it needs to be underlined that the mutual recognition of baptism in Austria is

---

• 375,581 members, 7 dioceses, 200 congregations, 1 bishop, 250 pastors.

a significant sign for the interpretation of baptism as a common act of incorporation into the body of Christ. The gift of baptism finds expression in a very meaningful way in II.A of the Lima texts.

4. Throughout the Lima texts *holy communion* is referred to as "eucharist". This begs the question whether the very term does not imply different interpretations. The biblical term is "Lord's supper", while the evangelical churches use "holy communion" or "sacrament of the altar". That these are not interchangeable terms is made clearly visible by the fact that "eucharist" is understood as a prayer directed to the Father, and emphasizing the church's utter dependence on him. Prayer certainly is part of administering holy communion, yet it is not the constituting act thereof.

5. Indeed, the constituting act is expressed in the words of institution. As far as evangelical understanding is concerned the church's acting finds, on the whole, too much emphasis and is hardly differentiated from the acting of Christ. The invocation of the Holy Spirit upon the gifts of bread and wine, as well as the sacrificial offering, present further difficult differences of opinion.

6. There seems to be the danger that the universal view of salvation history (*Heilsgeschichte*) covers up or even eliminates the distinctive quality of what is "given for you and shed for the forgiveness of sins". This diminishes the assurance of tempted faith. As a consequence the unacceptable view may be held that the church will have to bring about the realization of the kingdom of God in as much as her participation in God's mission "takes everyday form in the proclamation of the Gospel, service of the neighbour, and faithful presence in the world" (II. E. 25).

7. The proclamation of the word of God, the priority of the Bible over against tradition, and the word-event in the sacrament is completely put into the background or does not even come into view. A church of the Reformation, determined by the word of God as the true vehicle and conveyor of salvation through the threefold structure of baptism, preaching and the Lord's supper, can observe this only with reservation. Any development which virtually places the word of God only second to the sacrament must be resisted. Preaching and the Lord's supper are two equally-ranking forms of the word of God.

8. Finally, the mutual participation in holy communion is an open question which meets with different judgments. As long as, and despite deep differences, open communion is not practised by all churches, one cannot speak of agreement, not even in the widest sense.

9. The questions related to the Lord's supper are so deeply linked up with the matter of truth that no decision must be taken against one's own conscience. There will be some areas where we can come closer to each other, while there are other areas where confessional positions will leave no room for this.

As a practical example we refer here to the reserving of the elements for later distribution among the sick and those who are absent. This practice is affirmed in the text. Would it not be proper for the churches exercising this practice to proclaim the words of institution and promise to the sick, and to those who have been absent, as they distribute the elements among them.

10. *Ministry.* This seems to be the principal item of the convergence statement. It may well be affirmed that in order to fulfill its mission the church needs persons who "are publicly and continually responsible for pointing to its fundamental dependence on Jesus Christ". This statement corresponds to the intention expressed in CA.V (ministry), CA.VII (church) and CA.XIV (church order and ordination).

11. It is a question whether the "ordained ministry" can be considered as the point of reference for the unity of the church as this is based on, and already present through, Jesus Christ. Striving after this unity remains an ever-present commission as we seek to attain truth. For this reason the linking of apostolic succession in a merely personal way to the office of the bishop cannot be accepted. The only requirement for true "unity" of the Christian church is that "the gospel is proclaimed of one mind in accord with plain understanding and the sacraments are administered according to the divine word" (CA.VII).

12. The presbyterial-synodal order of the Protestant churches has found only little attention in the text. This order, however, represents that form of church leadership which based on baptism and Christian confession gives expression to the structure of the church in a spiritual way. The ordained ministry is placed neither below nor above but rather side-by-side with the presbyterial-synodal ministry of the non-ordained in the common task of leadership.

13. The ordained ministry is made central to such an extent that the absolute authority of the Lord of the church is diminished. The ministry appears to be of the same rank as baptism and holy communion. The fact recedes into the background that the ministry has its place within the congregation by whom it has not been created, yet from whom it receives its function. The evangelical ministry of preaching does not become effective through ordination by a superior ministry, but is exercised because of the commandment of Jesus Christ. The actual installation takes place in duly ordered form through the congregation, i.e., through persons entrusted with supervision as well as through presbyterial authorities.

14. The Lima texts speak in favour of a threefold ministry: bishops (supervision), presbyters (in our terms, minister) and deacons (ministry of serving). This is quite realistic. The problem is, however, whether this is the only valid and unrenounceable pattern, or a *de facto* situation which does not correspond with any divine commission. One could think of a different terminology for ministries. This does not become clear in the Lima texts. They rather follow a hierarchical structure, namely bishop (head of a diocese), local minister (= presbyter) and deacon (= servant with partial responsibility). These ministries may well be accepted in as much as they

represent divisions within the ministry of preaching, requirements for an ordered service and support towards common responsibility.

As far as we can see there is no emphasis in the texts on rootedness in the common priesthood, and the resulting brotherly joint responsibility for the proclamation of the word of God.

15. The ordained ministry is a specific form of the common priesthood of all believers, i.e. the fundamental obligation for the proclamation of the gospel which they share through baptism. This obligation calls for an ordained ministry. It is the task of the ordained ministry to shape its patterns so as to do justice to its functions, especially in preaching the word and administering the sacraments. Among the churches of the Reformation however the ministry of leadership means a joint effort of people charged with this task, be they ordained or not. This is true for presbyters and all the way to the synodal level. The Lima texts seem to proceed in the opposite direction: the basis is made up by the ordained ministry, which in turn charges persons who are not ordained with participation in certain tasks.

16. There is a lack of reference throughout to the statements of the Reformation concerning the subordination of the church under Christ and his word. Justification of sinners solely through grace and faith does not find proper expression. The church is too closely identified with Christ, so much so that the irreversible position of the Lord vis-à-vis his people is lost sight of.

17. The universal ministry of unity (papal-petrine ministry) as seen by the Roman Catholic Church is not even mentioned. It is necessary to point out that, according to the Roman Catholic Church, unity cannot be realized without the petrine ministry as this is by definition substantial and constitutive for the church.

**Outlook**

The Lima texts represent a remarkable stocktaking of the present-day teaching and practice of baptism, holy communion and ministry among the Christian churches. They attempt to point out convergences without hastily claiming agreement. Their true value is to be found in their doing away with polemics and their asking the churches for cooperation.

One cannot overlook the insufficient appraisal of the discoveries of the Reformation. This calls for complaint particularly when fundamental elements are at stake such as the word of God as the real centre and driving force of the church, the ministry of preaching in fellowship with and as a function of the common priesthood, congregations and church leadership as a brotherly effort of ordained and non-ordained persons, and justification as it relates to all.

Nevertheless these texts have raised much attention, found a wide distribution and brought about intensive cooperation, and thereby advanced interchurch negotiations.

# EVANGELICAL LUTHERAN
# CHURCH IN BAVARIA (FRG)

**Statement of the general synod of the Evangelical Lutheran Church in Bavaria**
During the meeting of the synod in Bad Neustadt/Saale, a detailed response on the convergence document on "Baptism, Eucharist and Ministry" was jointly adopted by all the church's governing organs: synodal committee, bishop and governing board. The Commission on Faith and Order of the World Council of Churches had requested this response. It provides information as to the points:
— where the Evangelical Lutheran Church in Bavaria agrees with the contents of the convergence texts;
— what it sees as a challenge to clarify and elucidate its own teachings and practice;
— where it expresses misgivings, makes suggestions for further work and proposes reformulations.

It was not the task of the organs governing the church to accept or reject the convergence document on baptism, eucharist and ministry, but rather to comment on individual statements in it from the point of view of the Bible and confession. The convergence texts do not claim to be a binding, dogmatic basis for the church community. They attempt rather to describe the extent to which understanding and rapprochement are possible today between the various churches each with its own tradition. They are intended at the same time to reveal possibilities for further ecumenical dialogue.

In its response the Evangelical Lutheran Church in Bavaria welcomes the convergence statements as an important step on the road to unity in reconciled diversity. It regards the texts as a challenge to examine anew its own understanding of baptism, holy communion and ministry in the light of the Bible and guided by its own confession, and to consider its attitude to suggestions and critical queries from other churches.

---

● 2,560,000 members, 1,514 parishes, 6 district bishops, 2,032 pastors.

It asks the parishes to regard the response as an encouragement to further work on these topics. The knowledge thus obtained can lead to a deeper understanding of the insights of the Reformation, make the ecumenical dialogue more productive, and provide guidance for meeting the challenges of the time as Christians.

*Bad Neustadt an der Saale, April 1985*

**Introduction**

1. This response is the outcome of an extensive dialogue and discussion process in our church. Parish chapters and councils, ecumenical circles and groups, church organizations, theological faculties and individuals have all contributed their views and expert opinions. The Bavarian Church Council under the chairmanship of the bishop has prepared its own opinion in two closed sessions and forwarded it to the general synod. On receipt of these contributions, the two committees — for basic questions of church life and for world mission and oekoumene — discussed the convergence texts in detail. We submit the joint response of the church-governing organs as the result of these consultations.

2. We welcome the three statements on baptism, eucharist and ministry sent to us by the World Council of Churches as the fruit of decades of intensive theological endeavours by the Commission on Faith and Order in which representatives of our church also participated. The various ecumenical studies, declarations and comments of the churches, in particular those of Accra in 1974 as well as the results of the plenary sessions of the ecumenical council of the churches have been incorporated into this process. Results of bilateral dialogue have also been included. The Commission on Faith and Order has accepted the task of "evaluating the net result of all these particular efforts for the ecumenical movement as a whole" (BEM, preface, p. viii). This has advanced the ecumenical dialogue by a decisive step and created a new starting-point for ecumenical encounter.

Consequently, the convergence texts on baptism, eucharist and ministry carry considerable weight but we do not believe that the current ecumenical processes should be treated in isolation. This applies to the Leuenberger Concord and the doctrinal discussions following it. It applies to the bilateral discussions we are engaged in and from which we hope for a clarification of some of the problems touched on in "Baptism, Eucharist and Ministry" in a manner precisely respecting our specific ecumenical situation.

3. It is the goal of the convergence texts to promote "the visible unity in one faith and in one eucharistic fellowship expressed in worship and common life in Christ" (By-laws of the Commission). This corresponds to the ecumenical concept of reconciliation in diversity, as it has been developed

primarily by Lutheran ecumenists in the past few years. The concept of convergence acquires a twofold meaning on this road to unity. First, it opens up a historically dynamic view of the church's path towards unity. Jointly acknowledged and achieved agreement promotes new community in worship and in witness and service in the world. This opens up the possibility of new convergences developed step-by-step until complete community in consensus.

Second, it introduces a comprehensive concept of consensus and convergence in which the spiritual experience of a church, the holding of divine service, the ecclesiastical traditions and structures play a role. Agreement on points of doctrine is placed here in a wider context. Visible unity is thus intended to develop from common experience, the practice of worship and dialogue. We consider that this way of achieving consensus via convergence and common experience provides an opportunity and a challenge for the ecumenical movement. The encounter, readiness to listen, recognition of common features even in differing forms of expression can promote mutual understanding and rapprochement. When convergence is achieved a new solidarity develops. As against the view that convergence grows only out of the "abundance" of concurring statements, it is the responsibility of the Reformation churches in this process to call attention to the fact that agreement on essential articles of faith is indispensable. It is sufficient for unity of the church that the gospel of justification before God solely from mercy for the sake of Christ through faith is preached and that the sacraments are administered as they were instituted. This requires on the one hand a clear consensus on the basic tenets of faith and allows latitude on the other hand for various ways of expression and forms of this one truth. Accordingly, we believe that willingness to listen to the abundance of messages and aspects cannot replace agreement on basic principles.

An approach that we regard as very promising is through attempts to enter into open dialogue without immediately bringing into play well-known divergences, judgments and prejudices of the past, but rather by jointly engaging in a fresh search for the truth in the Bible and traditions. This must not, however, lead to a process of looking for points of convergence, ironing out differences through the number of aspects considered and omitting or only partially recognizing divergences. A unity that is to be obtained by bracketing out the question of truth is questionable and not viable in the long-term.

We are in favour of linking common experience and church teaching. This opens up a learning process in faith and life. Just because we welcome this process, we must in the future insist on a more accurate relating of factors.

On the one hand, the concept of experience used must be clarified, particularly in its relation to doctrine. The interpretation of an event as specific experience is always influenced by our understanding of God and

God's action of the world and of mankind, that is to say: doctrine. This excludes a unilinear view of the link between experience and doctrine.

On the other hand, particular emphasis in the understanding of experience is given to the liturgical aspect, whereas other forms of ecclesiastical practice such as witness and service here and now and the action of Christians and the church in the world are only mentioned without assessment of their significance for the development of a convergence.

4. The convergence document with its request for a reception process asks us to indicate the extent to which our church "can recognize in this text the faith of the Church through the ages" (BEM, preface, p.x). In this context, the decisive criterion for us is the apostolic faith as recorded in the holy scriptures and included in the church's creed and doctrine. For us, however, the sixteenth-century confessions of the Reformers are an essential part of the church's confession and doctrines. That is why we always also consider whether the convergence texts adequately respect the findings of the Reformation. The Reformational confessions were seen by their authors as resulting from obedience to the scriptures. They accept the basic understandings and decisions of the old church and are designed to give proper expression to the gospel in their time. In this respect they have binding force for us. At the same time they commit us to meet the challenges of our time through obedience to the testimony of the scriptures. A responsible commitment to the confession does not close our minds to other traditions and churches, however; it enables us rather to accept their experiences under the gospel in critical frankness and to take their questions about our practice and doctrine seriously. Hence we are treating this response also as an up-to-date and responsible answer to the judgments and questions of the convergence documents on the basis of our confession.

The Commission on Faith and Order asks for an official response from the "highest appropriate level of authority" (BEM, preface, p. x). In the Reformer's view the responsibility for correct doctrine and the unity of the church are ensured by obeying scripture in the light of the confession and engaging together in a struggle for the truth of the church as a whole. In this responsibility ministry and congregation stand side by side. Under the authority of the gospel it is the task of the entire church to formulate its understanding of the gospel and to accept responsibility for it in the situation. All members of the church thus represent the highest level of authority in the reception process. Accordingly, this response of the church-governing organs includes the various observations in our church.

5. In dealing with the convergence texts, it becomes evident that a response demands initially a clarification of our own understanding of baptism, eucharist and ministry and thus sets a process in motion in which a definition of Lutheran identity is called for. The convergence texts can help us to rediscover theological insights and forms of ecclesiastical practice which have retreated into the background or have been forgotten and to make them

fruitful for the present. They also demonstrate to us where uncertainties exist in our own tradition, or where our practice — measured against the requirements of our doctrine — has become questionable.

The convergence texts open up for us the wealth of theological knowledge and the variety of worship of other churches. They inspire us to accept new and unaccustomed elements and to give a more lively shape to our church life and for this we are grateful.

## I. Comments on the structure of the convergence texts

### 1. SELECTION OF TOPICS

The themes of the convergence statements represent a selection from the ecumenical questions mainly under discussion at present. Historical and objective reasons have dictated and justified this selection because it has been demonstrated in practice that the varying interpretations of baptism, eucharist and ministry have been a severe obstacle to closer community among the churches. The texts do not claim to develop complete theological discussions on baptism, eucharist and ministry, but rather relate only to those aspects which are connected directly or indirectly with the problems of mutual recognition. At the same time, the texts do contain Christological, ecclesiological and ethical implications. Both will be considered in our response.

### 2. LANGUAGE

The language mixes biblical images, classical doctrinal statements of dogmatics, and elements influenced by liturgics. Statements with differing contents are frequently placed alongside each other with relatively little linkage. Description and commentary are intermixed.

This procedure and the attempt to incorporate the abundance of messages from tradition give the text a certain liveliness and unifying capacity but also ambiguity. The use of biblical images makes the text appear familiar to many parishioners but the unintroduced use of technical theological terms creates difficulties in understanding.

With all respect for the special nature of convergence statements, we desire a clear language here and a more pronounced underlining of the theological decisions.

### 3. THE BIBLE TRADITION

The convergence texts always commence with a biblical foundation taking account of the findings of current biblical science. This is shown by the fact that biblical witness is regarded in a historical perspective proceeding from the pre-Easter Jesus down to the testimony of the second generation, in the process of which the basic statements are for the most part placed additively[1] next to each other.

It is clearly stated that the Bible is the foundation and starting-point for understanding the faith and all theological argumentation. The recourse to the biblical testimony in its breadth hinders a premature narrow interpretation. It is one of the basic insights of the Reformation that the abundance of the biblical messages can only be adequately understood where their interpretation is determined from the centre, from that "which moves Christ". The orientation of the multitude of biblical messages towards this centre is not always consistently made.

Just because the interpretation of the Bible is still difficult and disputed, a clear procedure and the revelation of the consummated theological decisions are necessary here.

The convergence texts make extensive reference to tradition. In particular the doctrinal statements of the old church enjoy high respect as being the ecumenical tradition common to all of us.

A coordination of Bible and tradition is attempted but without arriving at a more exact definition of the relationship however. In our view, openness towards tradition — while acceptable — must not reach the point where tradition is equated with the Bible. Where the truth of the gospel is concerned, all tradition and all experience must be measured against the Bible with respect to their authority and their limits.

### 4. The Trinitarian[2] orientation

The Trinitarian justification possesses great weight in the convergence texts. It is shown how baptism, eucharist and ministry are founded on the action in history of the Trinitarian God (e.g. at baptism, baptism as gift of God, baptism as new life in and through Christ, baptism as gift and work of the Holy Ghost). We feel that this form of justification arising from the old church tradition is an enrichment of our understanding of the faith.

The efficacy of the Holy Ghost is brought into discussion in a new manner in these texts (e.g. in the statements on *epiklesis* in the eucharist). We encounter a spiritual understanding, in which the action of the Holy Ghost and the life of the church are placed in close relationship. The convergence texts inspire us to renew our quest for the action of the Holy Ghost also and particularly in our church. But any claim to possession of the Holy Spirit in the church and in Christian groups must be definitely denied. The action of

---

[1] German "additiv". The term is defined in a glossary to the response, i.e., a procedure in which different statements are linked up without checking whether they are compatible with each other.

[2] German term defined in the glossary as implying the inseparable operation of the Triune God.

the Spirit is not in our possession, but is promised wherever the word of the Bible is heard and accepted for life.

## 5. SACRAMENTAL AND ECCLESIAL ORIENTATION

Heavy emphasis is placed in all three convergence texts on the sacramental and ecclesial elements. This emphasis challenges us to reconsider the place and the position of the sacraments in our faith and in our church practice. The emphasis on the ecclesial factor directs our attention to the church as a living community, which lives from the presence of the Holy Ghost. It summons us to responsibility for the form of the church, its testimony and its service in the present. The gospel must be concrete and visible in the faith and the life of the church.

In this connection, we believe it must be emphasized that the church has its foundation in word and sacrament, which rank equally. The church does not possess word and sacrament; it is commissioned to preach the gospel and to administer the sacraments in responsibility before its Lord, whose coming it awaits.

## 6. THE SOCIO-ETHICAL ORIENTATION

The convergence texts emphasize that God's gift at baptism and eucharist, in congregation and worship, has direct implications for the life and the action of Christians in the world. In the face of many a reduction in the claim of Jesus Christ (in particular in the case of individual ethical statements) the convergence texts can trigger off a realization of our world responsibility. The correct handling of this responsibility occurs in the tension between the already incipient sovereignty of God and its still outstanding final dominance and in the tension of our existence as sinners and saved.

In correctly distinguishing between law and gospel, we regard this duty of action as a fruit of the faith and not as an imposed law. Freed from concern for our existence before God, we can — as justified — dedicate ourselves to the service of humanity.

## 7. IMPLICATIONS FOR OUR TREATMENT OF THE CONVERGENCE TEXTS

We know that the convergence declarations originated in a long process and in manifold mergers from varying traditions. We therefore regard it as an appropriate approach if each achieved convergence is appreciated and the Reformation viewpoint brought in constructively for the further progress of dialogue.

## II. Section on "Baptism"

The convergence text on baptism has been largely accepted by us. Baptism is the sacrament of unity. Baptism is rightly displayed as a gift of God. It is performed in accordance with its institution with water in the name of the Father, the Son and the Holy Ghost.

1. Institution of baptism

Christian baptism is rooted in the ministry of Jesus Christ, his death and his resurrection (§1) and by command of the risen Lord given to the disciples of the church. With the acceptance of recent exegetic findings, the institution of baptism is spoken of in a comprehensive sense: baptism is founded and passed on to the church not just in a single act of institution, but rather in the history and work of Jesus Christ, the earthly and the risen.[3]

2. Significance of baptism

*A. Agreement*

The significance of baptism is objectively described by inclusion of a multitude of New Testament pictures and statements. Baptism grants participation in Christ's death and resurrection, effects forgiveness of sins, conversion and liberation to new life. It becomes the foundation of our certainty of salvation. In the power of the Holy Ghost, we are selected and preserved in faith until our final redemption. Baptism is understood as appointment to God's people, as incorporation into the body of Christ and as admission to the new covenant.

*B. Challenges*

In this evolution of the meaning of baptism, three aspects are placed in the foreground, which we should re-examine for our understanding of baptism and its practice:
a) Baptism is not just an occurrence between God and the individual, but rather it is placed into the community of the church, resulting in consequences for our baptismal practice.
b) Baptism as sacrament of unity is an appeal to the churches to realize this unity established in Christ and to overcome the separations.
c) We are approached in a new way with respect to the ethical consequences of the baptismal event. The holistic aspect of baptism is recalled. The dividing borders of the old world era are overcome. This should become visible among the baptized.

*C. Reservations and suggestions*

Even though the church acts in administration of the sacrament of baptism, the subject of the action always remains the Triune God.

The necessity of baptism for salvation and the connection between baptism and orginal sin are mentioned only marginally in the text. It must be more

---

[3] §1 (last sentence): instead of "The churches today continue this practice as a rite of commitment to the Lord who bestows his grace upon his people", suggested wording: "The churches continue this practice today as a rite of assignment to the work of the Lord, who endows his people with his mercy."

clearly brought out that God liberates us in baptism from the realm of the power of evil, places us in a new saving relationship and assures us of future redemption.[4]

### 3. BAPTISM AND FAITH

*A. Agreement*
The coordination of baptism and faith is important in this section. It opens up an affair with God. Baptism therefore is "not only related to a momentary experience", but rather to a lifelong growing into Christ" (§9). It places the baptized into lifelong responsibility for testimony and service in the community of God's people.

*C. Reservations and suggestions*
In place of the misleading wording in §8 "Baptism is both God's gift and our human response", the priority of the gift of God should be emphasized in line with the textual context of §8–10 and it should be made clear that faith is not only the human reply, but primarily the gift of God.

### 4. BAPTISMAL PRACTICE

*A. Agreement*
In this section, infant baptism and adult baptism are considered as equally privileged possibilities of church baptismal practice. This respects the differing baptismal practice in the churches. But just because baptism occurs on faith, it demands a personal profession of the baptized. The association of baptism and faith, which places the person being baptized into a lifelong process of growth, permits an understanding with those churches which advocate adult baptism without granting adult baptism a theological priority. In this connection we welcome the statement that baptism cannot be repeated. We consider a baptism without water as impossible. Water and spiritual baptism belong together and as we understand it can neither be torn apart nor exercised against each other.

*B. Challenges*
Adherence to the practice of infant baptism means that parents, god-parents and community must be more committed than hitherto to their task of guiding the baptized children on their path towards faith. The baptismal discussion with parents and godparents and the baptismal sermon must be

---

[4] §2 (first sentence): instead of "Baptism is the sign of new life through Jesus Christ", suggested wording: "In baptism Christ gives us new life". §3 (first sentence): instead of "Baptism means participating in the life, death and resurrection of Jesus Christ", suggested wording: "Baptism grants participation in the life, death and resurrection of Jesus Christ."

accorded greater importance. From the recognition that baptism is incorporation into the body of Christ and that the entire community is summoned to responsibility, it follows that baptismal ceremonies should be held publicly with the congregation present.

From the experience that there are more and more unbaptized children in our secularized world, adult baptism must be considered as a missionary possibility.

In connection with our infant baptismal practice, we have again become aware of the questions concerning confirmation (time, function, purpose) (§14 does not describe our confirmation).

Baptism is a basic prerequisite for participation in holy communion. In the endeavours to open up participation in holy communion for children before their confirmation, it must be assured that the children have an adequate understanding of the communion occurrence. Appropriate measures should be considered in the rules for Church Life of the Evangelical Lutheran Church in Bavaria.

## C. *Reservations and suggestions*

In III, a distinction is made between believer and infant baptism. This usage suggests the misunderstanding that the gifts of baptism and faith are joined only in believer baptism. Baptism occurs in faith in every case. Such faith is a gift of God and the response of the human all in one, and cannot be unequivocally determined by human examination. We therefore suggest that we speak of infant and adult baptism.

For our church practice, we affirm infant baptism as that act in which the promise and claim of the gospel are dedicated to the child and the child is accepted into a relationship with God and into the community of faith. This means that baptism is a sign that God is saying yes to us unconditionally.

In a society in which infant baptism is no longer self-evident, baptism of an infant can unexpectedly become a professional act for parents and godparents in the midst of the professing community.[5]

## III. Section on "eucharist"

The convergence statements on the eucharist express in manifold aspects what is bestowed on us as a gift in the Lord's supper. Accordingly this text becomes an enrichment for our understanding of holy communion.

---

[5] §13 Commentary: instead of "As the churches come to fuller mutual understanding and acceptance. . ." suggested wording: "To the extent that the churches come to a fuller mutual understanding and acceptance . . .". §16 (last sentence): instead of "The first may seek to express more visibly the fact that children are placed under the protection of God's grace", suggested wording: "The first may seek that children need the mercy of God."

1. INSTITUTION OF THE EUCHARIST

*A. Agreement*

The statements on the institution of the eucharist take into account the findings of modern exegetics in a balanced way. The historical institution of the supper by Jesus on the last night before his death forms the focus. The table community which Jesus granted even to sinners while on earth and the post-Easter experiences of the presence of the Lord in the disciples' breaking of bread are related in appropriate fashion. We are particularly grateful that the character of the Lord's supper is so strongly emphasized as a gift of the Lord to his followers. Also important is the reference to the salvation history, which connects the Lord's supper as feast of the new covenant with the passover and the outlook towards the eschatological communion congregation.

*C. Reservations and suggestions*

Use of the word "eucharist" is unexplained. The word is used in two senses, firstly to express the entire service of worship with proclamation of the word and administration of the sacraments, and secondly as a term for the administration of the sacraments within a service of worship. The term "eucharist" is alien to our piety tradition; we speak instead of the holy supper.

In the choice of language also, it should be made clear that word and sacrament stand with equal rank alongside each other and are constantly related to each other. Word and sacrament are the central content of our worship.[6]

2. MEANING OF THE EUCHARIST

*A. Agreement*

We welcome the introductory remark that the holy communion is understood as donation and gift of God and visible sign of his mercy. It grants community with Christ, is the promise of forgiveness of sins and pledge of eternal life.

On the presumption that Christ is present in the sacrament and gives himself to us for the forgiveness of sins, we regard the Trinitarian foundation and evolution of the eucharistic act as an enrichment. It sets the eucharistic event into the whole action of God in creation, reconciliation and perfection and thus expresses the reconciliation act in Christ in its significance for the entire creation.

---

[6] §1 (last sentence): instead of "Its celebration continues as the central act of the church's worship", suggested wording: "Its celebration remains the central act of the worship service of the church."

The efficacy of the Holy Ghost is spoken of in an unequivocally emphasized manner. In this we see expressed that the church does not control the gift of the sacrament, but entreats the presence of God. This wards off at the same time a magical understanding of the speaking of the "verba testamenti".

The central significance of Christ's work of salvation becomes clear. Also important for us is the emphasis on the real presence. Christ sacrifices himself for us, encounters us, invites us.

In the eucharist text the joyous character of the celebration of holy communion is moved into the foreground. This reminds us that wherever there is forgiveness of sins there is also life and bliss.

## B. Challenges

Preaching and holy communion belong together as forms of expression of the gospel and may not be pitted against each other. Hence we support the restoration of Sunday worship including sermon and holy communion. In this connection, it is important that the ranking of the sermon be preserved and strengthened and that holy communion retain its character as offer, and not be interpreted as a statutory demand. Considerations on the form of these services and the association of oral confession and holy communion are necessary at this point.

The direct linking of the gathering around Christ with the mission in the world seems to us desirable in principle. No pressure for action must come from the Lord's supper, however; its effect is rather to set us in motion (compare the statement on the ethical implications in Baptism).

## C. Reservations and suggestions

The text on eucharist contains a not completely clear definition of the relationship between Christ as subject in relation to the church and the church in action. The line in the text in which the action of Christ on and in the church is very clearly expressed (e.g. §29) should be strengthened.[7] The convergence text does in §2 touch on the aspect of the forgiveness of sins but (in contrast to other aspects) it fails to develop this thought in more detail. We would like this central feature for the lived faith of Lutheran Christians to be brought out more strongly in the ecumenical dialogue. Holy communion is inconceivable for us without the element of personal dedication to the forgiveness of sins.

---

[7] §8 (last sentence): instead of "In the memorial of the eucharist, however, the church offers its intercession in communion with Christ, our great High Priest", suggested wording: "In the memorial of the eucharist, however, the church presents its intercessory prayer to Christ, our great High Priest."

We believe that Christ's sacrifice on the cross realized in the eucharist has atoning significance. The idea of an additional atoning effect of the *memoria* of the victim Christ through the church is unacceptable for us.

In our opinion, the real presence of Christ is inseparably bound to the elements in the celebration of holy communion. Section II.E dispenses with a precise definition of the presence of Christ in relation to the elements of bread and wine. We hope that clearer formulations will be reached in the continuation of the dialogue on this point.

The considerations on the *epiklesis* in the text on eucharist appear to us to be helpful where they lead to an understanding of Christ's presence as a gift, and make us aware that, in the real presence of the crucified and resurrected in bread and wine, renewal of life occurs, community is endowed and the power to active love grows out of experienced reconciliation.[8]

3. CELEBRATION OF THE EUCHARIST

Components of the eucharistic liturgy mentioned in §27 agree largely with what is customary in the tradition of worship of our church. This is true even for *epiklesis* and *anamnesis*, which up until now have been provided for optional use in Lutheran worship rules, but were rarely used. We suggest that more importance be attached to these components in our communion liturgy in the interest of the oikoumene. However, the extent to which these liturgical possibilities are to be used in the organization of the communion celebration must also be determined by the circumstances of each community.

Under no circumstances may the prayer of thanksgiving, the words of institution, the elements of bread and wine and the words of administration be dispensed with.

In accordance with our own tradition of faith and our trust in the promise of Jesus Christ to be present in bread and wine, a reverent handling of the elements is necessary.

IV. Section on "Ministry"

The convergence text on ministry acquires special importance in the ecumenical dialogue because many churches regard the mutual recognition

---

[8] §20 (middle of the section): instead of "As participants in the eucharist, therefore, we prove inconsistent if we are not actively participating in this ongoing restoration of the world's situation and the human condition", suggested wording: "As participants in the eucharist, we therefore prove ourselves inconsistent when we do not commit ourselves for the preservation of God's creation and the living conditions worthy of a human being."
§22. Instead of "Signs of this renewal are present in the world wherever the grace of God is manifest and human beings work for justice, love and peace", suggested wording: "Signs of the renewal are present in the world, wherever the grace of God is manifest and people are thereby moved to champion justice, love and peace."

of the ministries as a prerequisite for church community. The question of the ministry has for us a secondary theological importance compared with the considerations on baptism and eucharist. Baptism and eucharist are gifts of God, through which he directly grants us salvation.

In the discussion, it has turned out that the "ministry" is the most disputed of the three convergence texts; it also became apparent however that within our own church there exists a considerable theological range in the understanding of the ministry. Thus the convergence text on the ministry represents a special challenge to us to arrive at a further clarification of our understanding of the ministry.

Such a clarification would have to include the entire broader field of the understanding of the church. The fact that the understanding of the church is only implicit in the convergence texts makes a clear answer difficult, especially since the distinction between the church as the community of true believers and the visible church is not taken into consideration.

1. On the calling of the whole people of god

*A. Agreement*

The convergence text commences with the unfolding of the calling of the whole people of God. The basis for all life and action of the church is Jesus Christ, who through "the good news of the Gospel and the gifts of the sacraments" gathers his church in the power of the Holy Ghost and sends it out to witness and service in the world. With this foundation of the understanding of the ministry as the calling of the entire people of God, the convergence text agrees with the Reformation positioning of the ministry, which is constituted in the church by the commission to preach the gospel and administer the sacraments. It is also in accordance with our Reformation thinking when the propagation of the gospel and the enhancement of the community in love are described as the central tasks of the church, by which all services and structures in the church are to be governed.

*C. Reservations and suggestions*

It is surprising that the church's mission of witness and service is substantiated in detail from the point of view of the history of salvation and the Holy Trinity, but not from that of baptismal theology. It is our understanding that the calling of the entire people of God occurs through baptism.

In the list of the diverse and complementary gifts we believe that the talent for distinguishing the spirits should be included.

We welcome the linking of the church's mission to the world (§4) also with advocacy for fashioning a better and more humane order in this world so that the tension between the dawning and the still-to-come perfection of the kingdom of God is endured.

2. THE CHURCH AND THE ORDAINED MINISTRY

A. *Agreement*

The public and constant responsibility for fulfilment of the church's mission is mentioned first as justification for the special ministry (§8). This accords with Reformed opinion, i.e. that the special ministry has its foundation in this constant and public responsibility for revealing the gospel in word and sacrament.

We can also accept the historical argument for the ministry, i.e. that people are summoned over and over again to particular responsibility for service of the word and the sacrament. The New Testament testimonies on the origin of special services ranging from the calling of the disciples through the role of the apostles up to the institution of special spiritual shepherds, teachers and leaders are presented in measured terms.

We are glad that the commentary on §11 mentions the complex historical development of the specific forms of the special ministry prevailing today and recommends that no direct attribution to the will and institution of Jesus Christ should be made.

It is also in accordance with our understanding that the ministry is characterized in the New Testament by its very nature as service satisfying the standard of serving instituted by Jesus Christ. This avoids an understanding of the ministry marked by privileges and status. The ministry is placed in the service of the entire people of God.

B. *Challenge*

The priestly service of the whole church, as distinguished from the "unique saving priesthood of Jesus Christ" (§17 and commentary) is aptly described in the convergence text as an intercessory service for the church and the salvation of the world and as commitment of the entire person in testimony and action. In this service, the special ministry and the community are associated with and related to each other.

In this understanding of the priestly service, we consider the following to be of particular importance:

a) The clear distinction between the unique priestly service of Jesus Christ and the priestly service of the church. Jesus Christ is foundation and goal of all services of the church.

b) The emphasis on the priesthood of all believers, which is founded in baptism. This "ministry" and the responsibility associated with it for all members of the church must be constantly emphasized. It is primarily the task of the special ministry to qualify and prepare the community for independent accomplishment of its responsibility for testimony and service.

c) The comprehensive understanding of the priestly service of the special ministry and the community. This service is performed in the revelation and transmission of the liberating action of God in word and sacrament, in intercessory prayer and in the succession of Jesus Christ, who vicariously accepted suffering, overcame enmity, granted reconciliation and thus opened up life and faith.

## C. *Reservations and suggestions*

It is biblical when the convergence text (§ 32) ranks the special ministry among the charisms, i.e. the gifts of the Holy Ghost to the church (1 Cor. 12: 28–30), and also when it assigns to the incumbents of this ministry special responsibility for the discovery and evolution of the further charisms present within the people of God (Eph. 4:11 ff.).

A certain lack of precision is unmistakable in the use of the term "charism", however, which is not without consequences for the understanding of ordination. When it is said that "persons who have received a charism in the ordination are appointed to service through invocation of the Spirit and laying on of hands (§7.c) this includes an understanding of charisms in the sense of talents, knowledge and skill which are recognized and confirmed by the ordination. On the other hand, at another point (§32) the ministry itself is called a charism, which is granted in the ordination and is taken into service for the edification of the body of Christ.

The convergence text not only cites constant and public responsibility for testimony and service as justification of the special ministry, but it also emphasizes that it is the mission of the special ministry to point to the "fundamental dependence on Jesus Christ" (§8) and to be a "point of reference for the unity of the life and testimony of the church" (§14, commentary). As against such justification of the special ministry, the following must be made clear.

a) The unity of the church is not *constituted* by the special ministry but by the gospel. All members of the church share the responsibility for the unity of the church. The unity of the church is not *represented* by the special ministry either, but by the common testimony and common service of the entire church. It is the task of the special ministry to serve this unity.

b) The fundamental dependence on Jesus Christ (§8) characterizes the entire church. In this sense, the *representation* of Jesus Christ is the task of all members. As the community of Jesus Christ, we are called on to point beyond ourselves to Jesus Christ, the foundation and Lord of the church, and "to become Christ" towards each other in the succession of our Lord. Incumbents of the special ministry are called on to make this visible and to live it in their public service.

c) When the convergence text states that it is especially in the eucharistic celebration that the ordained ministry is the visible focus of the deep and all-embracing community between Christ and the members of his body (§14), it must again be pointed out that, from the Reformers' point of view, ministry and congregation become this visible point of reference in the entire celebration of the holy communion. The special ministry must in its own way serve the community and this vivid celebration. We have the legal and basic principle that the ordained incumbent of the ministry guides the eucharistic celebration, but is not constitutive for the real presence of Christ in the elements of the sacrament. In the convergence text the special ministry and the community are referred to each other. In their independent responsibility they are called upon for "mutual dependence and cooperation" (§16). In our view of the basic understanding of the priesthood of all baptized persons, however, this cannot only mean that the community is accorded only an accompanying or confirming function.[9] Responsibility for guidance is entrusted to the entire church and performed in a process of mutual relationship and cooperation. This is also expressed in our constitution (Constitution of the Evangelical Lutheran Church in Bavaria, Art. 1, §2) according to which the laity participates in the office of church supervision at all levels (parish board, superintendency synod, state synod and state church board).

We expressly affirm the wish that further thought be given in joint studies between the various churches and traditions to the question of ordination of women, and that in this process theological and non-theological (e.g. historical and cultural) points of view be clearly distinguished. We cannot however follow the line of argument that the "ordained ministry of the church lacks fulness when it is restricted to one sex" (commentary on §28); this played no part either when female ordination was introduced in our church. The justification for ordaining women in the church to the special ministry is not to be found in arguments of creation theology, which are irrelevant in this connection. The deepest reason for ordination of women is that the comfort of God's justice comes to pass in Jesus Christ and thereby all people receive the same dignity and can be called on in the service for testimony and mission.

## 3. FORMS OF THE ORDAINED MINISTRY

### A. *Agreement*

We welcome the clear statement that there is no uniform New Testament ministerial structure laid down as a standard for the church and for the recognition in principle that the church, trusting the guidance of the Holy Ghost, has the freedom to develop forms of the special ministry which are appropriate to the particular historical context (§§19,22).

---

[9] §12 (last sentence) Instead of: "They cannot dispense with the recognition, the support and the encouragement of the community", suggested wording: "They require the recognition, support, encouragement and *criticism* of the community".

*B. Challenges*

The freedom in organizing the special ministry described in the convergence text is for us the indispensable prerequisite for our agreeing to consider the threefold pattern of ministry as an expression of unity.

We recognize that the threefold division of the ministry — bishop, presbyter, deacon — was of great importance in the church of the early centuries and that it also possesses considerable weight today in some churches. On the other hand it is evident that the definition of the content of the three forms of ministry has changed so greatly in the course of the centuries even in those churches which have retained this structure that a purely formal recognition of the threefold pattern will not create unity, but only conceal actually existing differences.

Nevertheless, we can accept the relevant passages in the convergence text as indicative of the task assigned to us in the ecumenical context of reconsidering the various ministries and services in our church with reference to their theological foundation, to their agreement without understanding of the nature of the church, their association with the central worship event and their relationship to each other (§25). For this, insights and historical experiences of other churches can give us important help.

Such a reconsideration would have to start with the question of our understanding of the episcopal office and the deaconship.

a) As regards the episcopal office which has been widely reintroduced in the churches of the Reformation in the last few decades, we regard service towards the unity of the church as one of its essential tasks (§29). In conformity with the theological insight of the Reformation, which we cannot abandon, we must adhere to the view that the episcopal office is not an echelon hierarchically set over the other ministries by a special consecration, but a specific form of what is the single ministry as determined by its particular service mission (episkope).

b) The deaconship rediscovered by our church in the last century has been developed primarily in its socio-caritative form.

The convergence text points out to us the necessity of organizing the service of the deaconship in such a manner that the "interdependence of worship and service in the church's life" (§31) can be made visible.[10]

---

[10] §50 (first sentence): instead of "Churches which refuse to consider candidates for the ordained ministry on the ground of handicap or because they belong, for example, to one particular race or sociological group, should re-evaluate their practices", suggested wording: "Churches which refuse to consider candidates for the ordained ministry because of handicap or because they, for example, belong to one particular race or sociological group, should change their untenable practice."

*C. Reservations and suggestions*

The convergence text does not—either as part of the discussion of the three-level ministry or anywhere else—deal with the problems which the office of the Bishop of Rome presents to the ecumenical dialogue. We are convinced that these problems cannot in the long run continue to be bracketed out even as part of the multilateral dialogue, since the question of the mutual recognition of the ministries cannot be discussed without inclusion of the papal primacy claim.

In our church also the mutual recognition of the ministries is a primary goal on the road to closer community. We are grateful that this goal has been formulated so clearly (§51). We emphasize in this connection that willingness already exists on our part to recognize the ministries of other churches and in many cases is already practised provided that they clearly and unequivocally satisfy what according to the Reformation view is the central task of the ecclesiastical ministry: preaching the word of God and administering the sacraments as instituted. We hope that more and more other churches will find themselves willing to recognize that in the ministry of our church the commission of Jesus Christ has legitimately gained form.

4. SUCCESSION IN THE APOSTOLIC TRADITION

*A. Agreement*

We are glad to see that a clear distinction is made in this section between the succession in the apostolic tradition and the succession of bishops (§34, commentary and §36) as *one* form of the apostolic succession. In this connection, the apostolic succession is unequivocally designated as the primary and determining factor. In this we see acceptance of our Reformation tradition in which the *successio evangelii* is the prescribed standard for all church traditions and structures. It is in this sense that the churches of the Reformation have existed through the centuries also in their understanding of the ministry in the continuity and tradition of the church.

*C. Reservations and suggestions*

If the distinction between the succession in the apostolic tradition and the succession of the bishops is made in this way, we can respect the episcopal succession as a very important symbol for many communities of the faith. This means, however, as historical experience has proved, that there is no warranty for preservation of the doctrine according to the gospel.

5. ORDINATION

*A. Agreement*

We are able to recognize the features of our Reformed understanding of ordination in the description of the significance of the ordination (§§9, 41 to 44).

It is an act of calling (vocatio) in which the ordained person is bindingly subjected to the commission of Jesus Christ (§44); it is an act of blessing (benedictio), which is consummated under the visible sign of the laying on of hands (§43); it is finally an act of mission (missio).

We are particularly glad that the relation of the ordination to the church is clearly emphasized: it is "an act of the whole community and not of a certain class in it or of the ordained individual" (§41).[11]

### B. *Challenges*

It corresponds to our understanding of the basic unity of the special ministry when the presumption of the unity of the ordination is made and simultaneously the possibility is left open of giving it various orientations in view of the specific tasks of those to be ordained (§39).

We regard this as a stimulus to shape our ordination practice more flexibly.

When the convergence text strongly emphasizes the character of ordination as a personal commissioning by Jesus Christ and an initiation into the responsibility towards him, this is a challenge to reconsider qualification for ordination. Our Reformation tradition has very consciously attached importance to preparation through a theological scholarly education. It could be however that it has not sufficiently taken into consideration other more strongly spiritual aspects of the preparation (§47).

Passages in the convergent text (e.g. §46) can further inspire us to reconsider the relation between the ordination as a spiritual event and the service and appointment concerns.

### C. *Reservations and suggestions*

When ordination is described as "sacramental sign" (§41), we understand this in the sense that the ordained is made aware through a visible event of God's promise applying to him. However, theological clarifications are necessary on this point which must be connected with a reflection on the understanding of the sacrament.

### Closing remark

All of us are grateful that the convergence texts have inspired new theological encounter in the ecumenical dialogue and in our church.

---

[11] §7. c: instead of "The term ordained ministry refers to persons who have received a charism and whom the church appoints for service by ordination through the invocatio of the Spirit and the laying on of hands", suggested wording: "The term ordained ministry — cf. Note 7 — refers to persons who have received a charism and whom the church installs to service through the ordination, through invocation of the Spirit and the laying on of hands."

In all critical queries and suggestions for the future, we have endeavoured in our response to seek to understand and respect the theological concerns and insights as well as the worship experience of other churches.

We regard the convergence texts as an important step on the road to unity in reconciled difference.

Bad Neustadt an der Saale     General synod
April 1985          Synod committee
               Bishop
               Church board

# ESTONIAN EVANGELICAL LUTHERAN CHURCH

We are very grateful for the very important step forward the Faith and Order Commission of the World Council of Churches has made in the Lima document. We share your hope that the BEM document will be a great help in drawing the churches into closer communion.

## 1. Baptism

1.1. Although we agree to your declaration generally, we have (in spite of §12) an impression that the baptism of adults is taken as a norm in this document (for instance, §4: " . . . and are given as part of their baptismal experience a new ethical orientation" is impossible in the case of infants), and that more importance was attached to the baptism of adults than to infants' baptism. We also baptize adults if they make their personal confession of faith but we are still convinced that infant baptism must have theologically the same rights. In infant baptism we see the prevenient grace of God (*gratia praeveniens*). Where baptism will be considered as a seal of the covenant, it consciously puts children into the sphere of influence of the community's faith. God's promise precedes the personal confession and God's gift precedes our human response.

1.2. We admit "the necessity of faith for the reception of [the] salvation" in baptism. Nevertheless we can only agree with the sentence: "Baptism is both God's gift and our human response to that gift" (§8) in the case where the faith itself is a gift of God and only as such is "our human response". According to the evangelical understanding we can describe baptism only as a work of God where his justifying action is most clearly expressed. Only God is the giver; human beings are the recipients of the gift. Their response — faith — has no constitutive significance for the act of baptism, nor does it add anything to it.

---

● 200,000 members, 142 congregations, 90 pastors.

1.3. The conception that the unity of the church is created through our common sacrament of baptism (§6) is not accentuated enough. Namely baptism shows us that the body of Christ is not separated. The unity of the church must be recognized, not re-established. From supporters of believers' baptism we expect the recognition of God's action in every validly performed baptism, not taking age and other conditions of the person to be baptized into account. The presence of faith in a human being is not an established, certain fact. The certainty does not depend on the age of the person to be baptized but on the action of God.

## 2. Eucharist

2.1. The declaration that "the very celebration of the eucharist is an instance of the Church's participation in God's mission to the world" (§25) seems to us very problematic. Isn't there a risk that the celebration of eucharist turns into self-exhibition (compare §22: "The eucharist opens up the vision of the divine rule which has been promised as the final renewal of creation")?

2.2. Our theology hardly accepts the knowledge, in the convergence declaration concerning the eucharist, that the Christian church is a subject of the action. The statement that "the eucharist is the great sacrifice of praise by which the Church speaks on behalf of the whole creation" (§4) creates doubts that the church is placed at the centre of the eucharist (also in the Lima liturgy what we do is emphasized: "our eucharist", "we celebrate", "we bring before you", etc.). "In thanksgiving and intercession, the Church is united with the Son, its great High Priest and Intercessor": here, does the eucharist-celebrating congregation not take over the place of the High Priest and Intercessor?

2.3. The declaration that "the eucharist is essentially the sacrament of the gift which God makes to us in Christ through the power of the Holy Spirit" gives rise to a question which will be more concrete in the sections on the *epiklesis* (§§14–18): Is the Holy Spirit really a mediator in the celebration of the eucharist? Doesn't Christ himself give us the gifts in the ceremony of eucharist? (§29 – Ministry §14: "It is Christ who invites to the meal and who presides at it").

2.4. "The whole action of the eucharist has an 'epikletic' character" (§16). But this statement is relative because of the division of "epiklesis" into "epiklesis of gifts" (§15: "It is in virtue of the living word of Christ and by the power of the Holy Spirit that the bread and wine become the sacramental signs of Christ's body and blood") and "epiklesis of person" (§17). So we have an impression that the "epiklesis of gifts" brings about the transformation of the elements (as a matter of fact the words in the hymns of praise in the Lima liturgy are like a "narrated predicate" and not like a principal item of the biblical eucharistic liturgy). The great importance of *epiklesis* is not clearly demonstrated; there is also no biblical proof. We would like to emphasize the Christological dominance shown by the holy communion. This is delivered in remembrance of Christ; it means that faith in the death and resurrection of Christ must dominate. We believe that in the sacrament the living Christ is coming to us. The prayer for the Holy Spirit is not constitutive of the sacrament of the holy communion.

### 3. Ministry

3.1. The point of departure of the statement of ministry is "the calling of the whole people of God" (§1). This introduction contradicts partly with the following chapters because they deal only with the ordained ministry (§§7–55). But it is not a biblical point of view that ministry in the church is restricted only to ordained ministers. On the other hand, it seems doubtful that the calling of God's people is explained through the passion and salvation of Christ—through the Trinity—and not through the baptism. The explanation of calling without baptism as a sign of conversion and absolution leaves the way open for the theology of triumph instead of the theology of the cross. In the charisma doctrine in §5 the activity of the person is too emphasized.

3.2. Although the connection between the ordained ministry and the priesthood of all believers is emphasized, the convergence declaration speaks exclusively about leadership of the congregation through ordained ministers. The aspect of personal responsibility of the congregation is not accentuated enough. It seems to us that the role of the congregation versus the ordained ministers is according to §§11–12 quite passive.

3.3 From the point of view of the Lutheran understanding of ministry, the declaration in §16 is hardly understandable. The ordained ministers "manifest and exercise the authority of Christ in the way Christ himself revealed God's authority to the world" (§16). The formulation that "the ordained ministry is the visible focus of the deep and all-embracing communion between Christ and the members of his body" (§14) is unfortunate, as it could be a third element between Christ and the congregation.

3.4. The statement of the BEM document that the threefold ministry of bishop, presbyter and deacon may serve today as an expression of the unity we seek and as a means for achieving it (§22) is not theologically proved. In our Estonian Evangelical Lutheran Church the threefold ministry is also practised and we know that the structure of ministry cannot be the basis for the unity of the church. It is a form without substance. The expression of the unity of the church from our point of view can be only in the harmony of the churches in the preaching of the gospel and in the delivery of sacraments.

3.5. We welcome the separation between *apostolic tradition* as a term meaning the church living in continuity with the apostles and their proclamation, and *episcopal succession* meaning transmission of the leading ministry of bishop like a chain throughout history. But while the churches having episcopal succession are asked in §53a only to recognize the apostolic content of the ordained ministry existing in churches which have not maintained such succession, and also the existence in the churches of a ministry of episkope in various forms, the churches without episcopal succession are required to recover the sign of episcopal succession. These two elements are not equal: their results will not be the same. Our church demands our ordained ministers to be in the continuity of the apostolic tradition, because their service of proclaiming the word of God and their administering the sacraments are basic signs of the church. We set great value on the appreciation of the apostolic tradition by the other churches, regardless of the external signs of the episcopal succession.

3.6. The orderly transmission of the ordained ministry as a "powerful expression of the continuity of the Church throughout history" (§35) opposes the understanding of the Reformation in which the continuity of the church is a gift of God through the word and sacrament. For the evangelical understanding of the church it is necessary to make the distinction between the ministry in the church, and the person and the structure in which the ministry is realized. As God has established the ministry, the persons and the historical structures are subject to historical changes.

3.7. The ordination, episcopal succession, hierarchical structure, episcopal authority of dogma and the responsibility of leadership are questions of order and not questions of substance of the church.

### Response to the four questions in the preface of the BEM-document

1. *The extent to which your church can recognize in this text the faith of the Church through the ages.*

According to the Lutheran confession it is sufficient for the true unity of the church that the gospel about the justification before God by grace for Christ's sake through the faith (cf. *Confessio Augustana* 4 and 7) is clearly proclaimed and the sacraments are correctly administered. Up to this degree the confession of our church offers wide possibilities for the various articulations of theological teaching and for the organizational forms of the church. On the other hand, we must follow with extreme consistency and sharpness the principle of toleration (*satis est*) which God has given to us. What will do for the salvation of the people will do also for the unity of the church and for that very reason nothing more is needed for the unity of the church than the word of God proclaimed and visibly expressed in the sacraments. If this argument is accepted, we can accept from the point of view of Lutheran confession the many elements and stimuli the declaration has given to us. When explicating this gospel we accept various suggestions, but they cannot be made preconditions for the correct hearing of the gospel.

2. *The consequences your church can draw from this text for its relations and dialogues with other churches, particularly with those churches which also recognize the text as an expression of the apostolic faith.*

As the Catholic Church speaks about the *defectus* in the holy sacrament at the churches formed during the Reformation (GA 75), so it is of course more difficult for the Catholic Church to recognize the ministry according to the BEM document than it is for the Lutheran church, which sees in the Catholic Church much superfluity but no deficiency in proclaiming the gospel and administering the sacraments. As the Leuenberg Agreement itself places the question of ministry among these, which in spite of the different dogmas of the Lutheran and Reformed churches call in question the unity of the church, then we don't see any church-divisive difference in dealing with the ministry in churches not issuing from the Reformation.

3. *The guidance your church can take from this text for its worship, educational, ethical and spiritual life and witness.*

In many places we find indications of where and how we could widen, open and re-value our practice, to correspond better to the holy scriptures. So we see a duty to connect baptism more obviously with the worship of the church and to administer it during a public service and not during the special worship, so that the members of the congregation may be reminded of their own baptism (§23). We accept the statement that "the symbolic dimension of water should be taken seriously and not minimalized" (§18). We proclaim in the eucharist "the Lord's death till He comes" (1 Cor 11:26). In this the future glory is promised, visualized and granted. The eternal life does not begin after that, but exists in the person who commits himself to the Lord. Death does not break up the community of believers — the church. Christ shapes unity in death as well as in life. For us the eucharist must be the sensible expression of unity, which is not separated by death.

4. *The suggestions your church can make for the ongoing work of Faith and Order as it relates the material of this text on baptism, eucharist and ministry to its long-range research project "Towards the Common Expression of the Apostolic Faith Today".*

The aim of our efforts is not to formulate an obligatory ecumenical consensus theology (it would provoke new differences), but rather mutually to recognize the characteristics and meaning of theological and socio-cultural traditions and to see and experience the unity of the Spirit in the diversity of forms. We also do believe, teach and confess that no church can condemn others for having less or more external ceremonies not prohibited by God. We must keep unity with each other according to the Formula Concordiae X5: *Dissonantia ieiunii non dissolvit consonantiam fidei.*

# EVANGELICAL LUTHERAN CHURCH OF HANOVER (FRG)

## 1. Fundamental considerations concerning the document as a whole

Our response is determined by the following fundamental considerations:

The *character of convergence* of the declarations means to us that they are of a preliminary nature which is orientated to an aspired, later consensus. Therefore, we start from the assumption that further steps will be necessary and that this procedure of finding an answer does not represent a final result. For the same reason we presume that pointing out certain aspects opposed to an adoption does not infringe upon the spirit and framework of the declarations.

Our response mainly centres on the purpose of the declaration as we understand it, i.e. on looking for *possibilities of a common expression* of the various ecclesiastical traditions. Therefore, we do not judge commonness by the degree to which our own tradition is represented but take up the questions of other churches included in the text and confront them with our own tradition. Thus, in our response, we first of all point to commonness and answer questions put to us and then put forth further inquiries and reservations.

In trying to find an adoptive answer we ask for *ecumenical criteria*. In the preface of the text one of the criteria mentioned is "the faith of the Church through the ages". In view of the diversity and divergence of traditions it seems to be difficult for us to define this factor "faith of the Church". We cannot but refer to the witness of the scriptures. In that case the question ought to be: Do the texts show the message and the witness of the Bible? And this again is related to the question: To what extent are this message and witness of the Bible preserved through the ages in the various ecclesiastical and theological traditions?

The confessional sanction of our church sets us the task of examining the relationship between the given truth of the scriptures and church tradition.

---

• 3,539,000 members, 8 church districts, 1,343 congregations, 1,867 pastors.

Our response is of no doctrinal nature whatsoever. We want to stress this explicitly, since the formulation in the preface "official response. . . at the highest appropriate level of authority" could suggest such an understanding. Our response is a *declaration* of the senate of our church which cannot replace the process of acceptance at all levels of our church. On the contrary, it forms part of such an adoptive process which is open inasmuch as no member of the church and no pastor can be forced to feel bound to the texts. According to our understanding the binding force depends on the pertinent evidence only.

## 2. Suggestions for further work

Suggestions for further work of the Faith and Order Commission, as requested in the preface to the texts, result from our response to the particular issues. In the course of our discussion of the individual topics two fundamental questions emerged, an answer to which we suggest to work out.

For one thing there is the question of the *relationship between the scriptures and tradition*. Apart from quotations from the Bible which of course might lead to problems of interpretation also within the context of the whole scriptures, the statements of tradition, such as the liturgies of the early church or the patristic theology, are used in the text to show convergences. Therefore, the question arises as to the relationship between tradition and the scripture. When further dealing with this question the difference between the object of faith and the witness of faith ought to remain clear.

In the discussion of the texts another question, i.e. that of *the understanding of the oneness of the body of Christ*, emerged to be of central importance. This aspect, too, should be further investigated in order to bring about further commonness in the understanding and differentiation of church unity and church fellowship. In this context the relationship between eucharist fellowship and church fellowship ought to be considered. In our opinion it is open to question whether the eucharist fellowship may be made subject to an open declaration of the church fellowship.

The question of the understanding of church fellowship should be linked to a further investigation of the ecumenical aim of a "conciliary fellowship" and a "reconciled diversity". In this context it ought to be clear that church unity is a reality which arises from the operative Spirit of God.

## Lima text on baptism

*I. Commonness*

1. In accordance with the scriptures our church teaches that baptism is rooted in ministry, death and resurrection of Jesus Christ, that it is administered according to his command, that it gives forgiveness of sins and new life, that it is administered with water which is "contained" in the promise of Jesus Christ and that in all these aspects it is God's operative grace

to the sinner, a sacrament on which the faith of the baptized relies and to which he responds.

2. We can recognize this understanding of baptism in the Lima text. We are convinced that the bond of baptism to Christ and its foundation in the witness of the holy scripture as it is to be taken from the Lima text form the basis of the ecumenical fellowship of the churches. Therefore, we acknowledge as being valid the baptism of other churches which is administered in the name of the Triune God by pouring water over a candidate or by immersing him. By acknowledging the baptism of other churches we bear witness that, despite confessional dividedness and independent of these churches' understanding of their own institution, the body of Christ is not torn, since by baptism we form part of the communion with Christ and his congregation.

*II. Questions to us*

There are justified questions in the Lima text regarding our way of practising and handling baptism. These questions can help us to come to a better understanding of the gift of baptism and of our Christian life resulting from baptism. These questions refer to:

a) the stress on the close connection between baptism and the admission to the holy communion (§14, Commentary);

b) the organic link between baptism and catechetical instruction or baptismal preparation respectively (§12, Commentary);

c) the close link between the celebration of baptism and public worship as well as the church year (§§12,23);

d) the identification of believers' baptism as a sign of a missionary church while fundamentally acknowledging infant baptism (§§15 and 16).

These questions seem to be justified and productive, since the Lima text shows the diversity of display and form of baptism as we come across it in the ecumenical fellowship of churches as an inner unity being rooted in its relationship to the person and works of Jesus Christ.

*III. Questions to the Commission and reservations*

1. Although the Lima text puts infant baptism and believers' baptism side by side as being of equal importance, the impression prevails that believers' baptism is considered to be the clearer indication of an inner connection between baptism and faith. We stick to the conviction that baptism of infants and of believers is a sacrament of the anticipating grace of God (despite §14, Commentary b). Therefore, we welcome the rejection of any form of "rebaptism" (§13 and Commentary).

2. Thus we ask whether the "apparently indiscriminate baptism" (§16) refers to our practice of baptism. In the Lima text, moreover, we miss reasons for private baptism in case of necessity, as it is practised in our church.

3. We can acknowledge a "symbolic dimension" of baptismal water (§18) only as a help for displaying the event of baptism in the baptismal sermon

according to the scripture. The water has no effect of its own, not even of a symbolic nature, but turns into baptismal water only by the promise given in God's word and by the faith relying on this word.

4. We do not see what the characterization of baptism as a "rite of commitment" means (§1), especially since this concept is apparently meant to mark the difference between the times of the apostles and fathers and the present churches. Even today the churches cannot but understand baptism as God's work among men, in which faith confides and to which it responds as did the apostles and fathers.

5. We ask whether the New Testament scriptures and the liturgy of the church (§2) are meant to be considered as authorities of equal importance for the understanding of baptism. This could mean that other churches consider all elements of their baptismal rite to be necessary for salvation, even those which have been added only in the history of liturgy. As against that we cling to the opinion that the proper understanding of the gospel and the celebration of the sacraments according to the word of God suffice for the unity of the Christian church.

## Lima text on the eucharist

*I. Commonness*

1. The holy communion (i.e. the eucharist in a narrower sense) as a *gift from the Lord* is adhered to. The verba testamenti traditioned by St Paul are explicitly quoted (1 Cor. 11:23–25). The sentence "The Church receives the eucharist as a gift from the Lord" (§1) clearly summarizes the present result of the exegetic and systematic-theological discussion of the holy communion as being a gift of the Lord.

2. The *uniqueness* of *Christ's sacrifice* accomplished on the cross for the sins of humankind is clearly stressed: "The eucharist is the memorial of the crucified and risen Christ, i.e. the living and effective sign of his sacrifice, accomplished once and for all on the cross and still operative on behalf of all humankind" (§5).

3. The *saving event* is linked to real eating and drinking. "In the eucharistic meal, in the eating and drinking of the bread and wine, Christ grants communion with himself" (§2).

4. The *proclamation of the word and the sacrament* within the celebration of the holy communion are considered to *belong together*: "The eucharist, which always includes both word and sacrament, is a proclamation and a celebration of the work of God" (§3). "The celebration of the eucharist properly includes the proclamation of the Word" (§12).

5. *Christ* himself forms the *centre* of the eucharist event. It is he who invites us to take part in the meal and who therein gives himself to us. "The eucharist is essentially the sacrament of the gift which God makes to us in Christ

through the power of the Holy Spirit. . ." (§2). "The Church confesses Christ's real, living and active presence in the eucharist" (§13).

*II. Questions to us*

1. The eucharist meal is especially stressed and displayed as creating communion: "The eucharist communion with Christ who nourishes the life of the Church is at the same time communion within the body of Christ which is the Church. The sharing in one bread and the common cup in a given place demonstrates and effects the oneness of the sharers with Christ and with their fellow sharers in all times and places" (§19).

2. The eucharist is seen within the *total context* of the saving acts of the *Triune God* in creation, redemption and fulfilment. Thus, it turns into an event which relates the church to the whole of the creation. In this way a universal understanding is stressed in the eucharist meal: "The eucharist thus signifies what the world is to become: an offering and hymn of praise to the Creator, a universal communion in the body of Christ, a kingdom of justice, love and peace in the Holy Spirit" (§4).

3. The *diaconic mission* of Christians and the church is brought into *close relationship to the eucharist*. Strength for the service to the world is taken from the communion with Christ in the holy communion: "Reconciled in the eucharist, the members of the body of Christ are called to be servants of reconciliation among men and women and witnesses of the joy of resurrection" (§24).

4. The *character of joy* of the holy communion is especially emphasized. In addition, it is considered to be an anticipation of the final communion and the fulfilment with Christ and thus it is brought into an eschatological perspective: "The eucharist is also the foretaste of his *parousia* and of the final kingdom" (§6).

5. The holy communion is the *food of the migrating people of God*: "The eucharist is precious food for missionaries, bread and wine for pilgrims on their apostolic journey" (§26). Therefore it ought to be *celebrated regularly*.

For the sake of the ecumenical fellowship a proper treatment of the elements has to be taken care of. "The way in which the elements are treated requires special attention. Regarding the practice of reserving the elements, each church should respect the practices and piety of the others" (§32).

*III. Questions to the Commission and reservations*

1. In connection with the eucharist the church is frequently made the *subject*: "The eucharist is the great sacrifice of praise by which the Church speaks on behalf of the whole creation" (§4). It is the church which "expresses its thankfulness for all God's benefits" (§3).

"In the memorial of the eucharist. . . the Church offers its intercession in communion with Christ, our great High Priest" (§8).

The acts of the church, it is true, are always related to the *operation* of the Spirit. It is the Spirit on whom the acts of the church depend. This close connection, however, may easily lead to dropping both at once. But then, Christ is no longer the decisive subject in the eucharist. Thus, Christ's relationship to the church needs to be defined more precisely.

2. It is true, as to the *forgiveness of sins* granted to the individual and the holy communion the following sentence is put down: "In accordance with Christ's promise, each baptized member of the body of Christ receives in the eucharist the assurance of the forgiveness of sins" (§2). This statement, however, lacks any indication that this is a central event in the eucharist.

3. The *understanding of God's word* is *not clear*. Sermon and sacrament are said to belong together, it is true. But this is inconsistent with a sentence like this: "Its celebration (i.e. the eucharist's) continues as the central act of the Church's worship" (§1). A special quality seems to be attributed to the sacramental event. As against that we must adhere to Christ's being present in the sacrament just as much as in the proclaimed word.

4. It is left open whether the *"invocation of the Spirit"* (epiclesis) refers to the elements of the eucharist or to the celebration as a whole (cf. §§14–18, especially §14 and commentary). It is the work of the Holy Spirit that in the eucharist Christ is received in faith among bread and wine. We pray for this work of the Spirit, but we consider a consecrating blessing by the ordained minister, even by an invocation of the Holy Spirit down to the gifts to be untenable. In this context the following formulation seems to be problematic to us: "It is in virtue of the living word of Christ and by the power of the Holy Spirit that the bread and wine become the sacramental signs of Christ's body and blood. They remain so for the purpose of communion" (§15). Thus, the Holy Spirit would become a means of consecrating the bread and wine.

5. We appreciate the fact that the *understanding of the holy communion is open towards the acts of the Christians in the world*: "The eucharist embraces all aspects of life" (§20). There must not be any sort of conditional dependency of the salvation received in the *eucharist* on the good works of man, however. Thus, a sentence like the following is extremely misleading: "As participants in the eucharist, therefore, we prove inconsistent if we are not actively participating in this ongoing restoration of the world's situation and the human conditions" (§20). The life in the Spirit is directed by the harvest of the Spirit (cf. Gal. 5:22f.). But we receive the eucharist meal only as sinners justified by the faith in Christ. Our works do not contribute towards salvation.

### Lima text on ministry

As to the chapter "Ministry" as a whole we feel it is necessary to point to the following question: When deciding to deal with the "ministry" as "saving means" in addition to baptism and the eucharist, wouldn't it be necessary, in accordance with the witness of the scriptures, to deal with the "sermon", the proclamation or witness of God's truth, besides or even before baptism and the eucharist, apart from the structures of ordained authority set up by men? When thinking over this question we came to the conclusion that, in accordance with the consistent witness of the New Testament, we ought to ascertain explicitly within Christendom substantial convergences in preaching or proclaiming God's truth.

In order to make clear the question raised and the point of view on which it is based we should like to express our basic understanding of the relationship between "sermon" (proclamation) and ministry in some sentences as follows:

I

1. The members of God's people, the new Israel, the community of those who listen to the gospel as the saving message proclaimed in the sermon and who believe in it shall and will, by means of their talents, witness (proclaim) the truth, by which they understand what they are, to all those who do not yet know this truth.

2. The "news" of God's saving mercy (i.e. the truth about God and humankind made clear in sermon and sacrament) brings about the new reality, the new creation, the one church wherever and by whomever it is made audible (or "visible), and wherever and by whomever God's Spirit creates faith.

3. Any notion according to which the witness (martyria) or proclamation (kerygma) of the truth is entrusted or given to certain members of God's people only (related to an authoritative or govermental function) misunderstands the immediate authoritative work of God through the gospel and thus possibly deprives listeners to the word of the saving certainty.

II

4. In order that truth, in accordance with God's will, be and remain audible to possibly all men at any time and at any place, Christendom (by God's truth understanding the conditions of human frailties and possibilities) orders a ministry which has responsibly to provide public proclamation. Theoretically and practically this ministry is to be differentiated from human regimental authorities which are meant to serve the order within the congregation.

5. The authority of those who fulfill the service (ministry) of public proclamation which may differ according to time, nature and amount, place and categories of persons, roots in God's will avowed and linked to the promise of his help to prevent disorder even in the field of proclaiming his word, since disorder hinders the free work of his Spirit related to this proclamation. It does not root in a *special* "authority" conferred by God (through men) to deal with God's truth or even to define this truth by an ability guaranteed by "ministry" or "Spirit".

III

6. In our opinion the quality of authority to preach in public described above must not be upgraded by concepts of priesthood (conferred by ordination or consecration and excluding unauthorized persons), "clerical authority", "representation" in accordance with God's will, or the like. In the same way the fact of such assessments in the history of the churches must not be interpreted as the work of God's Spirit. We want to emphasize explicitly, however, that in our opinion the proclamation of God's word and the sacraments still bring about faith, even where the concepts just rejected are adhered to.

On the conditions described above we give the following answer to the questions to what extent we recognize the "faith of the Church through the ages" and "an expression of the apostolic faith" in the chapter "Ministry".

*1. Commonness*

a) In part I, "The Calling of the Whole People of God", there are indications in §§1 and 2 that all members of God's people (without the mediation of an institutionalized church or a special ministry) are and remain responsible for announcing the gospel to the world (§14). To our mind this responsibility would be described more clearly if the expression "people of God" as a whole were not consistently employed and if the word "priesthood" were used already in this context. Instead, it is used for the first ime in §17 with the addition "corporate priesthood of the people of God".

b) In part II, "The Church and the Ordained Ministry", there is rightly made a difference between the authority of the apostles and that of the ordained ministers (§10). It is said there that the church has always needed persons who are publicly and continually responsible for pointing to the fundamental dependence on Jesus Christ (§8), but that the actual forms of ordination and the ordained ministry have evolved in complex historical developments (§11, Commentary). In the Commentary on §13 we feel it is also rightly pointed out that any member of the body of Christ by means of his charism may share in "proclaiming and teaching the word of God" and in the responsibility for leadership. Referring to the "ordained ministers" only, however, it is said that their authority is rooted in Jesus Christ, who confers it by the Holy Spirit through the act of ordination (§15) and that it is only them who manifest and exercise the authority of Christ (§16).

*2. Questions to us*

Within the Lima text we feel questioned especially by those statements which leave open decisions on the order of the ministry or the ministries. In

both fields, however, we are of the opinion that we have to stick to the
decisions we have taken here.

a) There do not seem to be biblical or other decisive theological reasons
   against ordaining women (§18). However, we do not think that "the
   ordained ministry lacks fullness" (§18, Commentary) where only one or
   the other sex exercises the ministry.

b) Although approving the statements on the historical development
   towards a threefold ministry of the church (bishops, presbyters and
   deacons) we cannot find cogent reasons in this development for taking
   over this structure, especially since differentiations or demarcations of
   functions seem to be problematic.

*3. Questions to the Commission and reservations*

a) To us the relationship or the connection between charism and ministry
   does not seem to be made sufficiently clear. On the one side the text speaks
   of the various charisms bestowed "on the community" by the Holy Spirit
   (§§5, 32). Besides it is said that there are persons who have received a
   charism and who are (therefore?) ordained (§7c) or whose charism is
   acknowledged in the ordination (§44), or else we read that the power of the
   Holy Spirit is invoked for the candidate (since, according to John 3:3 the
   Spirit blows where it wills). And finally the ordained ministry itself is
   called charism (§§32 and 48).

   In all these statements it remains open whether or to what extent the
   "gifts" acknowledged by the church and thought to be necessary for the
   exercise of the ministry are considered to be "natural" gifts (talents?) or
   "graces" (§45).

b) In order to distinguish between the effectiveness of the proclamation
   (sermon) of unordained and ordained members of the people of God we
   should like to point to our reservation in No. 3 of our positive statement
   (see above). Since, in any case, it is God's effectiveness (authority) in Jesus
   Christ brought about by the Holy Spirit, we feel qualitative differences do
   not seem to be possible here. We ought to stress this in view of the
   unordained members of God's people who share in the proclamation.

c) Ministry §11 (Commentary) speaks of the "complex historical developments" which lead to the evolution of the actual forms of ordination and
   the ordained ministry. Apparently this development is interpreted to be
   the work of the Holy Spirit. "As the Holy Spirit continued to lead the
   Church. . . certain elements from this early (New Testament?) variety"
   were "further developed . . . into a more universal pattern of ministry"
   (§19). This universal pattern is apparently understood to be the threefold
   ministry. Later on it is said that the Spirit has many times led the church to
   adapt its ministries to the contextual needs (§22). In view of the different

and frequently separate developments in many churches we have to ask whether it is possible to speak of a development determined by the Holy Spirit within *one* church only. In accordance with the scriptures we have to face the possibility of error and sin, i.e. of the spirit of men also within these "developments" of the different and sometimes opponent churches.

# EVANGELICAL LUTHERAN CHURCH OF ICELAND

The Church of Iceland has received with gratitude the Lima statement on "Baptism, Eucharist and Ministry". There we find ourselves challenged to consider the elements of Christian faith, worship and order. The concord of representatives from so many churches, which is evident in the statement, gives us joy and hope that a visible unity of all Christians is a relevant goal to strive towards.

The Lima statement is not a confessional document and does not outline a final doctrine on baptism, eucharist and ministry of the church. The purpose of the statement is rather to show how the churches place their disagreements in a new light when they study and contemplate their common heritage together.

The value of the statement is, to a great extent, found in the fact that it forces us to look at our own confession anew and re-evaluate its merit for us. At the same time, the statement gives us an opportunity to enlarge our inheritance when we consider factors which are not prominent in our confession, due to the prevailing situation in the church when our confession came into being.

In the preface to the statement, there are questions which the Commission on Faith and Order asks the churches to keep in mind when they give their official responses to the statement. We will try to give answers to the questions of the Commission, but as the Lima text was only recently published in Icelandic, it is necessary for us to stress that our response is an interim but not a final one.

Before we go further into responding to the statement in details, we want to explain in what way we understand the questions of the Commission.

The first question asked is to what extent does our church find "the faith of the Church through the ages" in the text.

---

• 219,091 members, 284 parishes, 126 pastors.

The second question asks us which consequences our church can draw from the text as it concerns its relation and dialogues with other churches, particularly with those churches which recognize the text as an expression of apostolic faith.

In the third question we are asked what guidance our church can take from the text for its worship, educational, ethical, and spiritual life and for its witness.

In the fourth question our church is asked to make suggestions for the ongoing work of the Faith and Order Commission as it relates to its long-range research project "Towards the Common Expression of the Apostolic Faith Today".

The first question is the most important one, and it seems to us that the answer to the second, third and fourth questions will follow as consequences of the answer to the first one. The first question is at the same time the most difficult one. We are not asked whether we recognize in the text the expression of our own faith, but "the faith of the Church through the ages".

What is "the faith of the Church through the ages"?

It seems obvious to conclude that "the faith of the Church through the ages" is the "apostolic faith" referred to in the second (and the fourth) question. In that case it signifies the continuity of the Christian faith which manifests itself in more than one way in the lives of the different churches. In the first question we are asked whether we find in the text an interpretation of the witness of the New Testament and the common Christian tradition, both of which are the basis under the tradition we have preserved. At the same time we are challenged to evaluate our own tradition and our willingness to enrich it by listening to questions of other churches.

Guided by this understanding, we will go about responding to the first question as follows:

To begin with we will look for the meaning of the text in each part of the statement and evaluate it in the light of the common Christian witness in the New Testament and of the common Christian tradition.

Then we will state what we find lacking in the text for it to become a true "expression of the faith of the Church through the ages".

The responses to the second and the third questions will follow as consequences of the response to the first question and we will give them separately.

Finally, we will give the response to the fourth question in our conclusion.

### Baptism

*1. To what extent does your church find in this text the faith of the church through the ages?*

The Church of Iceland rejoices in the fact that the text on baptism is so firmly rooted in biblical metaphors. Baptism is closely linked with the life, death and resurrection of Jesus from Nazareth as the most decisive event in the history of mankind. The life, death and resurrection of Jesus marks a new beginning in the relationship between God and man, a new covenant, and in baptism people become partakers in the new covenant. Both word and act of baptism point out this reality as a historical event which gives a new vision to the future.

The images of the New Testament containing the meaning of expressing baptism are rich and varied. To a certain extent they are based on the witness of the Old Testament, but they all have the same aim, to lead one to Christ. In baptism people become participants in the death and resurrection of Christ which seals the covenant between God and man. In baptism a new meaning is given to life. The Holy Spirit is poured over those baptized for their guidance on the new way which is Christ. This reality emphasizes the corporate value of baptism, expressed in the metaphor of becoming a member of Christ's body, the community of the disciples of Jesus Christ in history, the church, which confesses that Jesus Christ is Lord to the glory of God the Father.

All this is given in baptism, and baptism is therefore primarily a gift. At the same time baptism is a response to that gift, and the response is manifest in a life aiming at transformation into Christ's likeness by the power of the Holy Spirit. The life of Christians is a struggle, but in that struggle they are given a continuing experience of grace.

Those rich and important images of baptism call on the churches to reconsider their behaviour. Whereas baptism leads to a reconciliation between God and man in the life, death and resurrection of Jesus Christ and also to a future on a new earth and under a new heaven, the division of Christ's body becomes unbearable. The doctrine of baptism forces the churches to reconsider their practices. As the event of Christ is only one, there is only one baptism towards unity in one faith, one hope and one love.

In this exposition we find harmony between the apostolic faith and the Lima statement. We also find harmony between what the Lima text emphasizes and what the confessional writings of our church teach about baptism, not least the Small Catechism of Luther. Therein, baptism is also called participation in the death and life of Jesus Christ, the beginning of a new life which leads to a transformation into Christ's likeness, a life where the renewing power of the new creation is at work through the Holy Spirit.

At the same time we find reason to point out the necessity to deal more clearly with the role of God's word in the life of the Christian, and the relation between word and baptism. In the statement it is emphasized that Christian life is a struggle, yet also a continuing experience of grace for those baptized. It is, moreover, stressed that as the baptized grow in the Christian life of faith they will become a proof to the world that it can be liberated. We want to emphasize this more strongly and also point out the role of the word in this struggle of Christian people. The word is proclaimed in order to give comfort, admonition and edification. In the preaching of the word we are anew called to follow Jesus. The preaching shows Christ crucified as the universal reconciliation and renews our calling to take up the cross of Christ and follow in his steps. The coming resurrection will be after death but not a development from something good to something better.

*2. What consequences can your church draw from this text for its relations and dialogues with other churches, particularly with those churches which also recognize the text as an expression of the apostolic faith?*

The Church of Iceland recognizes whatever baptism administered with water in the name of the Father, and the Son and the Holy Spirit. We consider infant baptism in perfect harmony with apostolic faith since in baptism God gives salvation.

There are a few churches in our country which do not recognize infant baptism and teach that baptism of believers is alone in harmony with apostolic faith. Often they build their argument on the postulate that baptism primarily signifies man's obedience and is received to confirm the faith he confesses.

If these churches do recognize that God gives salvation in baptism, it seems to us that a part of our disagreement has been done away with. We need to begin a discussion with those churches in our country which do not recognize infant baptism and have rebaptized those from our folds who have joined them.

At the same time we want to express our willingness to reconsider certain aspects of our baptismal practices, and to avoid a careless administration of baptism. There we need to focus on the aspect of Christian education, the preparation of parents and the awareness of the congregation. But on the other hand, we cannot recognize anything which limits God's grace.

*3. What guidance can your church take from this text for its worship, educational, ethical and spiritual life and for its witness?*

If we to begin with look at the liturgy, it is necessary for us to integrate our celebration of baptism with baptismal theology; we need to stress further the promise of baptism, the dividing line between old and new, by renouncing the evil before we confess our faith with the words of the creed which we have always used. We also need to allow the symbolism to speak to us in more clarity.

Concerning other phases of the church life we can inform that the Lima statement has been used in a few congregations as a reading material in study circles and proved to be very valuable. Participants in small groups have found the statement to be of excellent use, particularly due to the fact that it forces them to ask questions about concepts they have always taken for granted. It is also important that it emphasizes that Christian life grows up from baptism.

If we look at our baptismal practice, we must admit that we have not used our doctrinal tradition as we should, but given in to thinking about baptism more or less as a custom to be respected. In the light of our own tradition and the apostolic faith, we must reconsider our baptismal practice, as far as this is concerned, and affirm that baptism leads from faith towards faith.

There has been a debate in our church on Christian nurture and catechetical instruction and also on the necessity to instruct parents of baptized infants about the meaning of baptism. We are grateful for the fact that the Lima statement challenges us to carry on such a debate and at the same time to reconsider the liturgy of baptism in order to make it clearer and more faithful to the meaning of baptism.

It is accepted in the statement that infant baptism and baptism of believers are equally in harmony with apostolic faith. Infant baptism has been emphasized in our doctrinal tradition and even taught that it only is in accordance with apostolic faith. We want to stress the value and necessity of infant baptism and we point out that Christian faith creates society, which is an entity which we are born into. This mystery is better expressed in the practice of infant baptism than in baptism of believers.

It is a fact, however, that due to social circumstances in Iceland, many of those baptized miss Christian nurture altogether. The moment of baptism is very important in the lives of people, but they think less about the living it leads into. Many of those who experience faith later in their lives have difficulties understanding that conversion is in reality conversion to baptism. What the statement says about confirmation (§14) seems to be useful in order to meet the needs of those. It is very important to us that we seriously consider the theology of confirmation.

On the other hand, we want to affirm in accordance with our tradition and on the basis of apostolic faith that the Holy Spirit is given in baptism together with all the gifts of salvation. We cannot recognize the need of another rite adding to the value of baptism. Most of the time confirmation has led to first communion in our country, but as in our neighbour churches the trend has been to admit children to the Lord's table on the basis of baptism only. This is even permitted in the new service book of the Church of Iceland.

Pastoral considerations should not hinder us in thinking of those who hear and heed the call of Christ, leading to radical change in their lives and orientation.

## Eucharist

*1. To what extent does your church find in this text the faith of the church through the ages?*

Obviously this text reflects the faith of the church through the ages. Parts of it are in accordance with the main issues in our doctrinal tradition. Other parts do certainly belong to the faith of the church through the ages, in spite of the fact that they have not had a prominent place in our heritage.

Here biblical images are used extensively as in the chapter on baptism, their richness draws our attention, but the central issues are always in focus. The eucharist is "the new paschal meal of the Church" prefigured in the Jewish Passover, it is "the meal of the New Covenant", "sacramental meal which by visible signs communicates to us God's love in Jesus Christ".

It is emphasized in this chapter that we receive in the eucharist the gift of salvation as Christ has promised. "In the eucharistic meal, in the eating and drinking of the bread and wine, Christ grants communion with himself. God himself acts, giving life to the body of Christ and renewing each member. In accordance with Christ's promise, each baptized member of the body of Christ receives in the eucharist the assurance of the forgiveness of sins (Matt. 26:28) and the pledge of eternal life" (§2). "The words and acts of Christ at the institution of the eucharist stand at the heart of the celebration; the eucharistic meal is the sacrament of the body and blood of Christ, the sacrament of his real presence" (§13). "In the celebration of the eucharist, Christ gathers, teaches and nourishes the Church" (§29).

This emphasis is central in the continuing reflections of the church on the eucharist. It is also a major point in our church's doctrine of the Lord's supper.

The development in our church has, however, been such that we have only focused on this point and at the same time not dealt with other aspects of the eucharist which are listed in §2 and elaborated on in §§3–26: the eucharist as thanksgiving to the Father, *anamnesis* of Christ, invocation of the Spirit, communion of the faithful, and meal of the kingdom.

We have become familiar with these aspects in the revision of the eucharist which has taken place in our church's denomination for the last decades, and some of them have found a way into the renewal of the liturgy in our church those last years.

We are grateful for the emphasis on the work of the Holy Spirit. Most of the time, Christ has been at the heart of the act for us, but the emphasis on the Trinity gives it another dimension, binds together creation and salvation, and opens the eschatological dimension.

This chapter touches on some sensitive issues of controversy among Christian people, such as those concerning the real presence of Christ and the sacrifice of the mass. It strongly affirms the real presence of Christ in the eucharist, but the churches are, however, asked whether they can accommodate this difference concerning the real presence within the convergence formulated in the text itself.

The Church of Iceland gives an affirmative answer to that question. We consider it important to express the presence in such a way that the act indicates what is recalled and that Christ brings the fruit of salvation into the life of the church in the Lord's supper.

In a commentary on §8, the question is raised whether it is possible to review the controversy on "sacrifice" in the light of the biblical concept of "memorial". The Church of Iceland is willing to study that point further, as it has always emphasized strongly the real presence.

It is noteworthy that it is emphasized in the text that the eucharist touches all aspects of life and looks to the future when God will be all in everything. We certainly find this exposition to be in harmony with all apostolic faith. Biblical and ecclesiastical images regard the Christian faith as an organic entity. Its beginning is a birth into life, a new creation, enlightenment, resurrection from death. This all affirms the fact that one looks from a viewpoint of reality where there is sin and death towards a new reality of freedom and life in Christ. The same way a child needs for its maturity nourishment and protection from whatever threatens its life, so the child of God needs for its growth the nourishment and encouragement given in the eucharist and in listening to God's word.

We find it, however, necessary to elaborate more on the connection between word and sacrament. It seems to us not possible to deal with the eucharist without its connection with the word of God in the holy scriptures and its proclamation in the preaching of the church. It has always been maintained in our church that the word of God is an active means of grace, and that stress must not be diminished.

This unity of word and sacrament is indeed affirmed in §§3 and 12, and also in §§27 through 29, but we think it should be made clearer in order not to de-emphasize that man receives in the sacrament the gift of salvation, the forgiveness of sins, according to the promise of God's word.

*2. What consequences can your church draw from this text for its relations and dialogues with other churches, particularly with those churches which also recognize the text as an expression of the apostolic faith?*

The Church of Iceland has an open fellowship of the Lord's table. It welcomes everyone who wishes to receive the sacrament and does not prohibit its members to take communion with other churches. It has also happened that ministers from other churches have participated in the celebration of the eucharist in our church. We consider such behaviour desirable. We urge all churches of the different denominations to attain a greater measure of eucharistic communion among themselves. Open altar fellowship affirms actively the validity of the sacrament in other churches. It is a prerequisite of a true unity of the church, indeed the primary condition, if striving for unity is not to become a theoretical speculation only.

*3. What guidance can your church take from this text for its worship, educational, ethical and spiritual life and for its witness?*

We find many of the same emphases in our doctrinal tradition as in the Lima statement. Word and sacrament are the means with which the Holy

Spirit creates faith. We refer to strong comments of Martin Luther about those who claim they can be without the sacrament. They do not only dishonour the sacrament, they also despise Christ and his salvation.

The place of the Lord's supper in our church has, however, not been such as our doctrinal heritage gives occasion for. There are, without a doubt, many reasons for this fact, for instance one-sided interpretation of the eucharist which bases the partaking in the holy communion on repentance and penance only, and maintains that careful introspective preparation is needed before communion: and an influential theological trend which diminished the importance of the eucharist. It is a fact that the celebration of the eucharist fell into neglect in our church during the last century and the first half of the present one, in spite of our heritage which gives us reason to take to heart the admonition in §31.

In the last few years we have experienced a change in this respect. The number of eucharistic services has grown and a liturgical renewal has taken place in our church. That renewal seems to have led people to rediscover the ever new inheritance of the church of all ages which is given in the eucharist. At the same time, some elements of the liturgy, which make it an act of thanksgiving, memorial, invocation and communion, were given anew their rightful place of prominence.

The Lima statement challenges us to continue studying the place of the Lord's supper in our church; the reason for this challenge is the fact that its exposition is so close to our tradition and moreover because of what it draws from our doctrinal tradition of other churches. The same way new ideas have led to a renewal with us, so continuing encounters between our church and other churches and their traditions can lead us further on the way of renewal.

The Lima statement challenges us also to continue with the renewal of our liturgy. We affirm the emphasis of the statement that a liturgical renewal is not a question of form but rather of content and nature of the Christian life. No certain liturgical form gives power to the eucharist, only the promise of Christ can do that (cf. §§2 and 13). We also agree with the words of §28 that a certain liturgical diversity compatible with our common eucharistic faith is recognized as a healthy and enriching fact.

The Lima statement emphasizes the role of the Holy Spirit in making Christ really present in the sacrament. This emphasis is new to us who have considered the presence of Christ in the sacrament to be based on his own word and promise. We have, however, never questioned the influence of the Holy Spirit in the lives of those who partake in the eucharist. Our confessional documents affirm that the Holy Spirit creates faith in the hearts of believers and uses word and sacrament as means to that end. We want to express a most sincere desire to deal thoroughly with the question which §§14 through 18 raise. According to §13, the words and acts of Christ at the institution of the eucharist stand at the heart of the celebration. It also says that Christ's real presence in the eucharist does not depend on the faith of the individual, but to discern the body and blood of Christ, faith is required. As far as this is concerned, there is an agreement here between the Lima statement and Luther's explanation of the sacrament of the altar in the catechism. There it is also stressed that the Holy Spirit kindles faith in the hearts of people, not the human power of reason. In the same manner it can be argued that no human power or quality can bring about the nearness of the risen Christ in the bread and wine, but only the word and promise of Christ by the life-giving power of the Holy Spirit.

Nevertheless, it has to be avoided that the discussion about the act of the Holy Spirit leads one to think that the Father and the Son are an expression of the distant God but the Holy Spirit the expression of the ever-near God. Nor should the words on the invocation of the Holy Spirit be based on ideas which make the crucifixion a distant event in time whereas the Holy Spirit would be the active agent who channels the effect of this past event into our lives. Contemplation on the liturgical heritage of the church of all ages proves to us that time and eternity are united in the eucharist. When the eucharist is celebrated on the day of the Lord, time is absorbed by eternity. The importance of the cross and resurrection of the Lord as an event in time and space is certainly the fact that the cross and the resurrection is an eternal event which is constantly exposed as memorial with God and given us at the same time when we eat and drink at the Lord's table, to strengthen us in faith, hope and love. By coming together to the Lord's supper, we cast all our hopes on him, bringing our invocation, prayers and intercessions, not putting our trust in our own merit but in the mercy of God. And who creates trust, who makes it alive and who kindles love? The Holy Spirit does.

As mentioned before, the Church of Iceland has an open altar fellowship. Through the ages we have considered confirmation an act of admission to the Lord's table. But today we allow children, who have not been confirmed, to come to the Lord's table with their parents. The Lima statement gives us another opportunity to study more intensively whether the Lord's table should be open to people on the basis of their baptism alone or admittance should be limited by age or other conditions.

It pleases us to see how the eucharist is put in context with the Christian life as a whole, but not kept as an isolated event. For a long time our emphasis has been very individualistic, we have looked at communion through the bond between God and the individual. We find reason to rejoice over the fact that the Lima statement considers communion in such a wide context. "The eucharist thus signifies what the world is to become: an offering and hymn of praise to the Creator, . . . a kingdom of justice, love and peace in the Holy Spirit" (§4). "In Christ we offer ourselves as a living and holy sacrifice in our daily lives" (§10). "The Church, as the community of the new covenant, confidently invokes the Spirit, in order that it may be sanctified and renewed, led into all justice, truth and unity, and empowered to fulfil its mission in the world" (§17). "Solidarity in the eucharistic communion of the body of Christ and responsible care of Christians for one another and the world find specific expression in the liturgies" (§21). "The very celebration of the eucharist is an instance of the Church's participation in God's mission to the world. This participation takes everyday form in the proclamation of the Gospel, service of the neighbour, and faithful presence in the world" (§25).

We have not stressed these aspects, and our debate on the connection between witness of faith and social ministry has therefore gone astray. In the statement we are challenged to reconsider those issues in order to affirm Christian unity of life, proclamation and witness.

## Ministry

*1. To what extent does your church find in this text the faith of the church through the ages?*

It seems important to us that the discussion on ministry begins by dealing with the calling of all God's people. The New Testament sees the church as one with a calling and a role. From that point of view only can we concentrate on the issue of different callings of different members of the church.

It is also important to underline the fact that the form of the church developed over a long period of time, and the New Testament does not serve as a norm for church order (cf. §19). The semantic explanation in §7 is very useful, both for the clarity of the chapter and also to assist us in defining the questions we need to keep in mind while contemplating on the issue of the ministry of the church.

We are content with using the general term "ministry" for the calling of the church as a whole and the term "ordained ministry" for the special ministry of certain people in the church. We did so in our translation and we consider it to be in accordance with the apostolic faith.

We agree with the argument for the existence of the ordained ministry in §8, which states that the church continually needs people who publicly point to its fundamental dependence on Jesus Christ. The apostles serve as a model for such ministry, and at the same time, they are a model for the church as a whole (§§9 and 10).

The evolution in the early church is here clearly accounted for, how the pattern on ministry developed into the threefold ministry of bishop, presbyter and deacon. Although it is difficult to discern the origin of this pattern and to describe in detail how it developed, it is known to exist everywhere in the church in the third century.

The statement emphasizes that this threefold ministry may serve today as an expression of the unity we seek and also as a means for achieving it (§22). It also points out that some churches which have not formally kept the threefold form have, in fact, maintained certain of its original patterns (§§24 and 37).

This comment concerns our church in particular. The historical apostolic succession of bishops was broken in our country in the sixteenth century, but the pattern of the threefold ministry has been preserved here till this day. An important point made in the chapter is the interdependence in the relationship between ordained and unordained ministers of the church. This emphasis is important because it prevents us from thinking of the ordained ministry as an independent order, high above the service of the unordained which would then be considered as of less value. With reference to that, it is right to affirm the emphasis in §15 that the authority in the church is rooted in the authority of Jesus Christ and therefore has the character of responsibility before God and only exercised with the cooperation of the whole community.

The statement discusses the charisms and stresses how their existence enriches the life of the worshipping community. It is also noteworthy that the ordained ministry is considered to be among the gifts of the Holy Spirit to the church and therefore a specific charism. We agree with the argument of §33 that the preservation of the gospel does not depend on a certain structure, and that the Holy Spirit has often taken unusual measures when admonishing the church. It is necessary for us to keep in mind that the life of the church is entirely dependent on God and his initiative.

The guiding principles for the exercise of the ordained ministry in the church are therefore very important.

The issue of apostolic succession is dealt with in §§34–38. We fully agree with the distinction made between "a succession in the apostolic tradition" which refers to the whole church, and "the succession of the apostolic ministry" which is primarily exposed in the apostolic tradition in the church.

Thus is the apostolic tradition in the church defined:

> Apostolic tradition in the Church means continuity in the permanent characteristics of the Church of the apostles: witness to the apostolic faith, proclamation and fresh interpretation of the Gospel, celebration of baptism and the eucharist, the transmission of ministerial responsibilities, communion in prayer, love, joy and suffering, service to the sick and the needy, unity among the local churches and sharing the gifts which the Lord has given to each (§34).

The primary manifestation of apostolic succession is said to be found in the apostolic tradition of the church as a whole. The succession is also said to express "the permanence and, therefore, the continuity of Christ's own mission in which the Church participates". Then it says so about the succession of the apostolic ministry:

> Within the Church the ordained ministry has a particular task of preserving and actualizing the apostolic faith. The orderly transmission of the ordained ministry is therefore a powerful expression of the continuity of the Church throughout history; it also underlines the calling of the ordained minister as guardian of the faith (§35).

Churches which see little importance in orderly transmission are therefore asked whether they need not change their conception of continuity in the apostolic tradition. The episcopal churches are asked, at the same time, whether their ministerial structures are not in need of reform.

Churches which have not kept the episcopal succession are asked whether they could respect that succession *"as a sign, though not a guarantee,* of the continuity and unity of the Church" (§38 our italics, cf. §53).

We affirm this distinction and declare our willingness to consider these questions as far as they concern us.

We are also in agreement with the definition of ordination, its meaning and practice (§§39–44). We are glad to find it in full harmony with the tradition in the church, and also with the tradition we have preserved in our church.

In the exposition of the chapter as a whole, we find an expression of the faith of the church through the ages.

To us, the statement seems to be in harmony with the tradition of our church, and we express our joy over that. Our doctrinal tradition maintains that the nature and aim of the church should have priority over its form and structure. According to our confession, the ministry of the church has the role of proclaiming the gospel and spreading the kingdom of God. The question of the ordained ministry has to be reflected in the question of the total ministry of the church. We are not of the opinion that there should be a clear distinction between the ordained minister and those not ordained, but we claim that baptism draws the decisive line in people's lives. We think the primary role of the ordained minister is to preach the word of God, distribute the holy sacraments and carry the power of keys in the confessional. We are glad to find those points emphasized in the Lima statement.

Our critical points concern primarily the pattern of the threefold ministry and the apostolic succession. We affirm that the preservation of the apostolic tradition in the church is of a greater importance than the apostolic succession. Succession in the apostolic tradition means first of all doctrinal succession. Since the ministry in our church has always been transmitted through ordination by the hands of ordained men, it is our opinion that an unbroken apostolic succession has been preserved in our church, in spite of the fact that the succession of bishops was broken in the sixteenth century.

Secondly, on the basis of our doctrinal tradition and in the light of the Lima statement, we want to comment on the wording in §12, where it says that the church seeks an example of holiness and loving concern in the ordained ministry. If all God's people are equally called to spread the kingdom of God, then the calling to holiness and loving concern is equal for all and not only for the ordained ministry. In history we find a host of evidences that the outstanding examples of holiness and loving concern were outside of the ordained ministry, women as well as men.

Thirdly, we want to emphasize the unity of word and sacraments. The role of the ordained ministry is not only to preside over the eucharistic celebration, but also to preach the word of God. Therefore, we see reason to affirm that the wording in §14 refers to the liturgy as a whole, where the fellowship of the Lord's table and preaching of the word of God go hand in hand.

Fourthly, we call for a more thorough consideration of the ordained ministry of women in the church. In our church women are ordained into the ministry and the number of women studying theology increasés gradually. The ministry of ordained women has proved to be of great value, and we maintain that we are by duty bound to make real what has been testified, that in Christ there is neither male nor female, with him distinction between people is made void. We affirm that if people want to look for scriptural arguments for the status of women in the church, they should quote the letter to the Galatians: "There is neither Jew nor Greek, there is neither slave nor free, there is neither male nor female: for you are all one in Christ", rather than the words of St Paul in 1 Corinthians 14:34, that "women should keep silence in the churches". The argument in Galatians is obviously a more important one. There we have a theological definition of the meaning of baptism for the Christian community, it expresses prophetical insight not dependent on social mores of passed times.

*2. What consequences can your church draw from this text for its relations and dialogues with other churches, particularly with those churches which also recognize the text as an expression of the apostolic faith?*

The Church of Iceland recognizes indeed the ordained ministry of other churches. Our fellowship is primarily with churches of the same denomination in other parts of the world of which some have different practices of ordination to ours. In some instances the Lutheran churches have preserved the apostolic succession, in others not, but our fellowship does not suffer from that fact. It is clear that if a Lutheran minister from another church would request to be accepted into the ministry of our church, he would not be ordained again. On the other hand, the question has not been dealt with whether an ordained minister from another denomination who would request to be accepted into our ministry on the basis of our doctrinal teachings, would have to be reordained.

We express our sincere will to recognize the ordained ministry of whatever church which accepts the apostolic faith and agrees with us that the ordained ministry is based on the vocation of all God's people, and we wish other churches to recognize our ordained ministry in a similar way. But here we need to state that the question of accepting ordained ministers from other churches cannot be solved by our church alone; it also concerns our parliament due to the ties between state and church in Iceland.

The apostolic succession was broken in our church in the sixteenth century, as we have already stated, although we have retained the form of episcopacy ever since. In spite of the fact that our church recognizes only one form of ordained ministry, the ministry of word and sacraments, we have indeed kept the form of the threefold ministry. A person called to the episcopate is always consecrated by his predecessor or someone else who is an ordained bishop. To secure that the country is never without a bishop, and an elected bishop would not have to travel to another country for ordination, we have since 1909 constituted the order of two suffragan bishops who have the ordination and title of bishops but stay in their ministries as pastors. That example shows how highly we regard the episcopate.

We have then also retained the diaconate in our church. In the first centuries after the Reformation it existed in the form of unordained assistants in the congregations. In later years a few people have received ordination to a diaconal ministry. At present there is one ordained deacon serving in our church, and some congregations have on their staff assistants who in reality render diaconal services. We have indeed no rules or guidelines concerning the diaconate, but we express a sincere will to begin a study of its nature and role on the basis of the Lima statement and apostolic faith. In the light of the New Testament there seems to be a need to give a careful consideration to the variety of ministries within God's people in the world. Yet it is unclear what distinguishes the ordained ministry of deacons and the unordained ministries of others, both in full service in the congregations and in other fields within the church.

*3. What guidance can your church take from this text for its worship, educational, ethical and spiritual life and witness?*

In the light of the issues which we found emphasized in the Lima statement and we referred to when reflecting on the first question, we find reason to ask ourselves whether we take our tradition seriously enough. It seems that when we talk about the ministry of the church we are only referring to the ordained ministry. The term "layman" has in our church developed the meaning "uneducated", "inactive", and seen in the context of our doctrinal heritage, that meaning has to be wrong. The term "layman" comes from the Greek word "laos" in the phrase "laos Theou" (God's people).

The participation of the unordained ministry in the government and leadership of individual congregations and the church as a whole has, however, grown in the last years. The Lima statement encourages us to carry on with that development and break the isolation of the ordained ministry in the life and work of the church by giving responsibility to all baptized members of the church, both concerning leadership, liturgy and the general work in the congregation. We need, therefore, to study carefully those paragraphs which deal with mutual responsibility and unity of ordained and unordained ministries in the church.

The mutual relationship concerns more than government and order. It also concerns the worship and witnessing of the church in our time. At that level we must strongly take into consideration the role of the unordained ministers in the church, called to be salt and light in their respective surroundings, supported by the preaching of God's word and the communion of the Lord's supper.

In the Lima statement there is an important emphasis on the inner connection between the ordained and unordained ministries. We have to pay a close heed to this, both with reference to the act of ordination and the order of the ministry, in order to strengthen this inner connection. For too long the official worship has been considered the responsibility of the ordained minister alone, whereas the congregation has been an inactive audience. This is changing, and in the Lima statement we are encouraged to carry on with liturgical renewal which leads to a greater participation of all present in worship.

The guiding principles for the exercise of the ordained ministry in the church are a necessary admonition for us, where the emphasis on the "personal dimension" takes precedence over other emphases.

The discourse on the calling of the whole people of God is also a constructive admonition for our church, to strengthen the education of all its baptized members about the vocation of all Christians in the world. With that in mind, we detect the continuity in the Lima statement. The life born in baptism grows and matures by hearing God's word and is nourished by the eucharist in order to be strengthened for the service to our Lord, in the world which he has created.

In a modern pluralistic society, where time is divided between work, leisure and social activities, and where religions and ideologies fight for the hearts of people, the church needs to strengthen its witness by making it clear to all baptized people that they have a calling as members of Christ's body, wherever they are. This should be the prime educational aim of the congregations. This does not only depend on the ministry of the church concerning special issues, but its ministry in the world is the witnessing of those called to be the salt of the earth and the light of the world.

The responsibility of the unordained ministers in the church is great, they have various duties in different circumstances. The responsibility of the ordained ministry is above all to be found in their special calling to strengthen the service of all members of Christ's body, wherever they live and work, through the proclamation of the word and the distribution of the sacraments.

**Conclusion**

In the conclusion of our response, we want to comment briefly on the final question of the Commission:

*What suggestions can your church make for the ongoing work of Faith and Order as it relates the material of this text on baptism, eucharist and ministry to its long range research project "Towards the Common Expression of the Apostolic Faith Today"?*

It is the role of Christ's church to bear witness to its Lord and Saviour to all generations. This role is never changing. But the situation in which the church finds itself is ever changing.

Pluralism marks modern societies. There is a great interaction between religions and ideologies. In the old "Christian world" people are ready to review traditional values, also the heritage of faith. They are faced with new religions and ideologies coming from sources not known to them. In other parts of the world nations do try to define their ideological independence against the rule of the Western culture. In this frame of reference Christians must be careful not to be accused of running errands for alien cultures.

If the churches are to express jointly the apostolic faith, they must face this situation. The main question to ask is: What is the identity of the Christian faith? That question needs to stand alone, not conditioned by any temporal or cultural covering.

The Lima statement affirms that Jesus Christ is the identity of the Christian faith, the Son of God who bids people to follow him and makes them members of himself, nourishes their communion of discipleship and strengthens them for the ministry. The question is, how does this affect the lives of people in a modern society, their worries and fears and also their joy and their earthly blessings.

When the content of the Lima statement is studied, the issue of the relationship between the holy scripture and the tradition in doctrine and worship becomes intrusive, and it is obvious that the churches, individually and mutually, must labour for an answer to that question.

There is a heavy emphasis on the Holy Spirit in all parts of the Lima statement, and it does not hesitate to use the rich images of the Bible about the Holy Spirit and his acts. The church has to pay attention to those images and, above all, be open for the guidance of the Holy Spirit.

The connection between doctrine and worship is affirmed in the Lima statement, which places the confession in the context of praise and adoration. This emphasis is correct in our opinion, and we agree that this should be studied much deeper. We want to point out, however, that Christian praise is an extensive concept and also concerns the moral conduct of Christians in their life situations. With reference to that, one may draw attention to Christian ethics as baptismal ethics.

And last, we want to affirm that the exposition of apostolic faith in the present has to be tailored for Christians in general, not for theologians and scholars only. The vocation to proclaim Christ and spread the kingdom of God is extended to all baptized people, not a few elected ones. At the present time it may be more important than ever before that this vocation be understood by all Christian, baptized people, which makes a strong demand on the educational effort of all churches.

# EVANGELICAL LUTHERAN
# CHURCH IN OLDENBURG (FRG)

## I. Introduction

Constituting as it does part of the one church of Christ, the Evangelical Lutheran Church in Oldenburg seeks fellowship with all Christian churches. Reference is made to this ecumenical purpose in our church constitution. The first fundamental article of this Constitution states: "The Evangelical Lutheran Church in Oldenburg is founded on the gospel of Jesus Christ, its only Lord, as attested in the scriptures of the Old and New Testaments" (Church Constitution, Art. 1 §1). Through the biblical gospel, Jesus Christ as head of the church speaks to all the churches. The more the churches heed this gospel, the more they are drawn together in unity by their Lord and the more they each have to teach each other.

Our church therefore does not cling narrowly to its tradition. The same first article of its Constitution states: "The church accepts its obligation constantly to re-examine its doctrinal position in the light of holy scripture and in doing so to heed the advice and admonition of its brothers and sisters in its own confessional tradition and of other confessions" (Art. 1 §3). In this sense, it recognizes its "joint responsibility for the growth of the one church of Jesus Christ throughout the world" (Art. 2).

Guided by these principles, our experience has been that conversation concerning our Christian faith with other churches in the worldwide Christian family increases understanding of the teaching and spiritual life of these churches and that fellowship with them is strengthened by obedience to the biblical gospel. This experience encourages us, therefore, to test and align all church traditions, especially our own, by the biblical gospel.

The Lima convergence documents on baptism, eucharist and ministry are the outcome of a prolonged study of more than half a century and represent a milestone in the ecumenical movement of the twentieth century. They

---

• 520,180 members, 13 dioceses, 120 congregations, 242 pastors.

reinforce the determination to express the spiritual unity of the one church of Jesus Christ in visible fellowship as well, or at least in a drawing together of all the churches, and so not to regard either the distinctive church order which has developed in our history or the theological and spiritual life of the individual Christian as unalterable.

Our church gladly accedes to the request made by the World Council of Churches and the Faith and Order Commission for an official response to the Lima documents. The text of the Lima documents has been studied by our synod and supreme church council, as the leading organs of our church, and their views are presented below. We recognize the effort made in the convergence texts to base their statements in the witness of holy scripture and to present the various traditions in line with that witness. We therefore recognize the Lima document as an important step along the road to the unity of the churches and gratefully accept it in principle. We are also prepared to accept the three documents even where they employ a language unfamiliar to us even though it has a biblical justification. In what follows, of course, we also draw attention to a number of points on which we find agreement impossible.

## II. Four questions on convergence

In this official response we answer the four questions posed in the preface, to the best of our ability. Since, however, these questions themselves presuppose a conception which is of fundamental importance for the convergence process, we must begin with a few remarks concerning these questions.

1. Firstly, the Commission wishes to know "the extent to which" our church "can recognize in this text the faith of the Church through the ages". Our church recognizes that the Lima documents assemble and weld together many statements which seek to express the faith of the one church of Jesus Christ in different historical situations. But far more important for the ecumenical goal, in our view, is the extent to which it is possible to recognize in the Lima documents the faith attested in holy scripture.

2. The Commission then asks our church "what consequences" it can "draw from this text" (*sc.* the Lima documents) "for its relations and dialogues with other churches, particularly with those churches which also recognize this text as an expression of the apostolic faith". Our church recognizes its duty to engage in ecumenical dialogue with other churches. If the common recognition of the Lima documents is based on the common recognition of holy scripture, relations with other churches will ripen into church fellowship.

3. The Commission next asks what "guidance" our church "can take from this text for its worship, educational, ethical, and spiritual life and witness". Our church owns its duty to hear and heed the advice and admonition of its brothers and sisters in its own and other confessional traditions. For us, the

Lima documents are advice and admonition which prompt us to examine the present ordering of our life and witness as a church.

4. Finally, the Commission asks "what suggestions" our church "can make for the ongoing work of Faith and Order as it relates the material of this text on Baptism, Eucharist and Ministry to its long-range research project 'Towards the Common Expression of the Apostolic Faith Today'". Our main suggestion is this: that in their ecumenical discussions the churches should examine whether it is not essential to differentiate between the few necessary biblically based doctrinal affirmations which make church fellowship possible and the wealth of historically developed and diverse traditions which ought not to hinder church fellowship. In the hope that this distinction will prove possible, our church looks forward eagerly to the findings of the said research project. But, since these findings are not yet available, we consider it premature to give any detailed answer to this fourth question in the next three sections of this response.

### III. Baptism

1. Holy scripture has always been the basis of the church's faith throughout history, even if this basis has not always been equally recognizable in every period. But our church recognizes its special calling from Reformation times constantly to draw the attention of all Christians to this basis.

The convergence text on baptism also appeals to holy scripture (§1). Just as the New Testament itself reflects more than one interpretation of baptism, so too the Lima text sets various interpretations alongside each other. In this way it seeks to reflect the witness of the New Testament as fully as possible.

The question of the relation between baptism and faith (§III) has more than once in church history given rise to theological controversies and even to confessional divisions. The Lima text on baptism is an attempt to produce a statement which the churches can make together. We recognize here the relationship between baptism as a gift of God and faith as a human response (§8) in the sense that faith itself is rooted in the gift of God (§§1 and 2).

2. The text encourages our church to renew its dialogue with Christians inside and outside our church who—like the Baptists, for example—contest the validity of our baptism. The Lima convergence text on baptism can help us here to reflect together on the meaning of baptism and, above all, on the relationship between faith and baptism. The objective should be the mutual recognition of baptism. On the road to this goal, our church has decided not to make the administration of baptism dependent on the candidate's age.

3. The sacrament of baptism is highly cherished in our church. The Lima document can help us to reaffirm this tradition with renewed force in our preaching and in our religious instruction and nurture, and to attend to it in our spiritual life (e.g. regular celebration of the anniversary of baptism).

## IV. Eucharist

1. We welcome the way the convergence document on the eucharist emphasizes the New Testament basis in the section on the institution of this sacrament (§1). Especially important is the description of the eucharist as "the gift which God makes to us" in the church. As with baptism, so too in the case of the eucharist, respecting both its institution and its significance, the convergence document sets different aspects side by side. We recognize here the various interpretations of the eucharist in church history and in the different confessions. Different interpretations need not necessarily be divisive of the church but can be understood as complementary and thereby become a biblically warranted enrichment of our own theology, spirituality and church practice. In the Reformation churches, special emphasis is laid on the dimension of the forgiveness of sins (e.g. in Luther's *Small Catechism*). The importance of other dimensions is coming more to the fore today (e.g. fellowship). The Lima document tries to envision the different aspects not as contradictions but rather as parts of the one celebration.

At two points, however, it is impossible for us to accept the proposed document.

*A. The identification of Christ's intercession and sacrifice with the intercession and sacrifice of the community.*

The Lima document properly refers to the explicit mention of thanksgiving in the words of institution. The description of this as "thanksgiving" or "sacrifice of praise" (§§3,4) is certainly biblical. And although the sacrifice of praise has not up to now been especially emphasized in the Protestant tradition in connection with the bread and wine, thanksgiving is wholly consonant with the gospel and is accepted as an enrichment.

Besides this, the Lima document applies the term sacrifice to the unrepeatable saving work of Christ our High Priest; it speaks of the "sacrifice" as "accomplished once and for all on the cross" or of "the unique sacrifice of Christ" (§§5,8). The biblical doctrine of Christ's sacrificial death and high priestly office has always been central to eucharistic spirituality in the Protestant church.

Finally, the Lima document recalls the intercession of Christ, our High Priest and Advocate, who, according to Rom. 8:34, represents us and saves us from condemnation and, according to Heb. 7:25, intercedes for us that we might be saved and come to God.

But we cannot regard it as biblical:

a) to confuse the intercession of Christians for one another with the saving intercession of Christ our High Priest (§8);

b) to define eucharist as a sacrifice in two senses — in one sense, as sacrifice of praise (§4), in the other sense, as effective sign of Christ's sacrifice on the cross (§§5, 8, Commentary) — without carefully differentiating between the content of the two concepts of sacrifice;

c) to describe the contemporary celebration of the eucharist not only as the offering of God's gift (§2) on the basis of the sacrifice of Christ on the cross (§5) and of his unfailing intercession (§8), but also as the living and effective sign of his sacrifice;

d) to make the efficacy of Christ's sacrifice as God's work dependent on its being celebrated by God's people in a liturgy.

The biblical doctrine of the eucharist knows no sacrifical or intercessory cooperation of the community in Christ's redemptive work. It was for this reason that the Reformation rejected as unbiblical all attempts to define the eucharist as a sacrifice in this sense.

*B. The differentiation between Christ's presence in word and faith and another sort of presence in the eucharist.*

The presence of Christ in the eucharist is developed in the Lima document in two directions.

Emphasis is placed, firstly, on the presence of Christ's body and blood in bread and wine. Secondly, it is pointed out that the church "confesses Christ's real, living and active presence in the eucharist" (§13). Special emphasis has been laid in the history of doctrine and the liturgy on the first of these two directions. Christ's presence in the word of proclamation and in faith was regarded as less real than his physical presence in the elements.

But the biblical doctrine of the Lord's supper puts a stronger emphasis on the personal presence which Christ promises to his disciples even today. Christ's presence in the eucharist, therefore, is his presence as Lord of the banquet to whose table we are invited. The *Leuenberg Agreement* to which our church has given its official endorsement affirms this personal presence of Christ in the Lord's supper.

But we cannot regard it as biblical:

a) to define Christ's presence in the eucharist — i.e. in bread and wine — as unique, real, living and active (§13), true and real (§14) and as such different from the personal presence of Christ in word and faith as if this presence were less real;

b) to connect the invocation of the Holy Spirit not to the community which is celebrating the eucharist but to the elements of bread and wine (§14 Commentary), which thereby "become" and, for the purpose of communion, "remain" something different, so that "Christ's presence in the consecrated elements continues after the celebration" and a communion of the sick with reserved elements is considered as possible (§32);

c) to define the eucharist as "the central act of the Church's worship" (§1) and to insist on its being celebrated frequently and even every Sunday on the ground that this deepens the Christian faith (§§30,31), as if a service of prayer, praise and preaching lacked the centre or the power to deepen Christian faith.

2. The wealth of aspects and dimensions of the eucharist opens our eyes to the tradition in other churches and to imbalances in our own church and encourages us — despite many unhappy experiences — to continue to engage in conversation. We affirm, therefore, the readiness in our own church to offer eucharistic hospitality to all baptized Christians.

3. The Lima document on the eucharist offers stimulating ideas for the ordering of our worship which can enrich our traditional practice (§27). It compels us to re-examine our own liturgical practices; above all, consideration must be given to ways and means of strengthening the understanding of the Lord's supper in our congregations so that it may be more frequently celebrated.

## V. Ministry

1. Our church approves the way the Lima document on ministry begins with the calling of the whole people of God and thereby underlines the fact that the whole church is called to proclaim the kingdom of God. In harmony with the Pauline letters in particular, the Lima document speaks of the different gifts in the Christian community, bestowed on the whole people of God by the Holy Spirit.

The development alongside this of an ordained ministry still corresponds to the practice of many churches today. Our own church, too, has need of the ministry. What is expressed here is the fact that the gospel comes to meet the human being and that the faith created by the gospel is a faith which works by love. This is why our church constitution affirms that congregation and ministry are mutually interdependent (Art. 4 §1). The multiplicity of the church's ministry can be clearly seen in the supra-congregational leadership of the church, in the proclamation of the word and the administration of the sacraments, and in its diaconal service.

Despite this general agreement, we note three points at which our church is unable to endorse the text of the Lima document on the ministry.

### A. *The threefold ministry*

The Evangelical Church regards it as essential that the congregation, as the people of God called to priesthood, should be constantly strengthened in love and obedience to its Lord by the holy scriptures, finding its authority in them and experiencing its unity in them. For the church's life and witness, therefore, the constitutive factor is the gospel attested in holy scripture and received in faith. When, therefore, the congregation holds its communal public services and appoints ministers to lead its worship, what becomes visible in the ministry of these ministers is the witness of the gospel and its unifying power.

But we cannot regard it as biblical:

a) to regard ordained ministry, and not the gospel as attested in the Bible, as constitutive for the life and witness of the church (§8);

b) to relinquish the diversity of New Testament ministries and offices, which express the freedom of the Spirit to order the life of the Christian community, in favour of the threefold ministry which only developed later in the history of the church (§§8,19), and the "claim" of that threefold ministry (§25);

c) to insist on the ordained ministry, instead of on the unifying power of the gospel, as focus (§§13, 13 Commentary, 14, 14 Commentary), expression and means for achieving the unity (§22) of the Christian community;

d) to derive the authority of the minister in the church from the authority conferred in the act of ordination (§15).

All members of the church who live in fellowship with God and together heed the authority of the gospel are called and equipped to confess their faith and to give an account of the hope that is in them (§4). They also have a common responsibility for the ordering of their worship and common life. This comes to expression in the fact that the responsibility for ordering the church's life is entrusted in our church to the congregations and their elected and appointed representatives in the parish council, the district synods and in the general synod. This congregational representation also has the right in principle, therefore, to call or suspend ministers. This presbyterial and synodical constitution, which brings out the calling of the whole people of God and constitutes the basis for the special ministries in our church, and the ministries of church elders (i.e. the presbyters in the New Testament sense) are mentioned in the Lima document only in the margin (§26 Commentary). We consider it essential that the recommendation of Lausanne 1927 should be adopted positively in the efforts to achieve convergence.

*B. The apostolic succession*

The church lives in continuity with the apostles and their preaching of the words and work of Jesus Christ (§34). In the early period of the church, when the New Testament writings were collected and the canon of holy scripture still had to be established, the personal transmission of the ministry of preaching was an important basis for assuring the congregation of fidelity to the tradition of the gospel (§36).

But since the New Testament was finalized and, along with the Old Testament, entrusted to the church as holy scripture, there is no other trustworthy tradition from apostolic times. For us, therefore, the holy scriptures, containing the apostolic preaching, are the source and standard of faith. They alone can help us to maintain the apostolic tradition.

But we do not consider it biblical:

a) to bind the continuity of Christ's mission maintained through the apostolic preaching, to the activity and orderly transmission of the ordained ministry (§35);

b) to assume that a church which lives without episcopal (apostolic) succession but in fidelity to the apostolic faith and its mission lacks the continuity of the apostolic tradition (§53).

## C. *Ordination, proclamation and eucharist*

By ordination, suitable and appropriately trained men and women are declared by the church to be equipped for the leadership of public worship. Part of public worship is the proclamation of the gospel and the administration of the sacraments. The Lima document also rightly stresses that ordained ministers have the task of preaching and celebrating the sacraments (§13).

But we do not consider it biblical when in other places in the document the act of ordination is connected especially with the leadership of the eucharistic celebration (§§14,41; cf. Eucharist §29) and a materially indispensable connection derived from what is actually a later development in church history (§14, Commentary §41).

Since there are biblical and other theological grounds for the full official cooperation of women in the ordained ministry, it is the practice of our church to ordain women. In doing so we have taken a decision in accordance with the gospel and one which we have no wish to cancel. We expect the churches which reject the ordination of women to recognize the ministry of ordained women in other churches.

2. Despite considerable difficulties, even the Lima document on the ministry can stimulate and help us to continue working on the question of ministry with churches of other traditions.

3. The document on the ministry compels us to reflect more deeply on ways in which the various members of our church who exercise an ordained ministry, who are colleagues in the congregation and the wider church or cooperate in elected courts of the church, participate in the three main functions which the Lima document specifies for the church ministry. It can also help us to rediscover the liturgical focus of all church activities.

Oldenburg                                               28 November 1985

# EVANGELICAL CHURCH OF THE AUGSBURG CONFESSION IN THE SOCIALIST REPUBLIC OF ROMANIA

In drafting its official commentary on the convergence document "Baptism, Eucharist and Ministry" of the Faith and Order Commission of the World Council of Churches, the method followed by the Evangelical Church of the Augsburg Confession in the Socialist Republic of Romania was that recommended in the document itself. After an introduction of the genesis of the official comments, and a few general remarks about the reception process of this ecumenical document, there follows the detailed commentary on the three texts on baptism, eucharist and ministry separately, using the four questions suggested in the preface to the Lima document and summarized in the following four headings: (1) agreement; (2) consequences; (3) guidance and help; (4) misgivings and suggestions.

We welcome the appearance of these convergence texts and their contents. They are the fruit of intensive theological work by the Faith and Order Commission over many years, and we regard them as a landmark on the road to the removal of misunderstandings and obstacles in relationships between the churches. We note a considerable number of shared insights and theological affirmations in these texts and also rejoice that they contain guidance to help the churches to overcome the differences which divide them. We accept these texts as a challenge to us to re-examine our relationships with other churches which likewise recognize them as an expression of the apostolic faith. We find in these texts a number of hints and helps for re-examination of our own views of baptism, eucharist and ministry and of our church's worshipping, educational, ethical and spiritual life at certain points. Finally, we also take the liberty of offering to the Faith and Order Commission one or two suggestions for continued work on these texts. These suggestions arise from misgivings deriving from our own theological tradition.

This official commentary is the fruit of a long and arduous reception process. The convergence texts were sent to pastors and other church staff

---

• 135,000 members, 174 congregations, 140 pastors.

and workers. The Lima document and the theological and ecclesiological questions connected with it were frequently discussed in clergy conferences and retreats. Already by the beginning of 1983, the professorial council of the German-speaking Evangelical branch of the Protestant Theological Institute (equivalent to a university faculty) had produced a commentary which was also distributed and widely discussed in the church. At the Interconfessional Theological Conference jointly organized with Reformed, Orthodox and Catholic theologians in November 1984, the questions arising were also discussed in depth with representatives of these churches, and agreed theses were produced. Next, a draft of the official commentary was prepared by the member of the national consistory specifically deputed for this task; comments on this draft were secured from the professorial council of the Theological Institute and the national consistory itself; and the final revised and improved text was adopted by the national consistory at its meeting on 18 December 1985.

The favourable reception of this document was facilitated by the fact that it is based on the ecumenical concept of "reconciled diversity" which has been developed in recent years, in particular by worldwide Lutheranism. We are favourably impressed by the use of the term "convergence text" rather than the term "consensus document", because "consensus" exists only when "churches reach the point of living and acting together in unity" (preface). Where "shared convictions and perspectives" are to be highlighted and further steps towards visible unity are to be ventured, we can rightly speak of convergence. In our view, this attempt to achieve ultimate consensus by following the way of convergences and shared experiences is a golden opportunity for the ecumenical movement; and as such it should be welcomed, and seized with both hands.

In our view too, of course, for the unity of the church it is necessary to have agreement in essential points of belief and the administration of the sacraments in accordance with our Lord's intention in instituting them. According to our tradition, that still leaves room for a variety of ways and forms of expressing and ordering the one truth. Openness to the wealth of forms and perspectives presupposes agreement in the fundamentals of faith. The starting point for all our comments is the apostolic faith as deposited in holy scripture and in the confessions of the Evangelical Lutheran Church of the sixteenth century in general and in the *Confessio Augustana* in particular, which are accepted as legitimate interpretations of the ancient creeds of the church.

### The convergence statement on baptism

*1. Agreement*

We welcome the text on baptism and recognize in it the faith of the church through the ages (as expressed in holy scripture and in the confession of our church). We agree with the variety of New Testament images and statements which are used in the Lima document. The description of infant and adult baptism as equally legitimate options in the church's baptismal practice accords with the official practice of our church. We welcome particularly the recognition that baptism is an unrepeatable act, and the repudiation of practices which could cast doubt on the sacramental integrity of other churches or prejudice the unrepeatable character of the sacrament of baptism (§13, Commentary). We also endorse the significance of water for baptism and the unity of water baptism and Spirit baptism. We also consider important the statement that both infant and adult baptism require a similar and responsible attitude towards Christian nurture and that this by its very nature is never-ending. Acceptance of this standpoint can facilitate the mutual recognition of the different forms of initiation (§12, Commentary).

*2. Consequences*

The common statement on baptism and the mutual recognition of the rite of baptism are the basis of the unity of Christians and the Christian churches (§6) and an eloquent sign for expressing the unity of Christ given in baptism (§15). Among the WCC member churches in Romania the mutual recognition of baptism should no longer present any problem. In order to make this possible for other churches, our church has re-examined certain aspects of its baptismal practice and intends to make these even more conspicuous. They include the replacement of the mere sprinkling of the child's forehead with water, which can easily be confused with the sprinkling with holy water practised in other churches, by the much more distinctive sign of immersion afforded by pouring water over the child. We for our part must declare our willingness to accept expressly the baptismal practice of the other churches, even in those cases where there is already mutual recognition in practice.

From churches which only baptize adults, and endorse the convergence declaration on baptism, we, whose normal practice is infant baptism — though in some circumstances we also baptize adults—expect *recognition* of our normal practice as one possible form of Christian baptism — without repetition of baptism in the event of a transfer of membership from our church to theirs. This also applies to moves to supplement water baptism with a "baptism of the Spirit". On the other hand, greater attention needs to be given to the connection between baptism and repentance (or conversion) which is developed in the Lima document and is too little heeded in our churches. There should also be effort to achieve a responsible baptismal practice which takes into account the significance of baptism for the entire life of the Christian. This was something of great importance to Luther, and in the document it is described as a "life-long growth into Christ" (§9).

*3. Guidance and help*

Our church is challenged by the convergence text to examine its own baptismal practice in the light of its understanding of baptism. One question it will have to ask itself is, which aspects of the nature of baptism have been neglected in its doctrine and proclamation and need to be given a new emphasis? The statements about the connection between *baptism and confrontation*, and the accompanying commentary (§14 and Commentary), where the interposition of a "further and separate rite. . . between baptism and admission to communion" is suggested, prompt us to consider whether children might not approach the altar with their parents and there share in the celebration of the Lord's supper by means of some sort of blessing. We belong to churches which, while they baptize children, do not admit them to holy communion before some such rite has been administered, and perhaps have thereby failed to accept the full logic implicit in baptism. Yet any participation in the Lord's supper prior to confirmation seems inappropriate to our way of thinking.

The convergence text reminds our church of its obligation to aim at *a more responsible practice of infant baptism* (§§16, 21, Commentary §21b). The obligations of the parents in infant baptism must therefore be taken more seriously. The preparatory baptismal interview customary in many congregations should be given more force, and parents encouraged in the course of it to be an example to the children in their own lives and to let them take part in church worship from an early age. There should also be an opportunity of postponing baptism when the pastor is not convinced that the parents are taking it seriously. We should never lose sight of the pastoral responsibility of the ordained minister to the parents.

The list of essential elements in a comprehensive order of baptism (§20) prompts us to recommend to ministers to use for preference the first of the prayers proposed in the service book when conducting a baptism (this is the epicletic prayer, since this prayer includes the invocation of the Spirit as well as the theme of the renunciation of evil. Likewise to be recommended for use at every baptism is the confession of faith in the Triune God (which, in our service book is in brackets in the baptismal questions).

The recommendation that *the meaning of baptism should be explained* in the context of the baptismal service (§21), which is always done in our preparatory baptismal interviews, prompts us to recommend that other opportunities should also be used to explain the meaning of baptism in sermons on certain Sundays of the Christian year (e.g. first Sunday after Epiphany, Low Sunday and the sixth Sunday after Trinity).

The statement that baptism should normally be administered *during public worship* (§23) prompts us to recommend the extension of this practice — which is the rule almost everywhere in our rural congregations — to the urban areas — at least a few times in the year (analogously to the monthly celebrations of the Lord's supper). We are also urged to administer baptism at great festival occasions and recommend the examination of our administrative practice which conflicts with this particular recommendation.

*4. Misgivings and suggestions*

It seems to us that the document on baptism shows a distinct preference for the theology of redemption as liberation, rather than the theology of creation. A greater balance needs to be established here.

For example, in the statements on the meaning of baptism in the light of biblical images and metaphors (§2), baptism is equated with deliverance from bondage on the basis of a contested exegesis of 1 Corinthians 10:1–2. In connection with what is said about the symbolic dimension of water (§18), the commentary states that in some theological traditions the use of water conjures up "positive associations" with life and blessing. It will be necessary to remind people that in the New Testament water is a sign of death (Rom. 6:3f.), which is also indicated in the description of the meaning of baptism (§3), and that baptism is compared in the New Testament with the Flood (1 Pet. 3:20f.).

We believe it would be altogether better to speak rather of adult baptism than of believers' baptism. The use of the latter term in this context contains a view of "faith" which seems to us to be inadequate. Baptism always takes place on the basis of faith. Faith is at once divine gift and human response and its existence cannot be unequivocally determined by human verification.

**The convergence statement on the eucharist**

*1. Agreement*

In testing whether we can recognize in this text the faith of the church through the ages, we note that despite a different — in part fundamentally different — emphasis on how the doctrine and practice of the eucharist are regarded, the basic elements of a Protestant approach are discernible in the text, so that we can accept it unreservedly. We consider appropriate and concordant with our approach the acceptance as point of departure, of the New Testament tradition of the institution of the Lord's supper by Christ himself, and likewise the reference to the meals and feedings of Jesus' earthly ministry, the inclusion of the post-Easter experience of the Lord's presence in the disciples' breaking of bread, and the interpretation of the eucharist as the anticipation of the bridal supper of the Lamb (§1).

We especially appreciate the Trinitarian approach in the description of the eucharist as thanksgiving (to the Father), memorial (of Christ) and invocation (of the Holy Spirit); also the interpretation of the eucharist as the communion of believers and meal of the kingdom of God. This sets the celebration of the meal firmly within the total action of God in creation, reconciliation and consummation. We also welcome the attempt to use the central concept of recollective and anticipatory memorial (*anamnesis*) to settle interconfessional controversies about the sacrificial character of the eucharist. In this remembrance of Christ, the sacrifice accomplished by Christ once and for all on the cross is present and at the same time anticipated reality for us in the eucharist and benefits us as such.

We welcome the emphasis on the activity of the Holy Spirit, since this makes it clear that the church has no control over the gifts of the sacrament but prays for the presence of God. In this connection, we are delighted with the emphasis on the real presence of Christ in the Lord's supper. We thereby affirm our repudiation of any magical or mechanical view of Christ's presence in the eucharist (Commentary §14). Important also, in our view, is the emphasis on the character of the eucharist as the communion of believers, for this aspect has special significance in the tradition of our church (through the reconciliation rite associated with it). We likewise endorse the list of elements in the eucharistic liturgy (in §27), even though some of them are not highly profiled in our own tradition. We also endorse the view that the eucharistic celebration should be led by an ordained minister and that a more frequent celebration of the Lord's supper is desirable.

## 2. Consequences

To the extent that, on the basis of their own tradition, other churches can also approve this convergence text, it is possible to affirm the existence of an affinity of views which, in accordance with article 7 of the Augsburg Confession, permits us to recognize in them too the sacrament of the Lord's supper instituted by Christ. Eucharistic hospitality should be extended to the members of these churches. As occasion offers, negotiations on inter-communion and intercelebration should also be possible, though this still depends, of course, on the question of the mutual recognition of ministries. At ecumenical conferences, too, the eucharist should be celebrated together with members of these churches. These questions should lead to redoubled efforts to promote and intensify the discussion of the question of the recognition of ministries.

## 3. Guidance and help

The Trinitarian approach to the understanding of the eucharist (§2), to which reference was made earlier, prompts us to aim at a more comprehensive view of this sacrament, including also the aspects which fall under the heading of the theology of creation, i.e. to take into account the place of creatureliness and corporeality in the Christian faith. The tendency to concentrate the theological interpretation of the Lord's supper almost exclusively on the second article of the creed needs to be countered by an insistence on this cosmic aspect of the gospel and, specifically, of the Lord's supper, embracing the whole of creation. Even the elements of bread and wine acquire a new significance by the reference of bread and wine to Christ's body and blood, the significance of which as creaturely gifts should not be neglected. The words of §4, according to which "bread and wine, fruits of the earth and of human labour. . . are presented to the Father", prompt us to consider the implications of the fact that, in our own service book of prayers, there is not even a single offertory! This should make us remedy this defect by appropriate changes and the insertion of suitable prayers.

The statements on *anamnesis* (§§5–13) prompt us to reappropriate this concept, which in our traditional reflections has been interpreted quite differently, and in the light of it to rethink the celebration of the Lord's supper, with its foundation in the sacrifice of Christ, thus attaining a broader notion of the idea of sacrifice in the Lord's supper; as that idea also includes intercession (§8) and ultimately the basis and source of all Christian prayer (§9).

The statement (§20) that "the eucharistic celebration demands reconciliation and sharing among all those regarded as brothers and sisters in the one family of God" prompts us to ask whether our reconciliation rite could not also be given a new liturgical emphasis. Further thought should also be given to the significance of reconciliation among the brothers and sisters in the social context.

One of the elements of the eucharist listed in §27 is missing in our order for the celebration of the Lord's supper, namely, the "consecration of the faithful to God". (The sign of reconciliation is, of course, anticipated in the reconciliation rite.) In any development of the prayers in our communion service, we should include reference to the communion of saints and the prayer "Come, Lord Jesus!"

In connection with the point made in the commentary (on §28), that the church has attached the greatest importance to the continued use of the elements of bread and wine, we are prompted to insist that at the Lord's supper only grape wine — and as far as possible good pure wine — should be used.

The affirmation that the Christian faith is deepened by the celebration of the Lord's supper and that this celebration should therefore be more frequent prompts us to continue recommending as in the past — and even more forcefully — the more frequent celebration of the Lord's supper. But if this is to happen it will be necessary to rethink the connection between confession and communion and also to venture new steps in the practice of both.

Finally, prompted by the statements on the practice of reserving the elements (§32), we shall need to reflect on ways of ensuring the necessary care and reverence in the treatment of the elements after the communion service. In the case of our own eucharistic liturgy, this will require the addition of a clear form of consecration of the elements. The fact that the primary purpose of reserving the elements is their distribution to the sick and to others absent from the actual celebration prompts us to attach far more importance to the communion of the sick and communion in the home.

### 4. Misgivings and suggestions

The view of the Lord's supper in the convergence text seems to us to have certain differences of emphasis that are somewhat unfamiliar to us in the Protestant theological tradition, even if they are not opposed to the latter. Whereas Lutheran theology puts the main emphasis of the Lord's supper on the forgiveness of sins, which is mentioned only incidentally in the document (§§1–2), the latter strongly underlines its character as a sacrifice of praise and thanksgiving. This raises the question of the use of the term "eucharist" throughout. It is somewhat unfortunate that this term is used in two senses: on the one hand, for the total liturgical celebration, including the proclamation of the gospel and the administration of the sacrament and, on the other hand, to denote the administration of the sacrament within the setting of Christian worship. Even in our use of words, we should make clear the equal importance and inter-relatedness of word and sacrament. We should not give the impression that the eucharist as sacrament is considered more important than the word, as the convergence text seems to suggest when it speaks of the eucharistic celebration as "the central act of the Church's worship" (§1). Even when our purpose is to give the Lord's supper an important place in the church's liturgy, this should still not imply any unwillingness on our part to maintain the full and due importance of the proclamation of the gospel.

It also seems to us that the section on the real presence (§13) avoids a precise definition of Christ's presence in relation to the elements of bread and wine. In the Lutheran view, Christ's real presence is inalienably attached to the elements in the act of celebrating the Lord's supper. There is a real danger of spiritualizing here and the text should therefore be made somewhat clearer at this point.

Finally, an aspect already mentioned in connection with the text on baptism occurs again in the statements on the eucharist: namely, that in many places the document shows a distinct and one-sided preference for the theology of redemption in comparison with the theology of creation. From this angle, we find the section one-sided which speaks of the eucharist as embracing "all aspects of life" (§20). When it is asserted that "all kinds of injustice, racism, separation and lack of freedom are radically challenged" in the eucharist, it should surely also be affirmed at the same time that the eucharist, as representation of the kingdom of God, a kingdom which can never be fully realized in the world, gives us strength to remain faithful disciples of Jesus, to accept suffering and also to bear those things which we ourselves cannot alter in this world. The statement which affirms that "the grace of God is manifest. . . wherever human beings work for justice, love and peace in the world" (§22) needs to be supplemented also by a reference to the readiness of human beings to bear their cross patiently when need arises. This view is in any event not foreign to the document, as we can see from the passage in the text on the ministry (§34) which includes joy *and suffering* among the permanent characteristics of the church of the apostles.

**The convergence statement on the ministry**

*1. Agreement*

As in the case of the two previous texts, it is also with gratitude and basic agreement that we read the document on the ministry. This third text is of special additional importance because it is recognized that (as already noted in regard to the text on the eucharist) the future of ecumenical convergences in other questions too depends largely on growing convergence of views on the ministry. On the other hand, we are aware that the theological problem of the ministry is not assigned the same status in our own Protestant tradition as is given to baptism and the eucharist, because, unlike these, it is of only limited relevance to faith.

We especially welcome the fact that the statements about the ministry start from the calling of the whole people of God and, indeed, its relation to the Trinitarian communion of Father, Son and Holy Spirit. This calling is also rightly defined as a mission of witness and service in the world (§§4, 17). Laudable, too, is the way the document regains from the tracing back to institution by Christ himself of particular ministries that have developed in the course of history (§11). Even the reference to the public and enduring responsibility for the growth and mission of the church as the basis of the ministry is acceptable, inasmuch as this makes clear its ministerial function in the interests of the gospel and faith which are themselves constitutive for the church's life and witness. We are also grateful for the recognition that the New Testament does not describe a single pattern of ministry and that the church has freedom to develop forms of ministry appropriate to changed circumstances. Happy and helpful, too, for a balanced view of the episcopal office is the presentation of *episkope* under the three aspects: personal, collegial and communal.

The distinction between succession in the apostolic tradition and the succession of bishops (§34 Commentary, §36) as *one* form of succession is also a welcome aid to mutual understanding. Finally, we can go along with the description of ordination as calling, blessing and sending and are grateful for the interpretation of ordination as an act of the whole community and not of a certain order within it (§41). It is especially gratifying that the convergence text should also try to point the direction in which the mutual recognition of ordained ministries could become possible and that this is to be regarded as an explicit aim of the document.

## 2. Consequences

The way crucial statements are made in common about the ministry in this document — despite the differences on the subject that still exist — encourages us to declare our readiness to recognize the ministries of others in so far as these ministries serve the proclamation of God's word and the administration of the sacraments. We declare our support too for the initiation of negotiations with the object of achieving mutual recognition of the church's ministries and including all the ministries of all the participant churches.

We can also state our readiness to reflect on the description of the threefold pattern of ministry as an expression of unity and to examine whether this does not stimulate us to review the understanding and practice of ministry in our own church. Our own tradition seems to us to facilitate such a reflection since it already assigns an important place to an office of presbyter (elders, church fathers) and a diaconal office (in our neighbourhood structures) — though these offices are not ordained ministries. It remains to be seen whether this understanding also permits access to the threefold pattern of the ordained ministry in the sense intended in the Lima document, where presbyter means priest ( = pastor).

### 3. Guidance and help

The document on the ministry undoubtedly furnishes a whole series of hints and helps for the liturgical and spiritual life of our church.

As a church of the word we perhaps need to learn that an interpretation of the apostolic tradition as "pure doctrine" can be an undue restriction and that the apostolic tradition always means the church's form and order too. The concept of the ministry in other churches prompts us to examine whether our view of ministry really corresponds to the apostolic tradition and how far there have been accommodations to contextual needs (§22) in our own church life — such as, for example, improper borrowing of democratic examples and other secular patterns.

On the other hand, to have to deal seriously with what we often think of as the unduly strict distinction between ministry and laity in other theological traditions prompts us to reflect on whether we have not devalued the special responsibility of the ordained ministry, often mistakenly describing it as if there were no discernible difference between its responsibility and that of the unordained members of the people of God — our tradition of high respect for the pastor, who in spite of non-hierarchical community patterns is relatively strictly distinguished from the laity, can help us to move in this direction in our theology too.

Although the hierarchical version of the threefold pattern of ministry is undoubtedly incompatible with our tradition, we are nevertheless prompted to consider ways in which the specific differentia of the various ministries in the church can be more sharply profiled and their different functions more effectively coordinated. That might mean, for example, a greater emphasis on the spiritual nature of some of our so-called "lay ministries": the ministry of our church elders, for example, who have had and continue to have liturgical functions (the lighting of altar candles, the preparation of the eucharistic elements, the carrying of a protective cloth during the distribution of the sacrament, and so on), even though not ordained to this ministry. Consideration could also be given to the significance to be attached to the ceremonies of "induction" into these ministries and to whether — in our Protestant tradition in particular — the difference between these ceremonies and ordination is really as great as all that, since it is certainly here too a matter of calling, blessing and sending (though of course without the imposition of hands). Thus too, we are encouraged so to accept the episcopal office —

which among us is more personal than collegial in character — and in particular its special responsibility for the apostolicity and unity of the church's doctrine, worship and sacramental life (§29), that neither is it regarded as a superior hierarchical grade nor is the collective leadership and oversight called in question, which in practice exists. Similarly, our diaconal ministry, with the mainly charitable and social functions it has assumed in the Reformation churches, should be seen afresh in its spiritual dimensions and steps taken to highlight these.

As a church which has stressed intellectual abilities and a thorough theological training as a criterion in selecting candidates for the ordained ministry, we are, finally, prompted to ask in terms of the Lima document (§11) whether we take sufficient note of the fact that Christ "continues through the Holy Spirit to choose and call persons into the ordained ministry". More emphasis should be given here to the recognition of the gifts of the Spirit mentioned in the document (§§44 and 45) and awareness of the Lord's calling. By the same token, we need also to ask ourselves whether even stronger emphasis could not be placed on spirituality in the preparation for the ministry in our church (§47).

### 4. Misgivings and suggestions

Despite this wealth of agreement, help and guidance, we cannot pass over in silence a number of misgivings in respect both of the underlying approach and certain specific statements in this third text, nor our desire to make some proposals for consideration in future work on this document.

In criticism it must be said that, in view of the difficulty and importance of the problem of the ministry, both theologically and ecumenically, it is hardly possible to develop an interpretation of this theme of ministry independently of our understanding of the church. We need, therefore, a statement on ecclesiology, i.e. an agreed presentation on the nature of the church.

The mission of the church to witness and service is rightly developed in terms of salvation history and the doctrine of the Trinity, but, surprisingly enough, not on the basis of its roots in baptism. Yet according to the biblical witness, it is through baptism that the calling of the whole people of God takes place (Matt. 28.:20ff.).

We would go on to suggest further reflection on the term "charisma". This is defined, on the one hand, as gift, insight and ability (§7c) which are recognized and confirmed by ordination, but, on the other hand, is equated with the ministry itself when this is defined as a charisma bestowed in ordination. It is surely impossible to interpret ordination as the bestowal of a gift.

In basing the ministry on the need of the church for persons "to point to its fundamental dependence on Jesus Christ" (§8) and "to provide a focus for the unity of the life and witness of the church" (§14, Commentary), it is essential to warn against falsely interpreting this to mean that this unity is not constituted by the Gospel itself (Augsburg Confession 7), or that the whole church is not characterized by its fundamental dependence on Jesus Christ. We must not lose sight of the mutual dependence and cooperation which exists between ministers and the faithful. The question arises whether the convergence text does not unduly restrict the spiritual ministry to the ordained ministry.

In our view, it is also impossible in the context of the discussion of the threefold ministry to exclude the question of the office of the bishop of Rome from the ecumenical debate.

Finally, we wonder what is meant when ordination is described as a "sacramental sign" (§41). In the Lutheran view of the sacrament, this could not signify that ordination is a sacrament. Further study of this question is needed since ordination takes place at the command of Christ (John 20:21), with the apostolic sign of the imposition of hands.

Our question, therefore, is whether ordination cannot be regarded as a sacrament, as did Melanchthon for a time.

**Conclusion**

In conclusion we would stress that we welcome the appearance of the convergence texts on baptism, eucharist and ministry and register our support for further work on them, but also for the measures they recommend in the direction of a consensus. We have found in them a model of how common ground can be indicated by the different churches while retaining their different traditions. The Faith and Order Commission's study "Towards a Common Expression of the Apostolic Faith" should be presented in the same way and further steps ventured on the way to unity in this sense. We give God thanks for this document and pray his blessing on its ecumenical consequences.

# EVANGELICAL-REFORMED CHURCH OF NORTH-WEST GERMANY

Dealt with in the declaration of convergence of the Commission on Faith and Order of the World Council of Churches (Lima papers)

The Synod of the Evangelical-Reformed Church of North-West Germany acknowledges with thanks the endeavours of the Commission on Faith and Order of the World Council of Churches to help the Christian churches into a closer community with each other through these convergence declarations.

The Evangelical-Reformed Church of North-West Germany considers itself to belong to the "fellowship of churches which confess the Lord Jesus Christ as God and Saviour according to the Scriptures and therefore seek to fulfill together their common calling to the glory of the one God, Father, Son and Holy Spirit".

It tries to make alive this commitment in sharing the programmes of the World Council, in standing up for justice and peace and in entering into the dialogue of churches described in the Lima texts as a process of convergence.

Since congregational groups, presbyterial sessions and district synods have discussed the declaration of convergence thoroughly, the synod of this church now resolves as follows:

It is only by a new readiness to listen to the Lord of the church and to the sisters and brothers in the One Lord that we can break through our confessional narrowness to come to that ecumenical wideness and openness which Christ demands of us when he stands as our intercessor before the Father: "May they all be one: as thou, Father, art in me, and I in thee, so also may they be in us, that the world may believe that thou didst send me" (John 17:21).

The reception of the declaration of convergence is considered by us as the endeavour not only to discover and identify fundamental coincidences

---

● 200,000 members, 10 districts, 128 congregations, 140 pastors.

among churches in faith and life, but also to question critically our own position in the teaching and practical life of the church.

However, the search for unity does not aim at the wording of a minimal consensus. Special experiences of faith and theological insights should not be levelled out, but introduced into the ecumenical process of reflection. Therefore we consider ourselves to be called to direct critical questions from the Reformed point of view towards the declarations of convergence and to give useful hints for the future cooperation in the ecumenical encounter.

We give our comments on the topics of baptism, eucharist and ministry in the order of the following schedule of questions:
1. In which statements of the declaration of convergence do we recognize important *coincidences* of teaching and practical life of our churches?
2. Which statements of the declaration of convergence challenge us *to review critically* teaching and practical life of our church?
3. Which statements of the declaration of convergence give rise to *critical questions* which should be introduced into the ecumenical dialogue?
4. Which statements of the declaration of convergence are *helpful for the future cooperation* in the ecumenical encounter?


### The declaration on baptism

1. The good biblical exposition of part II, "The Meaning of Baptism", shows clear coincidences with the teaching and practical life of our church. The relationship between "baptism and faith" (part III) is correctly and appropriately described: baptism, as the gift of God, and faith, as the answer of man, belong together inseparably (§§8–10).

2. We are challenged to rethink our way of dealing with baptism, especially by the criticism of the declaration of convergence against a "manifestly indiscriminate distribution of baptism" (§§16 and 21, Commentary).

The preferred performance of infant baptism as a customary church rite inadequately expresses the truth that baptism not only "embodies God's own initiative in Christ", but is at the same time the response of faith made within the believing community" (§12, Commentary). A "life-long growth into Christ" is hardly stimulated (§9). Even the confirmation as the conclusion of pastoral instruction stands in the way of the insight that "there is always the constant requirement of a continuing growth of personal response in faith" (§12, Commentary). It appears as an additional rite which obscures the importance of the unique act of baptism.

The responsibility of congregation and parents for the baptized ones should be realized in a continuous catechumenate that is conducted in all stages of Christian life.

3. Agreeing in principle with the proposed statements on the meaning of baptism (§§2–7) — which is described in the Heidelberg Catechism as a

"visible sign and seal" (Question 66) through which the baptized are "incorporated into the Christian church" (Question 74)—we ask the authors of the convergence declaration whether they really carry through in all expositions the fact that Christ and not baptism is the sole agent of salvation. The question arises, for example, when it is said that baptism "makes Christians partakers of the mystery of Christ's death and resurrection" (§4).

4. When we turn from the divergencies which are still obvious in the performance of baptism and look at the theological statements in the declaration of convergence, we find that these are not only convergent, but even open to a full consensus. They could help—if taken as a frame of reference for other open questions of ecumenical dialogue—to overcome existing divergences in the declarations on the eucharist and ministry. In this sense we can underline the final sentence of §6 "therefore, our one baptism into Christ constitutes a call to the churches to overcome their divisions and visibly manifest their fellowship".

**The declaration on the eucharist**
1. The order of the exposition in the eucharist as: (A) thanksgiving to the Father (§§3–4); (B) memory of Christ (§§5–13); (C) *epiklesis* of the Spirit (§§14–18); (D) fellowship of the believers (§§19–21); (E) celebration of the kingdom (§§22–26); is a convincing description of the Trinitarian structure (A–C) with the present church (D) and the coming kingdom of God (E).

The statements about the eucharist as the "meal of the New Covenant, which Christ gave to his disciples as the anamnesis of his death and resurrection", as "sign" and "anticipation" of the kingdom of God (§1), in which he grants to us fellowship with himself, are biblically well founded. All this shows a high degree of conformity with our teaching, so that in specific cases it still seems possible to overcome remaining disputed points.

2. The comprehensive expositions on the institution and meaning of the eucharist are a helpful motivation for us to recognize and overcome a certain narrowness of our teaching and church life. Cautioning against an "unworthy" participation in the holy supper has led, in the Reformed tradition, to a "wariness of the eucharist" (*Abendmahlsscheu*) which has in many congregations obscured the insight that the eucharist has to be seen as a gift which makes clear that God is concerned about the whole person. We are called to rediscover anew the joy of the Lord's supper which Jesus Christ, who is at once the giver of the feast and the gift itself, offers us in the act of eucharistic celebration. The insight that the eucharist embraces all aspects of life (§§12–21), which is underlined several times in the Lima papers, can liberate us from an exaggeratedly individualistic interpretation of the meaning of the eucharist. However, we will have to learn to draw the consequences from this liberation for church practice: "The eucharistic

celebration demands reconciliation and sharing among all those regarded as brothers and sisters in the one family of God and is a constant challenge in the search for appropriate relationships in social, economic and political life." "As participants in the eucharist, therefore, we prove inconsistent if we are not actively participating in this ongoing restoration of the world's situation and the human condition" (§20).

3. On the background of our basic consent and in connection with some questions addressed to us, we do have questions to be directed at the declaration on the eucharist. If "God himself acts, giving life to the body of Christ and renewing each member" (§2) — how can a sacramental celebration itself "communicate(s) to us God's love in Jesus Christ" (§1)? How can it be said about the institution of the eucharist: "Its celebration continues as the central act of the church's worship" (§1) — even though the same Lord reveals himself through the gospel in preaching, in baptism and in the eucharist to his congregation?

Even though we consent to the statement "the whole action of the eucharist has an 'epikletic' character" (§16), it seems questionable to us, considering the biblical testimony, to call down the spirit on the elements (§27).

4. The connection of sacramental celebration and the recognition of our mundane responsibility according to the gospel, as underlined especially in the declaration on the eucharist, seems to be both essential and helpful for growing ecumenical fellowship. This is because it leads us to view the oikoumene as interconfessional dialogue about doctrinal questions just as much as it is a serious commitment for peace and justice, and to recognize and practise in a new way the unity of witness and service.

### The declaration on ministry

1. Under the heading "The Calling of the Whole People of God" the declaration on ministry explains in part I, in a Trinitarian order, how God calls (§1), Christ renders freedom, forgiveness and love (§2), and the Holy Spirit sanctifies persons and preserves the church. The paper points in a convincing way to the kingdom of God (§4), and the variety of talents in the congregation (§5), and thus describes the full fellowship which the churches have in view of their origin, their essence and their mission.

In the basic sentences of this first part it is said "that all members are called to discover, with the help of the community, the gifts they have received and to use them for the building up of the church and for the service of the world to which the church is sent" (§5). The same idea can be found in the 1934 Theological Declaration of Barmen, where Thesis No. 3 says: "The Christian church is the congregation of brothers (and sisters) in which Jesus Christ acts presently as the Lord in Word and sacrament through the Holy Spirit."

2. Starting from the statements of this first basic paragraph we begin by asking questions directed towards the concrete situation in our church: Is the

role of the ministry in our church really thought of within the framework of the "calling of the whole people of God"? In reality we have — in spite of sound biblical and reformational insights and the evoking of the Barmen Theological Declaration — a pastors' church (*Pastoren-Kirche*) where the church people are not only guided spiritually by their ministers, but very often intellectually patronized by the ordained incumbents of their parish.

In our church the "proportion of the gospel" and the "sharing of communal life" — and not the apostolic succession — are fundamental (§35). Not yet clarified is the question whether a singular ordination should be valid for a variety of commissions, or whether ordination should be repeated when a new commission in the church is being accepted.

Our concrete church life is put into question by descriptions of the task of the congregation like these: members of the church "are to identify with the joys and sufferings of all people as they seek to witness in caring love. The members of Christ's body are to struggle with the oppressed towards that freedom and dignity promised with the coming of the kingdom" (§4). We are reminded by these words of the comprehensive service of the Christian congregation put in words by the Barmen Theological Declaration: "As Jesus Christ is God's assurance of the forgiveness of all our sins, so in the same way and with all seriousness he is also God's mighty claim upon our whole life. Through him befalls us a joyous deliverance from the godless fetters of this world for a free, grateful service to his creatures. We reject the false doctrine, as though there were areas of our life in which we would not belong to Jesus Christ, but to other lords — areas in which we would not need the justification and sanctification through him" (Thesis 2).

3. On the basis of the fundamental explication of the calling of the whole people of God, we question the statement on the ordained ministry also in another way. In this paragraph we find sentences like these: "The church lives through the liberating and renewing power of the Holy Spirit" (§3). If this is correct, then with what right can it be said about the ordained ministry that it is "constitutive for the life and witness of the church" (§8)? Christ himself is, according to his promise, present by word and spirit in the assembled congregation. Where two or three are gathered in his name, he is there among them (Matt. 18:20). He himself gathers, protects and preserves the congregation chosen from the whole human race for eternal life through his spirit and word (Heidelberger Catechism, Qu. 54).

The fundamental insight that the whole people of God are chosen to serve God is not carried through in the statements about the ordained ministry. In spite of various references to the "active participation of all members in the life and decision-making of the community", which should be underlined clearly (§27), the ordained ministry is given an undue emphasis over against the community. If the Holy Spirit himself donates to the fellowship various complementary gifts (§5), if the Holy Spirit unites those who follow Christ in "one body" (§1), is it really fitting to say then that the ordained office bearers have to gather and guide the scattered people of God as shepherds? What is gathered and united into one body by the Holy Spirit cannot be scattered (§11)!

The clarification offered in the text: "The New Testament does not describe a single pattern of ministry which might serve as a blueprint or continuing norm for all future ministry in the Church" (§19), is not given due consideration in the expositions on the "forms of the ordained office". The ministry, as developed in the ancient church, experienced not merely an extension of functions, but also a new quality over against the community. The bishop was now seen in an opposite role to the congregation, which finally led to the idea that he alone and exclusively was in possession of the fullness of the sacramental power of consecration, and able to authentically hand on the apostolic succession (§§35–36). In spite of some restricting remarks, the paper accepts this type of ecclesiastic office as standard. The questions we have to ask towards the various forms of the ordained office are not aimed mainly against the threefold structure of the ministry and the functions connected therewith. These forms can be found in the Reformed tradition too. We ask about the evaluation of these roles: are these functions of equal rank, or are they connected with a hierarchical order presupposing various levels? According to Reformed understanding the ministry in the church — which certainly has to be structured according to different functions — should not be filled by members of the "clergy", but by the duly appointed members of the people of God. As pastors, elders, deacons and teachers they are provided with equal rights and take care collectively at the local level of the presbyterial administration of the church. On the larger scale the same duty is ascribed to the synod for a community of congregations.

According to the declaration on the "Forms of Ordained Ministry" synods and councils have no right to exercise supra-congregational or supra-regional leadership functions. They are merely permitted to assemble to express "the collegial and communal dimensions" (§27). Only the bishops are recognized as "representative pastoral ministers of oversight, continuity and unity in the church" (§29).

4. In contrast to the attitude of the authors of the paper, the collegial rule of persons of equal right seems to us to be the most fitting form in which the "calling of the whole people of God" is made real, and in which the service entrusted and commissioned to the whole congregation can be realized in the most appropriate way.

We stress this point not only because of the biblical insight we have gained and the traditions from which we come, but also in view of many free churches sharing these structures and of the World Council of Churches itself, which has developed the vision of church unity in the form of a "conciliar fellowship of churches".

In order to reconcile the widely divergent understandings of the ministry we accept as helpful what is said in the convergence document itself: "As they engage in the effort to overcome these differences, the churches need to work from the perspective of the calling of the whole people of God" (§6).

26 April 1985

# NETHERLANDS REFORMED CHURCH AND REFORMED CHURCHES IN THE NETHERLANDS

BEM has spread throughout the whole world and churches from various origins and confessions have studied it as a valuable contribution towards the overcoming of disagreements.

The Reformed Churches in the Netherlands together with the Netherlands Reformed Church have prepared a response. In it one finds considerable appreciation, though no secret is made of the fact that questions still exist especially on the part of the "Gereformeerd" tradition.

## Unclear issues

From the introduction of the Lima texts it appears that the World Council has offered a *convergence text* with the intention of stimulating *consensus* in the churches. The relationship of these concepts to each other is, however, not always clear. It is suggested that the churches seeking a *visible unity* should be in basic agreement with each other. Mention is made of an *ecumenical process of reception* and the search for *universal consensus*. *Promising convergences*, indeed even significant theological convergences in various areas have been reached. But this does not alter the fact that difficult questions that still divide the churches have not been solved. Indeed they have not or hardly been looked into (e.g. the Pope and his cardinals, female

---

● NRC: 2,700,000 members, 1,800 parishes, 1,775 pastors. RCN: 844,427 members, 823 congregations, 1,168 pastors. This text has been prepared following separate treatment in the general synods of each church. Both churches had nominated a committee of theological and ecumenical experts to introduce the BEM text to the different assemblies. Both synods decided to give a common response. The general synod of the NRC then asked the boards for church and theology, for relations with other churches, for liturgy, for catechism, for the relation of church and Israel, and for the diaconate to draw up the "hervormde" contribution. In the last stage, three sessions were held of an ad hoc committee in which four theologians of the Reformed Churches participated. The final proposal of this committee was dealt with in the synods of both churches separately in spring 1986. Both churches agreed with the proposed final text.

ministry, the ministry of those who are not theologically trained and do not work full time).

The questions which are asked of the churches are consensus questions aimed at a gradual *reception* of the texts that are suggested in the report. The members are asked what consequences they see in the text for their relationship and dialogue with other churches. Especially important is whether they can see these as an interpretation of the Apostles' Creed. The churches are also asked to what degree they will allow themselves to be led by the Lima text in their liturgy and in their catechetical, ethical and spiritual life and witness.

RCN and NRC have interpreted the questions asked by Faith and Order in such a way that they expect an answer to the question if and to what degree the suggested convergence texts could stimulate a return to visible unity in the community of churches.

**Translation problems**

Certain key words in the report are difficult to translate accurately because they do not have a Dutch equivalent. The English word eucharist can be translated with the Dutch words "eucharistie" and "avondmaal"; the word ministry by both "ambt" and "dienst". Those people who are busy studying and assessing the reports should therefore carefully investigate the correct interpretation of the words that are used. Otherwise there is the danger that the report will be misunderstood and as a result the contents misjudged.

But there is more to it than this. The word eucharist literally means thanksgiving. However, in ecclesiastical and theological discussions such as those held in the World Council, the word has a much broader meaning. It not only denotes the Supper of the Lord, but word and Supper are seen as an indivisible whole, "the eucharist, always *including both word and sacrament*, is the proclamation and celebration of God's work" (§3, italics ours). Words and their usage are not as innocent as is sometimes supposed. By defining "eucharist" as the indivisible whole of word and sacrament, a twofold decision has been taken:

— in accordance with early Christian practice proclamation of the word and celebration of the supper form a whole which must not be divided;
— the report looks at the worship service from the viewpoint of the Lord's supper in particular; therefore the worship service as a whole has a sacramental character; for that matter this second decision need not necessarily flow out of the first.

**Questions concerning Israel**

In the reading and studying of the Lima documents, the question could arise as to whether justice has been done to the unity of scripture. Biblical arguments are taken exclusively from the New Testament and as a result no special theological attention is given to the continuity of God's people in the

Old and the New Covenant. Those who take the Old Testament seriously and as a result of the dialogue with Israel are prepared to read the New Testament as having its origin in the Old Testament, will begin to see interconnections which were previously hidden and will encounter questions which, in the light of the BEM report, cannot be ignored. One could imagine, for instance, that the meaning of the fact that the supper of the Lord was instigated in the framework of the Jewish Passover could be further investigated, and that the offices of prophet, priest and king used in the Old Testament could be looked at when dealing with the structure of the church's ministry.

**Agreement on baptism in the Netherlands**

This is not the first time that our churches are preoccupied with the questions of baptism, Lord's supper and ministry in an ecumenical context. In the sixties representatives of four Reformation churches (NRC, RCN, Evangelical Lutheran and Remonstrant) began a discussion with delegates from the Roman Catholic Church episcopacy about the possibility of recognition of baptism in each other's churches. These discussions were bilateral and resulted in four agreements on baptism between the episcopacy and each of the four Reformation churches (1968–1974).

The discussion in which the Dutch "Hervormd" Church was involved resulted in agreements which were concerned especially with the manner in which the baptism would take place (running water) and the *scriptural Trinitarian formula* that would be used with it. The discussion between the episcopate and the "Gereformeerde" Churches in the Netherlands resulted in an agreement on a number of biblical-theological assumptions which indicate the saving reality of baptism — baptism is a sign and seal of the unique covenant with the Triune God. As a result the connection between baptism and the church community becomes manifest and also the relationship between cleansing with water and purification by the blood of Christ. Other matters which also came up for discussion were the position of the person administering the sacrament, the limits to private baptism, whether baptism as incorporation into the body of Christ cannot be repeated, and the possibility of transition from one church to another. The discussion between Roman Catholics and Lutherans gave the consensus greater liturgical depth because both churches signed each other's form for baptism.

The episcopate showed some reservation with regard to the administration of baptism in the Remonstrant Fraternity because of the Trinitarian formula. If this is lacking the baptism is not recognized.

The recognition of baptism led to a renewal of the baptismal community in the Netherlands between the Roman Catholic Church and a number of churches from the Reformed tradition. This was done on the basis of a few documents which paid more attention to formal than theological and liturgical criteria. This applies to the agreement between the Dutch "Hervormd" Church and the episcopate in particular. To a lesser degree it applies to the agreement in which the "Gereformeerde" Churches in the Netherlands and the Evangelical Lutheran Church were involved because the former requested attention to the covenant as foundation of baptism and the latter wanted attention given to the liturgical form used in the administration of baptism. These agreements have had effect. Examples of "twofold baptism", as was suggested in 1964 when Princess Irene was accepted into the Roman Catholic Church, have not occurred again, as far as we know. The mutual recognition of baptism by the churches has helped towards the formation of a kind of *baptismal community* whose significance may not be underestimated. An example that can be given is that the bishops, in the solemnization of a mixed marriage, carry out a different policy of dispensation when a baptized member of one of our churches is involved than when a Roman Catholic marries a non-baptized non-Catholic.

### Declaration on the ecclesiastically mixed marriage in the Netherlands

Although the discussions on the ecclesiastically mixed marriage in the Netherlands that resulted in the drafting of a communal declaration of the Roman Catholic episcopate on the one hand and four Reformed churches on the other (NHK, GKN, Rem. Br., Ev.Luth.) fall outside the framework of the Lima reports, we would still like to note that this discussion also resulted in a settlement that was operative from 8 May 1971. The declaration assumes that the mixed marriage qualifies as a "marriage in the Lord" (see §3 of the Declaration). Despite the existing differences, the churches are convinced that these marriages are a communion with the Lord (preamble of the Declaration). During the wedding ceremony the non-Catholic partner is involved in a Roman Catholic sacrament which he/she offers to his/her partner. Within the framework of the Lima reports it is not necessary to describe in detail what the consequences for the restoration of the church community would be if two estranged churches are prepared to carry the responsibility together for the (performance), the solemnization and the blessing of a marriage between two people who come from different church backgrounds. One should still be mindful of the fact that not only convergence in baptism, Lord's supper and ministry open the way towards more communion between the churches, but also agreement on the ecclesiastically mixed marriage.

### Discussions on the Lord's supper and ministry in the Netherlands

Not only baptism, but also the Lord's supper and church ministry have been the subject of extensive and searching discussions in the Netherlands between representatives of the Roman Catholic Church, six Protestant churches and the Old Catholic Church. The results can be found in two communal statements on "The Celebration of the Lord's Supper" and "Church Ministry".

In the statement on the *Lord's supper* it was noted that a number of biblical concepts can clarify its meaning, namely: the supper in Israel, its place and socio-religious dimension; the relationship between the day of the Lord and the Lord's supper; invocation of the Holy Spirit (*epiklesis*) through whose sanctifying power the past becomes a present reality (*anamnesis*); the prayer for the coming of God's kingdom (maranatha); ministry to the other and to the world (diakonia).

As thoughts and reflections on the subject of *ministry* developed, an obvious convergence of thought became apparent. One can note the following: the service of Jesus Christ as origin of church ministry and at the same time its boundary and permanent standard; the congregation as the people of God; the unique ministry of the apostles which cannot be repeated; the missionary character of ministry; the apostolic succession as being in substantial agreement with the tradition of the apostles, which found concrete shape in the New Testament as a commission to the whole church and especially those people in office. In the apostolic succession, therefore, the aspect of content is never divorced from the personal aspect nor the personal aspect from the aspect of content. Those in agreement with these statements will not speak disparagingly about the apostolic succession, nor will they feel the need to make the legitimacy of office dependent on an unbroken chain of ministries that should be historically provable.

### Response to the Lima texts

If one compares the first part of the Lima report about *baptism* with the agreements on baptism that were made in the sixties, then one can conclude that "Lima" has added important biblical-theological ideas to the agreements on baptism that were realized in the Netherlands. Baptism is called incorporation into Christ, entry into the New Covenant, sign of the new life through Jesus Christ, participation in Christ's death and resurrection, renewal by the Holy Spirit, etc. It is true that there is no further elaboration of the covenant relationship between God and man in the way that "Gereformeerd" Protestant circles deal with it and this is a pity. On the other hand the Lima report obviously does not intend to present a complete theology of baptism.

The description in the Lima report of the relationship between faith and baptism with its implications for church practice is in concordance with the contents of a report on baptism by the Dutch Council of Churches in which representatives from our churches also cooperated. It suggests that the symbolic character of the water during baptism demonstrates the participation of the one who is being baptized in the death and resurrection of Jesus Christ.

If one reads the Lima reports against the background of the reports published in the Netherlands then a marked congruence strikes the eye.

The paragraph on baptism in the Lima report is biblically and theologically more profound than the agreements on baptism made in the Netherlands. Even though the covenant theme, which does occur in the Lima report (see §1), does not play a leading role here, the point is whether that which is strongly professed regarding the redemptive function of baptism is not sufficient to restore the baptismal community. RCN and NRC are of the opinion that that which is strongly professed regarding the redemptive function of baptism is sufficient to restore the baptismal community because the faith of the church through the ages is recognizable in as much as it was based on the books of the Old and New Testament. Therefore, those churches which recognize the faith of the churches in this can acknowledge the baptism of the other and so the baptismal community can be restored and/or supported.

The reports made in the Netherlands also show a noticeable congruence with the results of the study by Faith and Order in relation to the *Lord's supper*. There are six scriptural/theological pillars on which the Lord's supper rests:

— the supper is placed in a wider framework together with the other meals that the Lord shared with his followers;
— preaching and celebration are indivisibly joined together, even though the BEM report puts more emphasis on the Lord's supper than on the preaching of the word;
— the uniqueness and unrepeatable nature of Christ's saving work in his birth, life, death, resurrection and ascension into heaven clearly emerge;
— during the celebration itself, remembrance (*anamnesis*) joins believers with the salvation brought about in Jesus Christ;
— the Spirit is described as the one through whom we can share in the saving gifts of the Lord who is present at the celebration of the Lord's supper;
— the Lord's supper is placed within the perspective of the kingdom of God.

The theological reflections of the Lima report on the subject of the Lord's supper rest on these six pillars which show a remarkable convergence with a number of biblical starting points that are fundamental to the "Gereformeerd" tradition. One thinks especially of the uniqueness of Christ's saving work and the unrepeatable nature of his offer. In addition one thinks of the position and work of the Holy Spirit in the sacrament. Those who are serious about the freedom of the Spirit, whose presence is called for, should no longer be preoccupied with the moment and the manner in which Christ reveals his presence in the gifts of bread and wine. Those who profess the uniqueness and unrepeatable nature of Christ's offer, will acknowledge that answer 80 of the Heidelberg Catechism cannot be applied to those who agree with the relevant passage in the Lima report.

Two additional observations can still be made. One could ask oneself whether justice is being done to the basic structure of the holy scriptures when at the congregational gathering preaching is seen as part of a sacramental activity. Does not the word go into the making of the sacrament? Does it not precede the celebration as a matter of principle? One should ask this question in the realization that in our tradition many people do not really see the sacrament as an instrument of salvation that feeds our faith and enriches life. Many people have only come to see something of this saving activity of the sacrament in their contact with Catholics, just as many Catholics have only come to realize the importance of the preaching of the word for one's religious life as a whole in their discussions and communal celebrations with Reformed Christians. In this matter there are obvious differences of emphasis between Reformed, Roman Catholic and Orthodox spirituality. But these are not so important that they should still block the way to communion.

The second difference in emphasis is contained in the cosmic interpretation that the Lima document gives to the celebration of the Lord's supper. The eucharist is called the supreme thanksgiving to the Father for all that he has done in creation, redemption and salvation . . . (§3). It is the supreme offer of thanks spoken by the church on behalf of the whole of creation. Reformed Christians cannot easily express themselves in such a way about the celebration of the Lord's supper. Here the Lima report has taken over ideas that are borrowed particularly from Eastern Orthodox spirituality. To our ears they may sound speculative because, leaving the preaching of the word aside, it gives the eucharist worldwide dimensions. This does not mean, however, that there can therefore be no communion at the Table. Also for Reformed Christians it is an established fact that salvation through Christ reaches beyond the borders of our earthly life in time and space. But we must beware here of speculations that proceed beyond the scriptures.

If we compare the basic theological ideas of Lima in the paragraph on the Lord's supper with the reports on the eucharist and the Lord's supper which were prepared in our country in the framework of the Council of Churches in the seventies, then once again the conformity in the basic theological position and biblical spirituality stands out. At that time our churches were very positive about the concept agreement that was drafted, in the assumption that a foundation was being prepared "for a communal celebration of the Lord's supper and as starting point for the development of other church activities" (Gereformeerd answer). It appears to us that this section on the Lord's supper which corresponds so well with the theological assumptions which are regularly to be found in our own tradition would make a good basis for the renewal of communion in the Lord's supper on the way to ecclesiastical unity.

The section on ministry in the Lima report gave many Protestant readers a pronounced "Catholic" impression. This is especially due to the substantial attention given to questions about continuity, succession and consecration. The section as a whole puts emphasis on a number of items which would normally not be of decisive importance for Protestant churches, while on the other hand all sorts of typically "Protestant" problems—such as for instance a non-hierarchical office structure or the specific service of the congregation member — get no attention or at least very little.

For this reason it is remarkable and gratifying that at the start the report tries to develop the biblical idea of the vocation of all of God's people as the presupposition for all that follows. The election of Israel (§1) and the life of the church, which is based on Christ's victory once and for all over the powers of evil and death (§2), precede the duties of the office bearer which are determined within the congregation. Thus it is stated: if the churches want to overcome these differences (that is with regard to ministry) then they will have to start with the vocation of all God's people (§6). This forceful introduction, however, does not lead to a convincing convergence. The report does make a serious attempt to break through a classical deadlock in the ecumenical discussions by adopting a middle course between the historical episcopate on the one hand and the rejection of any structural connection with tradition on the other. This attempt does not succeed, however, mainly for two reasons.

The most important reason is that the historical development towards a generally more acceptable pattern of ministries, in particular towards the threefold office of bishop, presbyter and deacon, gains a normative influence which a historical development should not be given. As a result the suggestion, that the threefold ministry be accepted as an "expression of the unity we seek and also as a means of achieving it" (§22), takes on a surplus value which then makes its acceptance more difficult. The normative influence of historical developments is decreased, it is true, by observations about other ways of discharging one's ministry (§§22, 32–33) and about the necessity of looking critically at the actual functioning of the threefold model (§§24–27); but the dominant thought behind the recognition of ministry remains the communal bond with a historical fact.

There is a second reason why one cannot speak of a convincing convergence and that is because a hierarchical ordering becomes apparent in the development of the threefold model of bishop-presbyter-deacon, especially where the tasks of ministry are described (§§28–31). The possibility of explaining the threefold model as three tasks that could be distinguished in the different systems of ministry – also "Gereformeerd" – is removed in the report itself because a hierarchy is introduced in the job description. Admittedly the importance of both sides amplifying the personal, collegial and communal dimensions of ministry is stressed (§§26, 27) – an important passage for the ecumenical discussion. In the rest of the report, however, these corrective remarks are not maintained to a degree that the opportunity arises for a non-hierarchical concept of ministry which emphasizes the relationship with colleagues and community, as is the case in the "Gereformeerd" tradition. If that had been the case, then there would also have been a place for the elder and deacon who take part in the work of session and other meetings for office bearers.

Summarizing it can be said that the section on ministry did not remove any of the real barriers that block the road to communion and unity between the churches. In order to achieve that there will need to be more definite pronouncements on the normativity of historical developments and the meaning of non-hierarchical forms of ministry. In addition questions such as the universal Petrine ministry and (especially) the admittance of women to office can no longer be left out of consideration.

**Summary and conclusions**

The RCN and NRC greatly appreciate the work done by Faith and Order that, after sixty years, has led to the drawing up of a report which has really contributed to the renewal of communion between the churches. The committee greatly appreciates and often agrees with the biblical/theological starting points which are contained in the introduction to each section of the report.

The inclusion of the theme of covenant in the report on baptism would have made it more meaningful for the "Gereformeerd" tradition. With regard to the theological reflection on the meaning of the Lord's supper, Lima has managed to connect the various church traditions by putting the emphasis on anamnese and epiklese.

The indissoluble bond between word and sacrament, preaching and celebration in the eucharist (§3), which Lima assumes, should be seen as a lesson for *all* traditions. In this one should see the *word* as anterior (not superior) to the *sacrament*. For the word constitutes the sacrament (Augustine).

In the section on ministry the charismatic character of the congregation is not consistently recognized, nor is justice done to the pluriform nature of the ministry which is in agreement with that character.

Historical developments should never be seen as normative, no matter how venerable they have become by their age (§22). In the continuing discussion between the churches, special attention should be given to the following points:

— the position of God's people in the election of office bearers;
— the position of the elder, deacon and session in church life;
— women as office bearers;
— ministry for a limited term;
— non-local representation of office bearers (primate of the bishop of Rome).

**It was decided to send the following answer to the questions posed by Faith and Order**

In the reports on baptism and eucharist we are pleased to recognize fundamental elements of the church's faith through the ages. Even though our churches, in some cases, would have put the emphasis differently or would have used different terms, we regard these reports as a stimulus towards further development of our understanding of the church and as a good starting point for discussions about this material with other churches. In the report on ministry we discovered less of these fundamental elements. It is true that the report offers important viewpoints which could be constructive in developing our understanding of ministry and our ecumenical contacts (given the fact that our churches do not have a detailed conception of ministry), but it does not show sufficient progress in the fundamental points of discussion. Therefore we cannot accept it, as we did the other reports.

For many years already our churches have been involved in interchurch discussions which take place in the framework of the Council of Churches in the Netherlands. The results have shown that our churches are drawing closer together in the expression and experience of faith with regard to baptism, Lord's supper and ministry. Especially the mutual discussion with representatives of the Roman Catholic Church has led to convergence on very important issues. These discussions will be continued.

Both the Dutch "Hervormde" Church and the "Gereformeerde" Churches in the Netherlands have set up working groups, both nationally and locally, which study developments and issues in relation to liturgy, catechism, ethics and missions. A few of these working groups have included the text of the Lima reports in their programme of study and will try to make them usable by the congregation (e.g. in the liturgy).

Our churches believe that it is very important that the Lima texts on baptism, the Lord's supper and ministry be of use to the Commission on Faith and Order in the work it is doing on the study "Towards the Common Expression of the Apostolic Faith Today". They would like to make the suggestion that in the above-mentioned study an attempt be made to do justice to the Old Testament, the Jewish background to the New Testament and the present Jewish tradition. They hope and expect that the work done by Faith and Order will result in increasing communion between the churches, on the road to unification.

# EVANGELICAL CHURCH OF CZECH BRETHREN

## Introduction

The 23rd synod of the Evangelical Church of Czech Brethren (1983) expressed its gratitude to the Faith and Order Commission of the World Council of Churches for its efforts to express the faith of the church on baptism, the Lord's supper, and ordination; it accepted the Lima text as the basis for conversations at all levels of the church and recommended that work-meetings of preachers and presbyters representing all the presbyteries be organized where the text would be the subject of concentration. This stimulated a consultation which took place 15–19 April 1985, in Chotěboř. It placed before the synod its evaluation of the Lima text.

The interest aroused by the text both here and around the world testifies that the questions it deals with reached a broader perspective than would have mere specialized material on the problematic of baptism, the eucharist, and ordination. In the ecumenical community the document from Lima is recognized as an outstanding contribution on the way of the church towards internal integration and unity.

However, if it is to serve in this sense, we are convinced that it should neither omit nor weaken a complex of great consequence which for us are the ministries of the word and the questions relevant to it; among these belongs the question of the authority of the scripture and its relation to tradition in the church. (The notion "apostolic faith" itself is regarded as dependent in principle upon biblical criteria.)

We affirm the effort towards a united church which the "documents of ecumenical convergence" desire to serve. We understand this unity as a fellowship of Christians under the word and at the table of the Lord and as a missionary and diaconal ministry of the church in the sense of Jesus' words "that they may all be one; even as thou, Father, art in me, and I in thee, that

---

• 240,000 members, 271 parishes, 288 preaching stations, 246 pastors, 35 lay preachers.

they may also be in us, so that the world may believe that thou hast sent me" (John 17:21). This understanding grows out of our indigenous Reformation traditions and from our current situation. Reformation churches in Czechoslovakia had a special sensitivity for the question of power (Chelčický), which relativized any kind of clericalizing Constantinian notion of Christian universalism. The approach of the Czech Reformation is once again actual today in a situation of radical secularization where we are discovering anew the missionary purpose of the church.

The Chotěboř consultation produced a document which was distributed to all the congregations of the Evangelical Church of Czech Brethren and whose text we present here.

## Baptism

We are grateful for those places in the Lima text which aid in clarifying complicated questions. Among them belongs the formulation that the Holy Spirit is at work before, in and after baptism.

Likewise we welcome the introduction of motifs in the notion of baptism which for us, until now, had been obscured for one reason or another, and the calling to mind of those domestic traditions which had been either forgotten or distorted.

In this way the emphasis on the cosmic range of Christ's work challenges us to a deeper study of the scripture as it is attested to by the symbolism of water in baptism. The mention of renunciation, which belonged to our Reformation tradition but which has not been preserved, leads towards the biblical consideration of the reality that the one baptized enters into the space of the government of the Holy Spirit, where the power of evil and forces opposing God (Eph. 6:12) are broken. Through personal commitment and the responsibility of faith, the baptized points towards the rebirth and liberation of all creation. The text underlined for us as well the eschatological scope of baptism to which the Bible testifies. This correlates with the understanding of baptism as the implanting into the body of Christ, which is more than individual piety. And that leads to the placing of baptism into worship which enables the congregation to recall more often the covenant which baptism signifies. With grateful joy we accept the call for mutual recognition of baptism.

We are of the opinion that confirmation (§14) is not a sacrament or rite which could be interposed between baptism and the Lord's supper to make baptism complete. For us confirmation has its place in the catechetical and pastoral ministry to children in the church.

With all gratitude to the Lima document, we believe that in the testimony of the scriptures, there is more emphasis on the fact that baptism is the real incorporation of an individual into the people of Christ (1 Cor. 12:13). The people of Christ, however, is not a mystical/invisible entity but a concrete congregation. In representing the congregation, the presbyters (a question to the presbyters should not be missing from the formulation of baptism) and the godparents (the witnesses of the baptism) bear responsibility for the one baptized and their function in the missionary church takes on a new meaning. The responsibility of the congregation towards the one baptized lies not only on the level of pastoral care, but in the real fellowship of faith as such. In that way faith confessed during baptism (or following it) loses the character of a mere personal confession and the subject of baptism and the congregation becomes the living Christ attested to in the witness of the scripture.

In a society where the number of those who were not baptized in childhood forms an obvious majority, a catechumenate directed towards baptism receives a new relevance. We would take it as valuable assistance if the Faith and Order Commission could provide for an exchange of experiences in this area, which is an outgrowth of the missionary task of the church.

The question of the conditions for recognition of baptism performed in charismatic (pentecostal) groups by the unordained is becoming pertinent for us.

The use of water in baptism requires clear biblical substantiation and kerygmatic clarity if it is to be well understood in faith as a sign. Similarly this applies to the use of other symbolic forms which signify the gift of the Spirit, and these are questions we want to deal with.

### The Lord's supper

Our conversation on the chapter on the Lord's supper brought us to the hope that motion towards unity implied by the text has the promise of the Holy Spirit and will lead us forward. The Lima text places before our eyes what a wealth of expressions of faith Christ fills the church with at his table. In agreement with the document, we can testify that also in our churches through discussions of its theses and through our recently published agenda, this wealth is becoming a reality. An underscoring is in order here of the pneumatological, koinonical and eschatological character of the Lord's table, the missionary motive (§§23, 24, 26), just like of the Trinitarian framework in which the eucharist is set.

The Lima text proceeds from patriarchal traditions which are not very common in our church. It understands the celebration of the Lord's supper as the "central act of the Church's worship" (§1), while in our tradition the centre of worship is the resurrected Christ; the word and sacraments for us are only "things ministerial" — the word as the source of faith, the sacraments as faith's reinforcement (Brethren Confession 10:3; 11:2, 3).

We accept the text as it deals with the eucharist as a valuable enrichment and a challenge to examine a number of significant questions according to the norm of the scriptures and their central message: justification of the sinner by faith and grace alone on the basis of Christ's perfect sacrifice. Christ is and remains the subject of the eucharistic feast; he himself is present in it (§6), he himself is acting there (§7). We are grateful that the treatise sees in the Lord's supper "the sacrament of the unique sacrifice of Christ" and points out that God does not repeat that which was according to his intention realized "in the incarnation, life, death, resurrection and ascension of Christ. . . . These events are unique and can neither be repeated nor prolonged" (§8). However, we would ask if the formulation which follows, that "in the memorial of the eucharist, however, the Church offers its intercession in communion with Christ, our great High Priest", does not place into the hands of the church something which belongs to Christ alone. Reformation faith is extremely cautious to make sure that the perfection and singularity of Christ's sacrifice be neither obscured nor diminished. The above-mentioned remark about the *anamnesis* and offering of intercessions of the church can lead to such obscurity. As Calvin so emphatically reminds us, a life of sacrifice and praise can be the only response from the human side (Heb. 13:16). However, the centre and core of the Lord's supper remains the once-and-for-all sacrifice of Christ.

The text points out that the crucified and resurrected Christ, glorified and seated at the right hand of the Father to whom he intercedes for us, is present at the eucharist. Here it would be necessary to clarify biblically (particularly from the Epistle to the Hebrews) the relation of faith in Christ who is interceding on the right hand of God in the historical event and once-and-for-all sacrifice of Jesus of Nazareth.

We welcome the calling of the "anamnesis of Christ" the very content of the preached word and eucharistic meal; we share the opinion that sermon and sacrament reinforce each other and that the celebration of the Lord's supper has every right to include the proclamation of the word (§12). We agree that "faith is required to discern the body and blood of Christ" (§13). All of this enables us to draw closer to our Catholic brothers and sisters and to overcome the consequences of the stringent language of the Heidelberg catechism (par. 80) on the mass.

We are enlightened about the nature of the presence of Christ in his supper by the New Testament exposition of the notion *soma* as "person" and *haima* as "the pouring out of life". According to this, the content of the confession about the body and the blood is the personal sacrifice of the life of that Jesus Christ who is present at his table as Lord. We recommend that this biblical approach be adopted as the point of departure for a common interpretation of Christ's presence at the eucharist. It would enable the problematic of "elements" and all those dogmatic and philosophical notions connected with it, with which our forefathers from patristic times to Neo-Orthodoxy attempted to grasp the nature of the eucharist in categories suitable to their age, to be put aside. The centuries-old debate about transubstantiation and the permanence of the presence today appears irrelevant if we bear in mind that Christ's presence is given to the congregation in the entire feast and not only in its elements. We welcome commentary 13 of the text which is headed in that direction: "The deepest reality under the signs of bread and wine is the total being of Christ, who comes in order to feed us and transform our entire being".

All of this culminates in the formulation "the bread and wine become the sacramental signs of Christ's body and blood" (§15), which corresponds with the nomenclature used here in the sixteenth century by the Unitras Fratrum.

We hold as adequate the witness of the scripture that the Lord's supper is the gift of fellowship with Christ and with each other (§19). This union anchored in the Holy Spirit and expressed in *epiklesis* liberates not only the individual from concentration on himself, but puts the local congregation into the one church of Christ.

In our situation we relate the portions concerning the results of the eucharist for life in the world mentioned in §20–§25 and §26. It seems particularly important to us in a situation where humanity and all creation are endangered. Likewise valuable is the remark that division in the church seriously weakens its service to the world, especially its missionary ministry (§26).

We understand the reference to the saints and martyrs (§11) as a reminder to the triumphant church and would have rather placed it into part D "The Eucharist as Communion of the Faithful". The motif of the new covenant, only cursorily indicated in §11, in the above-mentioned context should be duly broadened on the basis of the New Testament.

Our discussions underscored the clear tendency to celebrate the Lord's supper more frequently. In our church the decision concerning this is in the hands of the elders of the congregations.

The fact that the communion "under both kinds" is taken for granted in the text is for us, who live in the country where the question *sub utraque* was raised for the first time in the Middle Ages and led to difficult spiritual struggles, encouraging and hopeful evidence on the way to convergence.

### Ordained ministry in the church

We have concurred that the text on "ordained ministry" is also beneficial for the way towards convergence. The question of ordained ministry is complicated not only because of the number of various forms of ministry which have developed historically, but also and in particular because of the unequal theological import attributed to ordination in individual traditions.

Together with the authors of the document we are convinced that the most profound basis of ministry of the church and ministries in the church is the movement of God in Christ towards all of humanity for its salvation (§1–4). That provides the normative direction for the form of ordained ministry in the church. Its aim is not the preservation of the church nor its rule over the world, but rather the kingdom of God to which we refer by the Christlike ministry of proclaiming the gospel and works of love. We fear that the point of departure clearly expressed in the introductory paragraphs is not sufficiently respected in further formulations about special ministries, and so one gets the impression that building up the body of Christ (*oikodome*) and the unity of the church are the most innate aim of the ordained ministry.

In concurrence with the witness of the New Testament (for example, Eph. 4:7ff.) we emphasize that the resurrected Christ himself calls people to the ministry when he imparts special gifts of the Holy Spirit (charisms). The church, and that means a concrete community, acknowledges this initiative of the Resurrected One, recognizes the appropriate charisms of individuals, and confirms this with ordination. Only after that fundamental presupposition of the ordained ministry can the four criteria enumerated in §8 follow.

The diversity of charisms in the church, however, extends beyond the range of ordained ministries. The call to the ministry, as the text emphasizes (§4), applies to all of God's people and no act of service should be underestimated because it does not receive ordination (§5). This mutuality (complementariness) of charisms is strengthened by the bonds of love. It guards against the presumption of bearers of ordination and edifies the body of Christ.

The number of individual ministries already attested to in the New Testament for the diverse environment of the apostolic church points out to us that the forms and structures of ministry of the church and in the church are dynamic and flexible, however always in such a way that they remain forms of service, not control, and contribute to the unity, not the division of the people of Christ.

We are grateful for the statement that ministry in the church has not been dependent only on ordained workers, but that "there have been times when the truth of the Gospel could only be preserved through prophetic and charismatic leaders" (§33). The entire church and its ministers should be attentive to these charismatic manifestations, for through them the resurrected Christ keeps the church in spiritual motion.

We accept the document's invitation to have understanding for other types of ordained ministries in the church, especially for those which in certain historical situations proved themselves stable and thus contributed to the maintaining of unity. Nevertheless, in our situation we see that it will be necessary to consider new ways and forms of ordination in the church, suitable to the activity of the Holy Spirit in a missionary situation. However, we are not able to suggest any ready-made model.

We are thankful that in the interest of convergence the document omitted mention of some elements which have divided and do divide Christians: the hierarchical arrangement of ordained ministries, papal primacy, the essentiality of apostolic succession for the validity of the sacraments, and the definition of ordination as a sacrament. We find helpful the remarks on the three methods of carrying out ordained ministries: personal, collegial, and communal (§26).

In the following paragraphs we would like to indicate how our church community could contribute to the ecumenical discussion of these questions.

While for us the point of departure for church ministry is the local congregation, if we understand it correctly, the Lima document concentrates more on the questions of ministries in the church.

We raised the question over the right of the designation "priest" for ordained ministry in the church. Although the commentary on §17 has clarified some obscurities, we are still apprehensive that the application of this designation might overshadow the unique priesthood of Christ and the common priesthood of all Christ's people. (We understand the priesthood of all people as their commission to the self-sacrificial ministry of witness, confession, and prayer.)

We think that the threefold ministry in church (§19 and so on) is in some way preserved in a number of churches where the terms bishop, presbyter, deacon are not so-called explicitly, or in cases where these terms are applied with meanings other than those found in the Lima text. For example, in Czechoslovakia the ministry which we could call *episkopé* is carried out personally (the synodal senior, the seniors), collegially (synodal council, the seniorate committees), and communally (the synod, convents). At the same time we gratefully accept the remarks of the texts that its unconditional component is also concern for unity.

We have become aware of the fact that here in our country the primary place of the ministry of the diaconate should be returned to it, as referred to in §31: what is involved is a ministry of love to the needy and lonely in the congregation and the constant reminder of the fact that the church is called by the Lord to minister to the world.

We appreciate the attempt to solve the complicated problem of succession divided on the one hand as apostolic tradition and on the other as the succession of apostolic ministry. We share the conviction expressed in §34 that to apostolic tradition belongs the witness to apostolic faith, the proclamation and fresh interpretation of the gospel, celebration of the Lord's supper and baptism, the transmission of ministerial responsibility, communion in prayer, love, joy and suffering, service to the sick and needy, unity among the local churches and the mutual exchanging of gifts the Lord bestows on each.

Concerning apostolic succession, we are grateful that it is not conceived as the only sign of unity and the apostolicity of the church, let alone as its guarantee (§38). This enables a greater understanding among churches which hold to apostolic succession of the episcopate and those who conceive of it as the transmitting of apostolic faith. For us the sign of this apostolic succession is the scripture and early Christian creeds; through them we are joined with the church of all ages and all places. We are glad that the new translation of the Bible into Czech brought about the cooperation of the three types of Christian church.

Regarding the ordination of women, which our church adopted over three decades ago, the 23rd synod in 1983 evaluated the experience gained from it like this: "This synod expresses its gratitude that it has been bestowed to the church to recognize that in Christ there is 'neither male nor female' in proclamation of the gospel. The synod expresses its joy that a number of sisters have entered into this ministry and that congregations are thankfully receiving it." However, we do not believe that before adoption of this policy the ordained ministry in our church was incomplete (commentary on §18).

In conclusion we cannot refrain from saying that in the text from Lima we missed a statement similar to the very instructive passage from Accra (1974) about the mutual recognition of the ordained ministry which would doubtless be helpful in clarifying these complicated questions in our congregations.

*A supplement of the theological advisory committee of the Synodal Council on the Lima text about ordination*

The historical development of the presbyteriate from the "college which surrounded the bishop" (§20) to the "leaders of local eucharistic communities" (§21) is described correctly in the Lima text without a doubt. However, for us the question arises whether or not it was a fortunate development. It led to the bishop's being deprived of the college of presbyters and to a presbyter's being without a college in individual communities. And so there was a shift from collegial to monarchical administration which burdened the church for a long time and stifled the consciousness of Christian community (congregation) as a fellowship. Therefore we hold the re-establishment of a college of laity as representatives of local congregations in Reformation churches (under the name of the presbytery, among others) as a step of indispensible renewal, which should be an inspiration for other churches as well.

24th Synod
20–23 November 1985

# WALDENSIAN EVANGELICAL CHURCH OF THE RIVER PLATE (URUGUAY)

**Introduction**

The Lima text on "Baptism, Eucharist and Ministry" (BEM) was received by the Waldensian Board which in turn sent it on to the congregations and presbyteries for study in accordance with synodal mandate 31/89/84. The Waldensian Board had previously appointed an Advisory Committee to study the document in depth. We should point out that we did not have the text in Spanish; we had to make our own translation. The text in Spanish only reached us in the middle of 1984, from Argentina.

By mid-1984 only a few congregations and presbyteries had made a study of it and for this reason the company of pastors (CP) postponed its final analysis in the hope that a larger number of congregations might be able to study it and present their reports. Finally at its February 1985 session the CP studied it in depth and nominated a committee to draft the final report to present to the European area of the Waldensian Church and to the World Council of Churches.

**General considerations**

Among the negative aspects we note that only a limited number of communities and presbyteries made a study of the document. Basically there are two reasons for this: (1) a language that proved difficult of access not only for the community but also for the more qualified of its (lay) leaders; (2) linked with this was its content. The community considered that it is a text for "specialists", which is explained by the fact that it is an internal ecclesiastical document dealing on the whole with matters internal to the church community and lacking connection with external reality, especially if the situation in Latin America is borne in mind.

Nevertheless we must emphasize the positive elements that the document possesses. In the first place we consider that it represents an excellent attempt

---

● 15,000 baptized members, 24 parishes and 49 local churches, 18 pastors.

at mutual understanding and mutual recognition of baptism, eucharist and ministry by the WCC member churches. Secondly, it is a valuable endeavour to remove the mistaken ideas, prejudices, taboos, which we have in regard to one another. This enables us to see ourselves as we are and reconsider our own thinking on the matter.

Finally, the text marks an important milestone in ecumenical discussion and understandings, and challenges us to continue along the road to unity and cooperation between the churches. We are conscious that the road still lies ahead and that it is a long one.

### The text on baptism

Looking at the three documents as a whole, we find that this is the most acceptable, and in general terms could be accepted by our congregations.

At any rate we think we must note the positive and negative aspects of the statement. In §1 we note a tendency to give more weight to the tradition of the church than to its basis in the gospel. The endeavour appears to tend to give grounds for the *institution* of baptism rather than base it biblically and theologically. In that same respect, the reference to Matthew 28:18–20 seems to be introduced to safeguard its Trinitarian formula. Apart from the fact that biblical criticism tells us that these final verses of Matthew are of later origin within the primitive community, it is clear that the emphasis of the text does not fall on baptizing, nor in the words of the Trinitarian formula, but on the *make disciples*.

If we relate this with §3, we see that the text falls into the danger of mechanicism, that is, of asserting that baptism operates independently of the person baptized. "Baptism unites the person baptized with Christ and with his people" (§2); we affirm that it is not the action in itself, but baptism *responsibly assumed* that unites the person with Christ and with his people.

We regard as very important the statement in §5: "The Holy Spirit is at work in the lives of people before, in and after their baptism. . . . The Holy Spirit nurtures the life of faith in their hearts until the final deliverance when they will enter into its full possession, to the praise of the glory of God."

In §22 we consider the term "normally" to be unfortunate and that it should be removed.

### The text on the eucharist

We concur with the statement of §1 that the eucharist is a gift, but we think that the passage in 1 Corinthians 11 speaking of Paul receiving something from the Lord, does not refer to the sacrament but to the teaching which he now wishes to share with the other believers of his time.

Paragraph 2 appears to make statements which lead to a mechanical conception (as we have already noted in the previous document), in affirming: "In the eucharistic meal, in the eating and drinking of the bread and wine, Christ grants communion with himself. [It is] God himself [who] acts [in the eucharist]. . . "

We note as important the statement in §5 that the eucharist is "the memorial of the crucified and risen Christ. . . accomplished once and for all on the cross and still operative on behalf of all humankind". Likewise, when it adds (§8): "What it was God's will to accomplish in the incarnation, life, death, resurrection and ascension of Christ, God does not repeat. These events are unique and can be neither repeated nor prolonged."

What we cannot accept is the Commentary to §8 when it says that "there is only one expiation, that of the unique sacrifice of the cross, *made actual* in the eucharist and presented before the Father in the intercession of Christ and of the Church for all humanity", because the sacrifice of Jesus Christ cannot be actualized, made actual, but only recalled (*anamnesis*), and it cannot be said that the church can "present", "offer" anything to the Father, but that it is God himself who offers in Jesus Christ and it is the church that receives and is sent to bear witness to Jesus Christ among other people.

On the other hand we reaffirm the statements that "in Christ we offer ourselves as a living and holy sacrifice in our daily lives. . . this spiritual worship, acceptable to God, is nourished in the eucharist. . . " (§10). "United to our Lord and in communion with all the saints and martyrs, we are renewed in the covenant sealed by the blood of Christ" (§11).

In §13 we again meet with a dangerous absolutization of the eucharistic sacrament by attributing a mechanical value to it. The passage appears to indicate that if everything is done in accordance with the liturgical text and the right words are uttered ("This is my body. . . " etc.), the real living and active presence of Christ will take place. The presence of the community and the necessity for faith appear to be relegated to a secondary plane.

Within the document as a whole we consider that the chapters on "The Eucharist as Communion of the Faithful" (§§19–21) and "The Eucharist as Meal of the Kingdom" (§§22–26) are the most successful, and express our own understanding of this sacrament. From them we stress the statement of §20: "The eucharistic celebration demands reconciliation and sharing among all those regarded as brothers and sisters in the one family of God and is a constant challenge in the search for normal relationships in social, economic and political life. . . All kinds of injustice, racism, separation and lack of freedom are radically challenged when we share in the body and blood of Christ. . . As participants in the eucharist, therefore, we prove inconsistent if we are not actively participating in this ongoing restoration of the world's situation and the human condition." And what it adds in §24: "Reconciled in the eucharist, the members of the body of Christ are called to be servants of reconciliation among men and women and witnesses of the joy of resurrection [whose source is the resurrection]." Consequently: "Insofar as Christians cannot unite in full fellowship around the same table to eat the same loaf and drink from the same cup, their missionary witness is weakened at both the individual and the corporate level" (§26).

On the other hand we cannot fail to express a query about the kind of eucharist presented by the order outlined in §27. All the elements of Christian worship are included in it, from which we conclude that it is something different from the biblical Lord's supper alone.

We do not like §29 as a whole, especially when it describes the function of the ordained minister in the eucharistic celebration and states for example that he is "the ambassador who represents the divine initiative and expresses the connection of the local community with other local communities in the universal Church". The paragraph implies that the presidency of the eucharist is exclusively the function of the ordained minister; furthermore, neither the ordained minister nor anyone else who presides at the eucharist can "represent the divine initiative", but only, as we have said, preside at the celebration.

Finally, we express a doubt in regard to the terminology. Why is the word "eucharist" used, which refers to only one aspect of the celebration, and not even the most important, instead of other words which better express the meaning of the action, for example, "Lord's supper"?

**The text on ministry**

In general terms we consider that this is the most controversial text of all and the one which presents most problems for our Church.

Nevertheless we must express our complete agreement with the first chapter "The calling of the whole people of God" (§§1–6), and so we fully share the biblico-theological basis which is given for the ministries. What is being defined here, in different words, is the universal priesthood of believers.

Our main disagreement emerges with the second chapter, especially with the concept of "focus". In §8 it is said that "in order to fulfill its mission the Church needs persons who are publicly and continually responsible for pointing to its fundamental dependence on Jesus Christ", which is certainly the case; but we cannot accept the rest of the sentence: "and thereby provide, within a multiplicity of gifts, a focus of its unity", and still less the statement: "The ministry of such persons, who since very early times have been ordained, is constitutive for the life and witness of the Church." The ordained ministry cannot be the "focus for the unity of the life and witness of the community" (Comm. 13), because the only possible "focus" is Jesus Christ.

We regard as inadmissible the statement (§14) that: "It is especially in the eucharistic celebration that the ordained ministry is the visible focus of the deep and all-embracing communion between Christ and the members of his body." The document itself acknowledges (Comm. 14) that "There is no explicit evidence [in the New Testament] about who presided at the eucharist", although it immediately adds that: "Very soon however it is clear that an ordained ministry presided over the celebration."

Further on it is said (§23) that "a ministry of *episkopé* is necessary to express and safeguard the unity of the body". Again we think it a strained proceeding to arrive at the unity of the church by way of acceptance of the ministry of the bishop. Even less can we accept the statement that: "Every church needs this ministry of unity in some form in order to be the Church of God. . . ." (§23). We do not find in the New Testament a single word that would support this assertion; on the contrary, it appears that it was when emphasis was laid on one of these important ministries that dissensions in the community arose (cf. 1 Cor. 1:10–17). Unity will exist precisely when we understand that all barriers, hierarchies, differences must disappear when we have put on faith in Christ Jesus (Gal. 3:26–29; cf. Mark 10:35–45; Matt. 20:25–28).

We note §17, too, as valuable in affirming that in virtue of the unique sacrifice of Jesus Christ for all, "All members are called to offer their being 'as a living sacrifice' and to intercede for the church and the salvation of the world. Ordained ministers are related, as are all Christians, both to the priesthood of Christ, and to the priesthood of the Church." We are in complete agreement with the Commentary on this §17 in maintaining that "the New Testament never uses the term 'priesthood' or 'priest' (*hiereus*) to designate the ordained ministry or the ordained minister." Consequently we cannot understand — or accept — that later on this commentary itself maintains: "In the early Church the terms 'priesthood' and 'priest' came to be used to designate the ordained ministry and minister as presiding at the eucharist." What does this mean? That the "early Church" is of "greater theological weight" than the New Testament? Nor can we accept the explanation that in regard to the terms priesthood and priest used in this sense — and their alleged biblical basis in Romans 15:16 — the "meaning differs in appropriate ways from the sacrificial priesthood of the Old Testament, from the unique redemptive priesthood of Christ and from the corporate priesthood of the people of God" (Comm. 17). Since the coming of Jesus Christ there are only two possible meanings of the term, that applied to Jesus Christ himself (Heb. 7:22–28) and that referring to the whole body of Christ (1 Pet. 2:9). There is no biblical basis for attempting to establish a difference between the ordained ministry and the people of God in terms of "priesthood" and "priest".

The same duality of criteria is applied to the forms of ordained ministry by the statements (§19) that "The New Testament does not describe a single pattern of ministry which might serve as a blueprint or continuing norm for all future ministry in the Church. In the New Testament there appears rather a variety of forms which existed at different places and times." We affirm our complete agreement with this and our endorsement of its biblical basis. But immediately it is added that: "During the second and third centuries, a threefold pattern of. . . ordained ministry became established throughout the Church." This statement and what follows is the basis for the option for the threefold pattern of bishop, presbyter and deacon to the detriment of other possible forms. (We must make it clear that we are not opposed to the threefold form of the ministry, seeing that in general terms it is our own system, but it seems to us that excessive emphasis is laid on the importance of the "threefold" pattern, giving the impression that it is a model that all churches should adopt.)

We must, however, be fair to the text, which itself counterbalances these statements by affirming (§§32–33) that a variety of charisms are manifested in the community and that in the history of the church there have been persons who played an important part who did not fall within the threefold pattern (the only important remark we have to make on these paragraphs is: what have the religious orders to do with variety of charisms, §32?). It is even pertinently stated (§23) that: "the ordained ministry, which is itself a charism, must not become a hindrance for the variety of these charisms." We consider that this is the correct procedure: to affirm the variety of charisms, in accordance with the operation of the Holy Spirit, and on that basis to define the type of ministry appropriate to the reality of each church, since ministry has an "instrumental" function, not an "indispensable" one, as the text maintains. For that amounts in fact to trying to "put the cart before the horse". We conclude that in view of the importance of these two paragraphs, they should be placed at the beginning of the text where it presents the theological basis of ministry.

Chapter IV on "Succession in the apostolic tradition" refers to a number of interconnected concepts which need to be clarified separately and their inter-relation made plain.

In regard to the apostolic tradition it states (§34) that: "The Church lives in continuity with the apostles and their proclamation. . . The Spirit keeps the Church in the apostolic tradition until the fulfilment of history in the Kingdom of God." It is defined in the following terms (§34): "witness to the apostolic faith, proclamation and fresh interpretation of the Gospel, celebration of baptism and the eucharist. . . etc." We are not going to enter into the age-old controversy about "tradition", but we do express our agreement with the characterization of the apostolic church (which is here defined as "apostolic tradition").

Where we must express our disagreement is in regard to the Commentary to §34 when it maintains that: "Within this apostolic tradition is an apostolic succession of the ministry which serves the continuity of the church. . . The ministers appointed by the apostles and then the *episkopoi* of the churches. . . testified to the apostolic succession of the ministry which was continued through the bishops of the early Church. . ." How can it be inferred so easily that: "Within this apostolic tradition is an apostolic succession of the ministry", that is to say, that the evangelical purity of the church is made to depend on the institution of the ordained ministry and not on the gospel? In §36 both are mentioned, together with the "life of the community", but the importance attributed to the ordained ministry — to the detriment of the other two — is clear and obvious as "a powerful expression of the continuity of the Church throughout history" (§35).

Apart from the reserves already expressed, we have a formal query to raise here. We assume that the commentaries express the opinion of some churches and/or persons, but that when no majority consensus was reached among the authors of the final text, they ended up as they are, namely a commentary on certain sections or paragraphs which does not have the same status as the former. If this is so, why as we read §§34 and 35 do we find a dissonance produced by the introduction of the concept "apostolic succession through the ordained ministry"? Was it because this concept was not accepted by all, and consequently is incorporated as a commentary but nonetheless conditions all the succeeding paragraphs? We affirm indeed that an apostolic church exists, the "marks" of which are well indicated in §34, but its "continuity" (we prefer this term to that of "succession") is expressed by fidelity to the gospel of Jesus Christ in its witness and work as proof of the action of the Holy Spirit.

As regards "ordination" (Chapter V), we consider that an exaggerated role is attributed to the church. The church prays to God, commends, but it is the Holy Spirit who provides and ordains, and always acts freely. The church cannot control or orchestrate the action of the Holy Spirit.

We regard as very pertinent the statement that the act of ordination signifies "an act of the whole community and not of a certain order within it" (§41), but we cannot accept the use of the term "sacramental sign" (§41). What does this mean? That the ordained ministry is raised to little less than the rank of a sacrament (cf. §43b)? It seems to us that §44c is the most appropriate and correct statement that can be made on the subject, and consequently we wholly subscribe to it.

Finally, in regard to the mutual recognition of the ordained ministries (Chapter VI), we find two recommendations. Churches which have not retained the form of historic episcopate have maintained "a continuity in apostolic faith, worship and mission. . ." (§37) and for this reason the other churches are asked to "recognize the apostolic content of the ordained ministry" of these churches (§53a).

On the other hand, the churches which have retained the episcopal succession maintain it as "a sign, though not a guarantee, of the continuity and unity of the Church" (§38). (Isn't there a contradiction between this and the expressions "powerful expression" — §35, and "serving, symbolizing and guarding" — §36?) The churches which have not retained it "may need to recover the sign of the episcopal succession" so that "the continuity with the Church of the apostles [may find] profound expression in the successive laying on of hands by bishops. . ." (§53b).

We cannot accept this because, in short, what is being asked is that the churches without episcopal apostolic succession should accept it so that they may feel themselves profoundly identified with the church of the apostles.

To conclude our comments on the document of ministry, we wish to express our approval of the first chapter on "The calling of the whole people of God" (§§1–6) in which a biblical and theological basis is given for the ministry of all believers in relation to "the building up of the Church and for the service of the world to which the Church is sent" (§5). We think that this chapter should be followed by the section on "Variety of charisms" (§§32–33).

On the other hand, however, we find that from §7 onwards the text concentrates its attention on the ordained ministry in its "threefold" form, narrowing it even further to the function of the bishop. Continuity with the church of the apostles is made to concentrate (or "focus") in an institution — the ordained ministry — and not in Jesus Christ who, through the Spirit, "keeps the church in the apostolic tradition until the fulfilment of history in the Kingdom of God" (§34), as the text itself affirms.

**Final remarks**

We once again emphasize what we consider to be the most valuable aspects of the text. It compares the various traditions and theological conceptions, showing where they coincide and reach agreement and where differences persist. It expounds their views and biblical basis (on the other hand we must note that the depth of exposition of this basis is rather uneven).

In its turn it suggests concrete steps to advance along the road to unity, in pursuit of the goal of "the common expression of the apostolic faith today". We think that the aspects which deserve attention have been indicated in our analysis of the three documents.

As regards questionable aspects, we have already lingered over them, especially when examining the text on ministry. We think we made our dissent plain there, so that it is unnecessary to repeat it.

We wish, however, to put some queries which arise for us and the reflections they prompt.

In the first place we notice that BEM frequently resorts to expressions such as "the earliest Church", "the early Church", "very soon, since very early times". At first sight the references are quite vague, but if we link them with the analysis we made of Commentary 17 and §19 (especially) of the text on ministry, we shall see that it is not so. There is a clear reference to the church of the second and third centuries and not just to the early church (first century), that is to say to the sub-apostolic, not the apostolic period. This leads us to think that greater theological weight is attributed to an ecclesiological criterion (the theologico-institutional form of the church of the third century) than to the biblical basis (the various "ecclesiologies" which may be found in the NT). We consider that the choice made by the text is not the most correct.

This leads to our second question. Why choose the church of the third century as ecclesiological model? The text itself implies that in that period the church became defined institutionally in regard to functions exercised within the community and the exercise of authority. This occurred in response to heretical movements that arose within the church; in other words, the church sought internal consolidation.

We presume that the choice and use of the church of the third century as model in the text is in line with the intention to seek in our time a church which will not be monolithic but can present "internal unity" in relation to its mission. It is true that Christendom is deeply broken and that it is necessary that "all may be one in order that the world may believe. . ." (cf. WCC motto).

The Lima text, however, points in a direction which we do not think is the most correct one, and accordingly we put our questions, which concern two basic points.

1. The three documents are imbued with a spirit which we for our part consider "excessively sacramentalist" (we emphasized this in dealing with the texts on baptism and eucharist). Our disquiet goes further still. Is the sacrament as it is celebrated in our churches in itself a Christian concept? Should there be two or seven sacraments? Was it the intention of Christ and the primitive community to establish rigid celebrations? Or, was the spirit that animated them not rather the creation of "signs" than of "sacraments" (and what is to be thought of the washing of the feet. . .)? Should we not today also leave the spirit free to give rise to other "signs" which would express the unique sacrament which is the life and death of Jesus Christ? We consider that it is in this direction, opening out spaces and paths for the expression of faith, that the church should advance, and not go narrowing and stereotyping the classical rutted tracks.

2. The question of the "focus". Behind the emphasis on the ordained ministry and concentration on the bishop and the apostolic succession, we suspect that there stands the problem of "authority" within the community. Even if there is no undervaluation of the function of the assembly of believers, we see that much emphasis is laid on the role of the ordained ministry in regard to governance and administration of the sacraments and pastoral functions generally.

On the other hand, §§41 and 43b of the statement on ministry attract our attention. Is it the intention to raise ordination to the rank of a sacrament? Would we have in the not very distant future a hierarchical church with three sacraments in which the ordained ministry would subsume and condition the other two? Is this the model which the text is projecting for the future? We do not think so, but we wish to call attention to the general approach which is being given to the discussion of these themes which are so important for the life of the church.

We do not want to conclude our contribution solely with criticisms and doubts, but with an affirmative tone. As the Waldensian Church we are engaged in the same project as the other member churches of the WCC: to seek ways to unity with the sole purpose of bearing witness to the coming kingdom of God. Consequently the important thing is to announce that kingdom rather than to consolidate and affirm the church, which is only an instrument for attaining that goal. In this perspective the internal structuration and the administration of the sacraments cannot be made uniform and imposed on all the churches, for they are only means to an end, and as such, exist in relation to the mission of the church in a given situation and epoch.

At the root of Waldensianism is the affirmation of a "poor, weak church" profoundly critical of any kind of "constantinianism". That means that the Church cannot depend on external political support or a hierarchical structure , but that by affirming a "poor and weak church" we maintain a church free from bonds of any kind, a church that is an instrument of the Spirit in order to be able to announce and live the liberating gospel of Jesus Christ.

We recognize that a large part of humanity is suffering from hunger and exploitation at the hands of a rich minority, which in many cases calls itself "Christian". It awaits and needs a church in solidarity with it and sharing its lot. Only in commitment to and solidarity with the dispossessed and those who suffer, in obedience to the gospel of Jesus Christ, will the church be able to find the path of unity. It is on this path, not by internal hierarchical reinforcement, that the church will be able to advance on the path towards unity. Paraphrasing the biblical text, we affirm that the church must "seek the Kingdom of God and his justice. . . the rest will be added to it" (Matt. 6:33).

> *Drafting Committee*
> Wilfrido Artús
> Hugo Gonnet
> Darío Michelin Salomon

# EVANGELICAL CHURCH IN HESSE AND NASSAU (FRG)

**Preliminary remarks**

1. We gratefully appreciate the efforts of the Faith and Order Commission of the World Council of Churches in assisting the member churches to find the unity given to us in Jesus Christ. We express our gratitude for having been presented with the convergence statements from Lima. We understand them not as new texts of confession but as an attempt to focus on the main points of church life in which the churches represented on the Faith and Order Commission want to come together. We have tried to answer the questions asked by the former director of the Secretariat on Faith and Order and the former chairperson of the Faith and Order Commission in the preface of the Lima statement:

— the extent to which your church can recognize in this text the faith of the church through the ages;

— the consequences your church can draw from this text for its relations and dialogues with other churches, particularly with those churches which also recognize the text as an expression of the apostolic faith;

— the guidance your church can take from this text for its worship, educational, ethical, and spiritual life and witness;

— the suggestions your church can make for the ongoing work of Faith and Order as it relates the material of this text on baptism, eucharist and ministry to its long-range research project "Towards the Common Expression of the Apostolic Faith Today".

2. Throughout the whole text of the Lima statement we have missed a definition of the relationship between the word and the church. According to our understanding the word of God, as testified in the holy scriptures, is the cognitive basis of theology and of the church. Traditions, not clearly testified

---

● 2,160,000 members, 7 districts, 800 congregations, 1,300 pastors.

to in the word of God, do not have the same status for us, for example traditions that developed later or doctrinal statements in church law, also those concerning the ministry.

It is also very important for us to make a distinction between God's acting in Christ and the actions of the church. Even though Christ is present in his members, he remains juxtaposed to the empirical church.

We are certain that many differences and inquiries are based on these questions. We would welcome a continuation of the discussion. The following groups should be more strongly heard: free churches, theologians and ways of life of the churches of the "two-thirds" world, today's knowledge of the history of the so-called heretics and experiences from the Jewish–Christian dialogue.

3. We do not want to conceal that we have difficulties with some passages of the convergence statements. This applies mainly to the third part, the statements about the ministry. We fear that there is too much emphasis on the ordained ministry, which we do not see as being threefold in the sense of the Lima statement. Finally, we would like to point out that in our opinion the statements of convergence from Lima are a real help for the empirical unity of the church if they lead to common celebrations of the eucharist crossing church boundaries. It is our hope and plea to God that this will soon occur.

## I. Baptism

*1. To what extent can your church recognize in this text the faith of the church through the ages?*

1.1. We appreciate how, by compiling the traditions of baptism of several churches, as presented in the statements of convergence, the wealth of the biblical understanding of baptism is expressed (§§2–7).

1.2. According to our understanding, too, baptism represents the "basic bond" of unity in the body of Christ, given to us by God through Christ (Eph. 4:3–6; §6).

1.3. Baptism in our church is also an unrepeatable act (Order of Life of the Evangelical Church in Hesse and Nassau No. 2; Baptism 13) because it expresses God's having turned to us once for all time in Christ. Therefore, re-baptism is not possible. It calls into question God's unmerited grace.

1.4. We emphasize that baptism should be celebrated in a congregational worship service and we have this practice as a rule (Order of Life of the Evangelical Church of Hesse and Nassau No. 3; §§12 and 23).

1.5. In conclusion we can assert, together with the Evangelical Church in Germany, that we, to a large extent, recognize in the statements of the text on baptism what has been accepted in our church as the teaching of the holy scriptures on baptism.

*2. What consequences can your church draw from this text for its relations and dialogues with other churches, particularly with those churches which also recognize the text as an expression of apostolic faith?*

2.1. As a consequence in our relations with other churches with whom we are also united by this statement, we hope for mutual recognition of baptism, just as we recognize baptism in other churches, when it is carried out according to the scriptures with water and in the name of the Father, the Son and the Holy Spirit (§14).

With regard to the recognition of infant and children's baptism, this applies above all to Baptist churches. We hope that the Orthodox churches will recognize baptism as practised in our churches, even if the baptismal rites differ (no participation in communion) and even if the baptism is performed by someone who is not recognized as an officially ordained minister by the Orthodox Church. The interconnection between the three main topics of the Lima statement — baptism, eucharist, ministry — is especially apparent in this case.

2.2. We emphasize the position of the statement that our one baptism in Christ is a call to all churches to overcome their divisions and to manifest their church fellowship in allowing the Lord's table, in principle, to be openly accessible to all baptized Christians.

*3. What guidance can your church take from this text for its worship, educational, ethical and spiritual life and witness?*

3.1. For the proclamation of baptism in worship services, we have received valuable ideas for biblical witness in the passages on the meaning of baptism (§§2–7).

3.2. We gladly accept the suggestion that a renewal of baptismal vows, for example on Easter eve or during the baptism of others, may be celebrated. Such a renewal of baptismal vows could also be celebrated together ecumenically. According to our tradition, the Sunday after Easter or the sixth Sunday after the Feast of the Trinity would also be appropriate occasions.

3.3. That baptism is viewed as a basis for participating in the eucharist (§14, Commentary B) is demonstrably practised in our allowing children to participate in the communion meal after having received the necessary guidance and instruction.

3.4. We are asking ourselves the question how can our church better guarantee its missionary and educational responsibility to its own baptized, above all to avoid an indiscriminate execution of infant baptism (§§16 and 21; Commentary 6).

This can be accomplished by:
— intensive preparation for baptism of the parents and godparents;
— aiding in the choice of godparents;

—Christian instruction must not be limited only to the time of religious education in schools and confirmation classes but should support a lifelong growing in Christ (§8);

—more guidance for a life based on faith, for example "Sunday schools" for adults;

—deferring baptism.

3.5. We consider it to be a part of the parents' spiritual responsibility to decide when their child should be baptized. If they at first desire the blessing for children and infants during a worship service, then this is only possible if the parents do not question the special meaning of baptism for their child but want to help him/her thankfully to affirm and accept his/her own baptism at a later time in life.

3.6. The questions raised by other churches about our own practice of baptism have given us the opportunity of reflecting more about the possibility of baptizing at various ages and to find an appropriate practice of baptism for each age. There should be no competition in baptizing children, teenagers or adults because in each form of baptism a different aspect of the biblical understanding of baptism is being revealed (compare §§11–14).

3.7. We expressly confirm the important idea that the dynamics of the baptismal event embrace and determine the whole life of the baptized (relationship between baptism and ethics; §10). This relationship is important for the proclamation of baptism, in confirmation classes and for church youth work. In perceiving our responsibility for the whole world, the Lima statement emphasizes an aspect of our baptismal understanding which demands taking the reality of being baptized more seriously (the congregation's mission).

*4. What suggestions can your church make for the ongoing work of Faith and Order as it relates to the material of this text on baptism, eucharist and ministry to its long-range research project "Towards the Common Expression of the Apostolic Faith Today"?*

4.1. The designation of Christians being the people of God (§1) as well as the expression "Christ and his People" (§2) need to be explained with regard to the significance of Israel in the history of salvation. The permanent calling of Israel, to whom the offer of baptism and the promise of the Spirit were first directed and continue to be, may not be concealed or substituted by the existence of the church composed of members from all nations.

4.2. We ask for more differentiated arguments when the term "faith" is being used, particularly in the passage on "faith and baptism". The whole document on baptism of the Lima statement must be phrased more clearly that it is God's action that creates, gives a basis for, and makes church and human action possible. The gap between God and human beings must not be levelled to a relationship of human beings cooperating equally with God.

Otherwise baptism could be misused in part simply as admission to church membership and in part simply as a motivation for ethical renewal.

4.3. It is true that baptism "initiates the reality of the new life" (§7), which is to make an impact in the midst of our world. This should not create the impression that baptism has a "dynamic" that slowly permeates the whole of life on its own and extends itself to all nations. God's gift in baptism is much more in correspondence with human beings admitting that God is right in his judgment about the present old aeon (Luke 7:29) and submitting to the dominion of Christ seated on the right hand of God. This is what gives a final seriousness to the proclamation of the gospel in the present; so far baptism is necessary for salvation.

4.4. We ask you to examine the possibility of speaking of the baptism of infants, children, youth and adults without grading them. In any case children's baptism and adult baptism must be recognized as two possibilities of equal rank.

4.5. The intensified nurture of children, confirmands and youth in the congregation should be evaluated as the church's attempt of taking its task beyond infant baptism very seriously.

4.6. Working under the conditions of a "territorial church (*Volkskirche*) in transition", we question the idea of a blessing being given when the parents decide to postpone baptism of their children; would this not weaken in public the validity given by the gospel to the baptizing of children? For this reason, we are presently not in a position to recommend an official liturgical form for this type of blessing.

## II. Eucharist

*1. To what extent can your church recognize in this text the faith of the church through the ages?*

1.1. We stress the character of the eucharist as a gift of the Lord, as "an assurance of the forgiveness of sins" and "pledge of eternal life". It is Christ who invites us to the meal (§§1 and 2).

1.2. We agree that the characteristics of praise and joy of the eucharist are extolled (§§3 and 4). Here we can learn from early Christianity and other churches today.

1.3. Important in the eucharistic character of the oneness with Christ is for us the community among the participants in the eucharist and sharing the eucharist with each other at all times and places (§19). This tradition may guard against individualism and strengthen community. We are thankful that Jesus' table-fellowship with publicans and sinners acts as a model for the solidarity of the eucharistic congregation with all large and small marginal groups (§24).

1.4. We welcome the view of the Lima text that the eucharist embraces all aspects of life (§20). We emphasize the social-ethical aspects of the eucharist as a challenge in our social, economic and political life (§21).

1.5. We understand anew in this all-embracing relationship the missionary character of the eucharist as participation in God's mission to the world (§§25 and 26). Based on the eucharist, the proclamation of the gospel, service of the neighbour and a faithful presence in the world create unity.

1.6. We need to rethink the Trinitarian and cosmic relations of the eucharist (§§4 and 23). "The world" and the "whole of creation" are present in the eucharist; the Trinitarian God is active in it.

*2. What consequences does your church take from this text for its relations and dialogues with other churches, particularly with those churches which also recognize the text as an expression of the apostolic faith?*

2.1. As a consequence of this text, we must examine whether our understanding of the eucharist in terms of ecumenics, mission and service is as broad as the convergence texts.

2.2. Moreover, we must examine whether our traditional, Protestant understanding of the eucharist goes far enough in incorporating the world loved and reconciled by God into the idea of the community of Christ (*koinonia*). The eucharist wants to make us able, strong, and ready to suffer so that we find peace, diminish "friend/foe" images and overcome divisions.

2.3. We hope that a consequence will be mutual admission and invitation to the eucharistic meal just as we have already expressed on the basis of the one baptism. For the sake of the unity of the body of Christ, we are expecting intercelebration very soon. Although we know full well that the entire unity of the churches remains a gift given by Christ through prayer, we do have before our eyes as the goal of the present ecumenical movement a covenant of historically grown churches who recognize each other fully despite persisting differences ("reconciled diversity").

*3. What guidance can your church take from the text for its worship, educational, ethical and spiritual life and witness?*

3.1. As an aid in our worship life, we accept the suggestion that the eucharist should be celebrated frequently, if possible every Sunday, to commemorate the death and resurrection of Jesus Christ (§§30–31). In some of our congregations weekly eucharistic celebrations are already taking place. We agree that the best way to unity in eucharistic celebration and fellowship of the churches is the renewal of the eucharist itself in the different churches (§28). We realize that it is not merely a question of increasing the number of eucharistic celebrations but much more of a deepening of our understanding of the eucharist and of gaining new experiences of lived community at the Lord's table (discussions about the Lord's supper, seminars, retreats, youth and children's work, new forms of celebrating together). Our eucharistic celebrations should be planned so that an increased participation of children, the handicapped, the sick and other disadvantaged is possible.

3.2. A respectful use of the elements of communion, which is expressed in the consumption of all gifts offered during the celebration of the meal (§32), is a result of our understanding of the meal being Christ's gift.

*4. What suggestions can your church make for the ongoing work of Faith and Order as it relates the material of this text on baptism, eucharist and ministry to its long-range research project "Towards the Common Expression of the Apostolic Faith Today"?*

4.1. For the ongoing work of the commission we would like to see the aspect of the forgiveness of sins for the individual as well as for the community more clearly stated at the beginning of future texts on the eucharist (§2) ("given for you" — both singular and plural). This aspect of the eucharistic celebration, based on a biblical heritage, is strongly rooted in the Protestant tradition.

4.2. Because of the uniqueness of the sacrifice of Christ, the danger of confusing the congregation's repeated sacrifice of praise with the unique sacrifice of Christ should be avoided when using the term sacrifice.

4.3. Future texts should more clearly maintain that Christ himself — and not the church — is the giver and gift of the eucharist as was stressed at the beginning (§§1 and 2) and in the Order of Life of our Evangelical Church in Hesse and Nassau.

4.4. With regard to the eucharistic liturgy (Lima liturgy and §27) we welcome the *epiklesis* as the invocation of the Holy Spirit on the community and the elements of communion. The whole "epicletic" character of the entire eucharistic celebration is important for us.

4.5. The Lima texts closely tie together the eucharist and the proclamation of the word with the idea of *anamnesis* of Christ. It is necessary to reflect anew on the connection between the word and the sacrament.

We feel that the passage about the eucharist being the central act of the worship service (§1) is in need of interpretation. The celebration of the eucharist continues to be the necessary central act of the worship service so far as the proclamation of the word and sacrament together contain the promise of the presence of Christ. The worship service and the celebration of Christ's meal remain in an indivisible relationship. They should not be juxtaposed: the worship service and the eucharistic meal, each celebrated for itself, refer to each other.

### III. Ministry

*1. To what extent can your church recognize in this text the faith of the church through the ages?*

1.1. We stress the calling of the whole people as the starting point for considering ministry in the church (§6). All who have been baptized are bearers of different ministries, no one is without a gift. The unity of the various ministries is founded in the calling of the one people of God, in the one sacrifice of Jesus Christ for all and in the work of the Holy Spirit uniting Christians into the body of Christ, which is understood as God's witness in the one divided world.

1.2. We welcome the emphasis on the variety of charisms in the community of the church. The ordained ministry should promote these charisms (§§19 and 32). It serves the charisms and therefore serves the building up of the body of Christ (Eph. 4:11ff.) and represents the focal point for the unity of the body.

1.3. We see the necessity for having ministries of leadership and guidance in congregations and in the entire church. However, no hierarchy among the ministries or in the ordained ministry should originate from the different ministries (§§8 and 9).

1.4. We agree with the presentation of the apostolic tradition (§34), although the succession of bishops, in our view, can only be a sign of the connection with this tradition (§34).

*2. What consequences can your church draw from this text for its relations and dialogues with other churches, particularly with those churches which also recognize the text as an expression of the apostolic faith?*

2.1. As a consequence we are hoping for a mutual recognition of the ordained ministry, for instance also the ordination of women. The whole of the biblical witness simply does not allow such a weighty difference between women and men in the church.

2.2. It is obvious (simply from the length of the text) that the greatest difficulties for the empirical unity of the church lie in the area of the understanding of the ministry. Here we must work intensively. The ecumenical recognition of the sacraments, baptism and eucharist, mentioned in this statement also depends on the mutual recognition of the ordained ministry (baptism with the Orthodox, eucharist with the Orthodox and with Roman Catholicism with regard to Protestantism). According to our understanding, every ordained ministry derives from baptism and not the other way around.

2.3. In some points we certainly have different ideas about the ordained ministry than our Catholic and Orthodox sister churches. We recognize their ministry as a ministry of Christian proclamation of the word and administering of the sacraments. If this recognition is lacking, then the very existence of a church is being contested by other churches.

*3. What guidance can your church take from this text for its worship, educational, ethical and spiritual life and witness?*

3.1. The reference to the ministries, especially mentioned in the Lima paper, leads us to ask ourselves along with the Evangelical Church in

Germany if we have in fact created a monopoly for the ministry of the proclamation of the word through the ordained minister.

3.2. It is important for us that there is no hierarchy of qualities among the ministries, because in our tradition the participation of non-theologians (laity) in leading the congregations and the whole church is essential. Our church synod, the highest directive body in the church, is comprised mostly of lay people (2/3), as specified in the church's constitution. When we hear the word "presbyter", we usually think of lay members of church councils rather than of ministers of different ranks. Deacons and deaconesses have their own professional status not derived from the ordained ministry of a pastor, and perceive their own tasks of service in the church.

*4. What suggestions can your church make for the ongoing work of Faith and Order as it relates the material of this text on baptism, eucharist and ministry to its long-range research project "Towards the Common Expression of the Apostolic Faith Today"?*

Our wishes for the ongoing work of the Commission have grown out of our reflection on our understanding of and the reality of the ministries in our church:

4.1. We would like to see more emphasis placed on cooperation with non-theologians (laity) in directive bodies. The synodal element is lacking for us in the Lima text. In this way the biblical tradition of the wandering people of God and the preliminary character of church doctrine and structures are neglected (2 Cor. 4:7).

4.2. We would like a coordination of the ministries according to their function without theological glorification, i.e. no hierarchies. This applies to all ministries in the church. The biblical texts critical of authority and power (for example Matt. 21:24ff.) also apply to the ministries and functions of the church.

4.3. We cannot see that either the unity of the church or an authentic interpretation of doctrine is guaranteed in the papal office alone.

4.4. The office of the *episkopé*, of "supervision", of visitation is important. This office in our church is administered in a collegial manner and includes the laity (§26 and Commentary).

4.5. We would like to see more clearly maintained that the call to the people of God, the priesthood of all believers, is the starting point for an ecumenical understanding of service in the church. The biblical tradition transmits a great variety of gifts of grace and services that cannot be put into a system.

Accepted by the Church Synod
of the Evangelical Church
in Hesse and Nassau
4 December 1985

# EVANGELICAL CHURCH OF WESTPHALIA (FRG)

## Introduction

1. The Westphalian general synod welcomes the convergence document of the Faith and Order Commission of the World Council of Churches on the subjects of baptism, eucharist and ministry.

We are gratified to see the extent of the agreement on central issues of Christian faith and life expressed in this text and the wealth of thought-provoking ideas from other churches which can help enliven our worship services and liturgy.

We see in this text an impressive description of the dynamic way in which the churches are drawing closer together.

When we speak of the "reception" of this text, we do not mean merely the official response of the highest body of the church government to the Lima text but rather a process in which all church members can participate. Thus in our opinion it is not sufficient for "the highest appropriate level of authority" to provide a response. Accordingly, many of our local congregations and district synods have demonstrated by working with the Lima text that they wish to participate in this process. Since 1982 they have occupied themselves with this text and have provided important ideas for the following response. The general synod as such concerned itself with the document at its meetings in 1984 and 1985.

In this way we have started down the path of listening to the witness of other churches, including those not having their roots in the Reformation. We ask the Commission to continue in the work it has been doing, in order that the unity of the church may become increasingly manifest and the fellowship in faith and life the churches have already achieved may be deepened.

2. Evangelical Lutheran, Evangelical Reformed and Evangelical United local congregations are joined together in the Evangelical Church of

---

• 3,600,000 members, 1,676 congregations, 1,600 pastors.

Westphalia. The church, its local congregations and its members are exhorted "bowing under God's word to serve the unity of the church on the basis of their own confession and thus also to listen to the witness of faith of the other Reformation confessions" (Church Constitution (CC) of the Evangelical Church of Westphalia, Fundamental Article IV).

In 1973 the general synod subscribed to the Leuenberg Agreement and committed itself to fellowship with the signatory churches. This fellowship in word and sacrament goes beyond the "listening" required by Fundamental Article IV. In it we recognize an expression of the ecumenical essence of our church. Through the Evangelical Church in Germany (EKD), the Evangelical Church of Westphalia partakes in the ecumenical fellowship of the churches of the world (CC, Article 3). We are grateful for the enrichment we have experienced in this fellowship. We recognize our obligation to further this fellowship and to make our contribution to it.

3. Thus we make our response:
— in the realization of the fellowship we have hitherto been granted;
— with the intention of also listening to the witness of faith of those churches which do not have their roots in the Reformation;
— in the hope that bowing under God's word will lead all churches "towards the common expression of the apostolic faith today" and will help them along the path to full fellowship (p. x, preface to the Lima text "Baptism, Eucharist and Ministry", *Faith and Order Paper No. 111*, 1982).

The basis for our response is the question of the extent to which the biblical witness and the fundamental concern of the Reformation confessions as well as the latter's historical impact find expression.

For this reason our responses concerning baptism, eucharist and ministry are each divided as follows:
a) criteria for our statement;
b) points of agreement with the Lima text;
c) questions the Lima text poses us;
d) our counter-questions and reservations.

We close our statement with an answer to the four questions posed by the Faith and Order Commission (cf. p. x, preface to the Lima text).

### Baptism

*a) Criteria*

1. Our understanding of baptism is founded upon the promise God gave us along with baptism, as expressed in Matthew 28:19 and Mark 16:16. We thus understand baptism as a washing of renewal in the Holy Spirit (Tit. 3:5); in baptism we are buried with Christ, so that we might walk in newness of life (Rom. 6:4).

2. The Leuenberg Agreement summarizes our understanding of baptism in the following words: "Baptism is administered in the name of the Father

and of the Son and of the Holy Spirit with water. In baptism, Jesus Christ irrevocably receives man, fallen prey to sin and death, into his fellowship of salvation so that he may become a new creature. In the power of his Holy Spirit, he calls him into his community and to a new life of faith, to daily repentance, and to discipleship" ("Leuenberg Agreement", as published in *Lutheran World*, 20, 1973, pp. 347–53, paragraph 14).

3. Our church constitution describes our baptismal practice accordingly: "Holy baptism is administered in accordance with Christ's commandment in the name of the Triune God, whereby water is poured three times over the head of the person to be baptized (CC, Art. 172:1).

"As a rule, the children of Christian parents are baptized in the course of the first few months after their birth" (CC, Art. 174:1).

Baptism at a later time is also possible (cf. CC, Art. 177).

"In the confirmation service, the children, who have been baptized and have received religious instruction, trusting in God's help confess with the congregation their faith in the Triune God" (CC, Art. 195).

This baptismal practice is based on the insight that "it is not our doing . . . [which makes] baptism" (Luther, *Large Catechism**) and that therefore in accordance with the traditions of other churches infant baptism should be the rule.

*b) Points of agreement*

1. We confess that baptism is a gift of the Triune God and that through it we are incorporated into the body of Christ as the New Covenant.

2. We agree with the view that for this reason the whole Christian church has been commissioned to practise baptism (§1).

3. We point, as does the Lima text, to holy scripture as the basis for any understanding of baptism.

4. We testify to the connection between baptism and faith and understand baptism as "lifelong growth into Christ". We, too, see in it the basis for the call to common responsibility and common witness (§§8–10).

5. We affirm the invitation to mutual recognition of baptism when it is administered in the name of the Triune God and with water and the confession of faith is made in the presence of the congregation by the parents (and, if applicable, by the godparents) or by the candidate (§§15f.).

6. We consider it to be of great importance that baptism be understood as an unrepeatable act and we reject any practice which could be interpreted as "re-baptism" (cf. §13).

*c) Questions posed us*

1. We accept the question for consideration of whether we ought not be more willing to regard infant, child and adult baptism as equally valid forms

---

*Translator's note: one asterisk in this text indicates my translation.

of baptismal practice. We expressly agree with the view that baptism must in any case be understood as "God's own initiative" (§12 Commentary).

2. We learn from the Lima text that baptism "needs to be constantly reaffirmed" (§14 c. Commentary) and that this could be done by renewing the baptismal vows.

3. We also learn from the Lima text that "the symbolic dimension of water should be taken seriously" (§18) and that the gift of the Spirit should be signified more clearly in additional ways (by the laying on of hands, by making the sign of the cross) (§19). We do not practise anointing or chrismation, for we feel it could distort the view of the fundamental essence of baptism.

4. We consider the reference in §20 to the "new identity as sons and daughters of God, and as members of the Church" acquired through baptism to be very important. We consider it imperative that in addition to the parents and godparents the whole congregation be reminded of this new identity and its validity here and of their responsibility for those being baptized (§23): We will attempt "to provide an environment of witness and service" (§12), in order to avoid the danger of "indiscriminate baptism" (§16).

5. We allow ourselves to be reminded that baptism has ethical implications. It has a dynamic which embraces the whole of life. Through baptism we are called not only to personal sanctification. As baptized persons we are also challenged to strive for the realization of the will of God in all realms of life (cf. §§4, 6 Commentary, 7, 10).

6. We agree that by its very nature baptism brings the person baptized into the fellowship of the Lord's table and is on the other hand the prerequisite for participation in communion. Although we cannot consider baptism to be incomplete if (e.g., in cases of infant baptism) participation in holy communion does not immediately follow the act of baptism (§20), and in our usual practice confirmation is prerequisite to participation in holy communion, we have nevertheless begun experimenting with allowing baptized children who have grown up in the church fellowship to partake of holy communion before confirmation after receiving appropriate instruction and guidance. This could help make manifest that through baptism one is incorporated into the body of Christ gathered around the Lord's table (cf. Eucharist §19 Commentary), since we, too, regard participation in the eucharist as a reaffirmation of baptism" (Preparatory Committee for the EKD-Synod 1983, "Gesichtspunkte für Stellungnahmen zu den Konvergenzerklärungen . . .", *EKD Texte*, 7, 1983, B. II. 5).

7. At the same time, however, this of course makes it necessary that we reconsider the significance and special character of confirmation, which up to now has taken place at the end of a period of instruction through the church and upon the confession of faith by the confirmand as the rite of admission to holy communion and to the rights and obligations of full members of the

congregation (§§14 and Commentary) (EKD: "Gesichtspunkte . . .", B. II. 6).

*d) Counter-questions and reservations*

1. The use of the term "baptism of believers", limited to the baptism of adults (cf. §§11, 12), does not aid convergence in the understanding of baptism. In our opinion, infant baptism is not devoid of belief. It is administered in the midst of the congregation, which confesses its faith in the Triune God, and it is oriented to the acceptance of the salvation granted in baptism (§12).

2. It should be made more explicit that even as "our human response" to God's gift to us (§8), baptism is not a second step which we ourselves effect, but is rather effected by the Holy Spirit and thus made possible by him.

## Eucharist

*a) Criteria*

1. Our understanding of communion is founded on God's promise expressed in the words of institution (Mark 14:22–24 and parallels; 1 Cor. 11: 23–25) that Christ himself will be present with those who in faith partake of bread and wine.

2. For a long time, celebrating communion with congregations of other confessions was absolutely unheard of for many congregations in our church. As a result of the Arnoldshain Theses of 1957 and the agreement of the Reformation churches in Europe (Leuenberg Agreement) of 1973, we now witness together:

"In the Lord's Supper [celebrated in conformity with the words of institution] the risen Christ imparts himself in his body and blood, given up for all, through his word of promise with bread and wine. He thereby grants us forgiveness of sins, and sets us free for a new life of faith. He enables us to experience anew that we are members of his body. He strengthens us for service to all men.

"When we celebrate the Lord's supper we proclaim the death of Christ through which God has reconciled the world with himself. We proclaim the presence of the risen Lord in our midst. Rejoicing that the Lord has come to us, we await his future coming in glory" ("Leuenberg Agreement", par. 15 and 16).

3. In our tradition the assurance of the forgiveness of sins receives particular emphasis: "What is the use of such eating and drinking? We learn that from these words: 'Given and shed for you for the forgiveness of sins'; namely, that in the sacrament we are given forgiveness of sins, life and salvation through such words; for where there is forgiveness of sins, there is also life and salvation" (Luther, *Small Catechism*, "Fifth Main Part, Second Point"*).

"It means . . . to accept the whole of Christ's suffering and death with a believing heart and thus to receive forgiveness of sins and eternal life" (*Heidelberg Catechism*, "Question 76"*).

4. Our church constitution directs us to celebrate communion as often as possible in worship services (or with the sick and invalids at home) with those who have received instruction in the sacrament and have professed their faith. It emphasizes the value of proper spiritual preparation (confession of sins) (cf. CC. Art. 179–182).

This communion practice is based on the insight that (here, too) it is not our doing which makes communion and that therefore first and foremost it is God's action and not the church's action which is decisive.

*b) Points of agreement*

1. In many cases the Lima text takes up, sometimes even using the same wording, the witness of the Arnoldshain Theses and the Leuenberg Agreement.

We agree that in communion Christ:
— "stands at the heart of the celebration" (§13);
— "grants communion with himself" (§2);
— "invites to the meal and presides at it" (§29);
— grants "the forgiveness of sins" (§2), thus "fulfilling the promise contained in the words of institution" (§14 in connection with §2);
— liberates us for witness and to a new ethics (§§24f.);
— unites to "communion within the body of Christ" and thus of the whole church (§19);
— guarantees the final coming of the kingdom of God (§22).

2. We consider the fact that the discussion of the Lord's supper takes the worship service as its starting point and that frequent reception of communion is encouraged to be highly important (§31).

3. We share the desire for "a greater measure of eucharistic communion among" the churches (§33) on the basis of mutual understanding, which grows from common faith.

*c) Questions posed us*

1. The Lima text links the eucharist with "the meals which Jesus is recorded as sharing during his earthly ministry" (§1) and comprehends it as a whole as Trinitarian: as "universal communion in the body of Christ", as "an offering and hymn of praise to the Creator" and as "a kingdom of justice, love and peace in the Holy Spirit" (§4). We see here a broadening and deepening indicated by scripture of our understanding of communion.

2. In the context of the concept it proposes, the Lima text emphasizes the term eucharist (thanksgiving). In the eucharist, the world, which God has reconciled with himself, is present. As the representative of a world which is not yet able to do so, this world which has already been reconciled and

renewed in Christ sings God's praise in thanksgiving and adoration. We gratefully accept the idea of the universal scope of the eucharist, of already being able to join in in the eternal song of praise of the world renewed by God.

3. Particularly in its clarification of the *anamnesis* or memorial of Christ, the Lima text refers to Christ's ministerial offices (cf. esp. §8). Usually, we mention them only when speaking of Christology. We gratefully accept this indication of their significance for the understanding of the Lord's supper.

4. *Epiklesis* is the invocation of the Holy Spirit. We accept the reminder in the Lima text (§16) that this invocation refers to "the whole action of the eucharist". This invocation grants us the possibility of overcoming the difficulties traditional to Western Christianity concerning the consecration (§14 Commentary).

The "epikletic" understanding of the whole action of the eucharist enables us to extend the liberation from the fixation on the elements achieved in the Leuenberg Agreement. Is it not possible that the emphasis on the invocation of the Holy Spirit in the eucharist (*epiklesis*) could help the churches develop a more common understanding of ministry?

5. The Lima text calls attention to the fact that "the eucharist embraces all aspects of life", that it is directly related to the diaconal ministry of the congregation and is the basis for "solidarity in the eucharistic communion" (§21). "The eucharistic celebration demands reconciliation and sharing among all those regarded as brothers and sisters in the one family of God and is a constant challenge in the search for appropriate relationships in social, economic and political life. . . . As participants in the eucharist, therefore, we prove inconsistent if we are not actively participating in this ongoing restoration of the world's situation and the human condition" (§20). We expressly agree with these statements and regard them as a confirmation of the articles on communion in the Leuenberg Agreement.

6. The Lima text places great emphasis on calling to mind the Triune God in the "eucharistic liturgy". We must ask ourselves how we can better comply with this desire in our celebration of communion.

7. "It is in the eucharist that the community of God's people is fully manifest" (§19).

We must critically ask ourselves whether all of the expressions of life in our church are thus related to the worship service and vice versa (cf. 1 Cor. 10 : 16).

*d) Counter-questions and reservations*

1. We cannot agree with the exclusive use of the term "eucharist". The terms "the breaking of bread", "the Lord's supper", "communion" are equally adequate expressions of what happens. The exclusive use of the term "eucharist" could convey the impression that the church, rather than Christ, is acting.

2. An understanding of communion in conformity with the words of institution cannot ignore that in addition to the bodily eating and drinking the words "given and shed for you for the forgiveness of sins" are "the main part of the sacrament" (Luther, *Small Catechism*, "Fifth Main Part"*). Is the eucharist really being understood as the gift of renewal when this fundamental aspect is not specifically elaborated? We suggest that "the eucharist as meal of forgiveness" (cf. §2) be treated in a separate section.

3. The statement that the celebration of the eucharist "continues as the central act of the Church's worship" (§1) requires interpretation through §12: the preached word and the eucharistic meal are intimately related. In the preaching of the gospel and in communion, Jesus Christ gives himself.

4. Does the formulation "It is in virtue of the living word of Christ and by the power of the Holy Spirit that the bread and wine become the sacramental signs of Christ's body and blood. They remain so for the purpose of communion" (§15) not place in question the proclamation character of the words of institution (§§3, 7, 12) and ascribe to the elements a permanent sacramental character (cf. also §32)?

Since Christ's presence is central to communion, in our understanding any independent significance of the elements bread and wine is impossible.

5. Anyone who does not admit members of other Christian confessions to communion denies the unity of the body of Christ. The formulation in the commentary to §19 does not express this with sufficient clarity when it uses the phrase "less manifest". Differentiated information ought to be given concerning the reasons for any refusal to admit others to communion. The churches should be called upon to increase their efforts towards more eucharistic hospitality.

6. Although the difficulties in Western Christianity concerning the consecration (§14, Commentary) can be overcome through a recovery of an *epiklesis* of the Spirit when attention is paid to the fact that the whole worship service has an "epikletic" character, it must nevertheless be pointed out that the document on the eucharist did not get beyond the division of the *epiklesis* into an *epiklesis* for the elements and an *epiklesis* for the people (§§14, 15). The thesis that the whole action of the eucharist has an "epikletic" character (§16) is not consistently upheld.

We consider it problematic that among other things the Lima text continues to presuppose the *epiklesis* for the elements (and that this is too obvious to be overlooked in the "Lima liturgy"). Paragraph 14 concentrates too much on the transformation and the recipient of the elements.

**Ministry**

*a) Criteria*

1. Although there are some differences of opinion between the Lutheran, Reformed and United congregations within our church concerning their

understanding of ministry, we all agree that it is "the ministry of reconciliation" (2 Cor. 5:18) rather than the order of ministry which is constitutive to the church.

2. Our view is oriented to the biblical witness, which knows no uniform structure of ministry. Instead, it subjugates the ministries and charisms of the congregation to the gospel. Ministries receive their binding force from the gospel. Their form must meet the requirements of the times (cf. *The Barmen Declaration*, 1934, Thesis III).

3. Accordingly, Article 1 of our Church constitution states: "In commitment [to the Gospel of Jesus Christ, the Lord of the Church] and in the freedom based thereon, [the Evangelical Church of Westphalia] confers its ministries, exercises its governance and fulfills its other tasks."

Concretely, the statement is made: "The ministry of word and sacrament is performed principally by ordained ministers. This ministry can be conferred on either men or women" (CC, Art. 18).

The governance of the church at the different levels and the oversight of the congregations is carried out by collegial bodies (presbyteries, synods, church government) consisting of ordained and non-ordained church members (cf. CC, Art. 54, 113, 137).

*b) Points of agreement*

1. We are in agreement with the Lima text that God the Father calls his people through Christ in the Holy Spirit and that the church lives through the liberating and renewing power of the Holy Spirit (§§1, 2).

2. Along with the Lima text, we, too, welcome the fact that it is possible to speak of ministry only in the context of "the calling of the whole people of God" (§1). Although the ministry of preaching the word and administering the sacraments is at times vis-à-vis the congregation, its place is nevertheless within the congregation.

3. We welcome the conclusion that manifold charisms are bestowed on the people of God through the Holy Spirit and that the ordained ministry can build up the church and carry out its service to the world only in community with them (§5).

4. We welcome the fact that the tasks of the ordained ministry are defined by the basic dimensions of the calling of the people of God. The ministry serves the building up and gathering of the community, its witness and its proclamation and its caring ministry in the whole world (§13).

5. We welcome the fact that on the one hand the "specific authority and responsibility" of the ordained ministry is mentioned (§9), which "assemble [s] and build[s] up the body of Christ by proclaiming and teaching the Word of God, by celebrating the sacraments and by guiding the life of the community in its worship, its mission and its caring ministry" (§13), and that on the other hand "these tasks are not" to be "exercised by the ordained ministry in an exclusive way" (§13 Commentary).

6. We affirm the understanding of apostolic succession formulated in the Lima text. We, too, confess that the church can live only "in continuity with the apostles and their proclamation" (§34) and that for that reason "the ordained ministry has a particular task of preserving and actualizing the apostolic faith" (§35). We subscribe to the opinion that "the primary manifestation of apostolic succession is to be found in the apostolic tradition of the Church as a whole" (§35).

7. We share the view that certain designated persons are ordained (through the laying on of hands) for the ministry of proclamation and of administering the sacraments (§39). We, too, understand ordination as "an action by God and the community" (§40). It takes place in a worship service (§41).

*c) Questions posed us*

1. The Lima text leads us to consider in more detail the relationship of the ordained ministry to the other offices and ministries involved in congregational leadership and diaconal work, as well as to the charisms given the congregation. The elevated position of the ordained ministry must not be allowed to detract from the necessity and dignity of the other offices and ministries nor of the charisms.

2. We accept the question of whether we ought not to reorganize the forms of the diaconate being exercised in our church and establish it as a defined ministry of the church (cf. Eucharist §21 and Ministry §31).

3. The Lima text points out that the "ordained ministry should be exercised in a personal, collegial and communal way" (§26). We are in danger of over-emphasizing the personal dimension of the ordained ministry.

4. We learn from the Lima text how important the promise and the invocation of the Holy Spirit are for the understanding of ordination (§§39ff.). In our tradition, this has not always been kept in mind with sufficient definitiveness.

5. The Lima text reminds us that church ministries are not first and foremost functions governed by carefully laid-out regulations but are rather a gift of God through the Holy Spirit.

6. In agreement with the Lima text, we recognize that there is no New Testament basis for limiting the ordained ministry to the triad of bishop, presbyter, deacon (§§19–25). However, in the structure of the ordained ministry developed in §19 we see the basic dimensions of the ministry which has been given to the whole congregation. We recognize the task of helping these dimensions find expression in the church as a service community and in the priesthood of all believers.

7. We particularly find ourselves confronted with the question of whether the ministry of *episkope* in the church (care that the proclamation, life and service of the church remain in agreement with scripture and confession and within the community of the whole church today) ought not be strengthened

at all levels of the church. This ministry for the unity of the church (§§20, 23) gains significance in the face of considerable differences of opinion and deep-running controversies at all levels.

*d) Counter-questions and reservations.*
 1. The Lima text treats baptism, eucharist and ministry as mutually dependent signs for the recognizable unity of the church. However, the impression must be avoided that in addition to proclamation and the sacraments, the ordained ministry is also constitutive for the church.
 2. Despite the biblically oriented statements on the calling of the whole people of God (§§1–6), it is possible to gain the impression that the ordained ministry is constitutive for the church (§§8, 14). Although the ordained ministry has an important function, it must not be allowed to stand between Christ and the faithful (cf. §17). In our tradition we put it this way: the focus for unity is Christ alone in his word and sacrament.

For this reason we are unable to concur with the special theological qualification of the ordained ministry (the representation of Christ through the ordained minister as put forth in §11).
 3. We are unable to support the conclusions of the Lima paper concerning the threefold pattern of ministry. It should speak much more freely of the variety of offices and services in the church, whereby the term "office" (*Amt*) places the emphasis on being commissioned to a service and the term "service" (*Dienst*) on carrying out this task.** In our understanding, the term "office" automatically includes the *rite vocatus*.
 4. We would have preferred it if the Lima document had expressed more clearly that corresponding orders of church offices and services (ministries) must not be a necessary prerequisite for the mutual recognition of churches as churches (cf. *Augsburg Confession*, VII and XV). That which makes a church a church is not dependent upon its order of ministries. A particular order of ministries does not bestow a higher quality upon a church.

For this reason, one should make a clear distinction between the theological and the structural levels. We are one in the "ministry of reconciliation". Freedom, on the other hand, should be allowed to reign where structures are concerned. If the apostolic tradition in the sense of a succession of word and sacrament is the common basis (§34), it should be possible for the churches to recognize each other independently of the structure of their ministries (EKD: "Gesichtspunkte . . .", D. III. 5–7).
 5. The New Testament does not dictate any particular church order (§19). However, all churches trace the basis and structure of their ministries to the New Testament. The presbyteral-synodal system of government is also based on scripture.

---

** Translator's note: both *Amt* and *Dienst* can be translated into English as "ministry".

We request consideration of whether it might not be possible through joint deliberations on ministry to reach a similar convergence between churches with episcopal, presbyteral-synodal and congregational systems of government as has been reached in the Lima text in the statements concerning adult and infant baptism between churches of the corresponding traditions.

The reason we make this request is that the Lima text calls upon those churches without the episcopal succession to subscribe to "the orderly transmission of the ordained ministry" as "a powerful expression of the continuity of the Church throughout history" (§35). Churches without the episcopal succession "are asked to realize that the continuity with the Church of the apostles finds profound expression in the successive laying on of hands by bishops" (§52).

However, at this point the critical remark is necessary that in those churches with the episcopal succession, the episcopate also embraces certain mandatory powers (consecration of bishops). Under these circumstances, the episcopal succession means introducing a new hierarchical element: the ordained ministry as such then has a hierarchical order (bishop, presbyter, deacon). It would not be possible for us to accept this type of pattern.

6. In §14 a connection is pointed out between an ordained minister's guiding the congregation and presiding at the eucharist. Reformation theology sees the living relationship between Christ and the congregation in the celebration of the eucharist as being independent of the person presiding. In addition, it is not only the ministers who guide the congregation; non-ordained members of the congregation (presbyters) also have their share of responsibility at all levels.

7. We cannot agree with the indecisive discussion on the ordination of women (§18). We know of no biblical or theological reasons for excluding women from ordination. For us the mutual recognition of ministries thus includes the recognition of the ordination of women and we hope that churches which do not allow the ordination of women themselves will recognize it in other churches.

### An answer to the four questions posed by the Faith and Order Commission

*Question 1: To what extent can your church recognize in this text the faith of the church through the ages?*

The guiding principle in our response was the question of the extent to which we could recognize the message of the Bible in this text. We find the faith of the church which is binding for us witnessed to in the "apostolic tradition" (M 34). The church has the task of keeping this faith through the ages and of herself transmitting it in witness and service. This understanding of the faith of the church led us to agree with certain points in the Lima text and to be critical of other points. But it also led to some self-critical questions, for according to Reformation insight the witness of holy scripture is always and ever anew the standard and norm for the teaching and life of the church.

*Question 2: What consequences can your church draw from this text for its relations and dialogues with other churches, particularly with those churches which also recognize the text as an expression of the apostolic faith?*

The Lima text awakened in us the hope that (perhaps already) in the not-too-distant future it will be possible to take concrete steps to achieve more church unity and unity of faith among Christian churches which belong to the World Council. We are thinking of a procedure whereby the churches choose gradual church unity and unity of faith:

— mutual recognition of baptism;
— mutual granting of eucharistic hospitality;
— mutual recognition of ministries in all their variety.

a) Confessionally related churches should enter into bilateral conversations and examine the possibility of entering into church fellowship. In this connection we gratefully call to mind the Leuenberg Agreement, which formed the basis for a church fellowship between the Lutheran and Reformed churches of Europe even though full agreement had not been reached on all questions of doctrine or of the external structures of church and parish life.

We also call to mind the church fellowship declared between the synods of the Evangelical Churches of the Union (EKU) in the Federal Republic of Germany and the German Democratic Republic (resolution passed in 1980) and the General Synod of the United Church of Christ (UCC) in the United States of America (resolution passed in 1981).

We hope that the efforts at church unions continue and that the common points of apostolic faith expressed in the Lima text also help churches to recognize their obligation to take steps towards church fellowship. "The world is too strong for a divided Church"* (Visser 't Hooft).

b) We have asked ourselves what conclusions we must draw for our own church, thinking especially of our relationship to the Roman Catholic Church.

What can we do to achieve the mutual recognition of our sacraments and the mutual recognition of our ministries? On the basis of our self-concept, we feel that the mutual recognition yet lacking is no obstacle to already, e.g. practising eucharistic hospitality at our communion celebrations. If Jesus Christ himself is the Lord of the meal, inviting all to approach in faith, we have no right to turn back members of other churches.

Have the discussions of the Lima text, especially on the eucharist, not made the question appear even more urgent whether it is not only permissible but even necessary to extend the invitation for guest participation at communion, especially with respect to partners of confessionally mixed marriages?

The mutual recognition of baptism would fulfill an essential prerequisite for such an invitation. For baptism, "as incorporation into the body of Christ, points by its very nature to the eucharistic sharing of Christ's body and blood" (B14 Commentary b). We regret that we are still some distance from a mutual understanding of ministry.

Further work is urgently needed on this point. Bishops and church governments, particularly, must not overlook the fact that within the people of God there is not only a deep longing for more unity among the churches but there also exists a genuine desire to listen to one another, to learn from one another and in a disjointed world to witness to and to live the spirit of reconciliation and love.

An encouraging sign of this is the agreement of 29 March 1985, between the Evangelical Church in Germany (EKD) and the Catholic Diocese of the Old Catholics in Germany concerning a mutual invitation to participate in communion.

c) We regard the Council of Christian Churches in Germany (ACK) as an important step in the conciliar process. However, we must seriously consider whether in the ACK questions of organization, representation, etc. are not being taken more seriously than ecumenical content. The ACK urgently needs to concern itself with the discussions and proposed goals of the ecumenical groups and initiatives and of the World Council of Churches.

The ecumenical service groups are to be found, among other places, at the "Kirchentag" church rallies and in the Council of Ecumenical Groups. As a rule, they are closer to the World Council of Churches and its special programmes and to local initiatives than to the established church. At the local level there are individual personal contacts with the congregations, but seldom joint worship services. Contacts and cooperation must be intensified at all levels.

*Question 3: What guidance can your church take from this text for its worship, educational, ethical, and spiritual life and witness?*

"We feel that the Lima text offers substantial help by presenting the great breadth and diversity of the ecumenical witness in the areas of baptism, the Lord's supper and the ministry in such a way that the dominant impression is not that of the disunion of Christendom; instead, it is made clear how this diversity is part of a greater unity through its orientation to Jesus Christ as he is witnessed to in holy scripture" (EKD: "Gesichtspunkte . . .", p. 18).

On the other hand, we encounter in the text some statements to which we cannot subscribe. They show us, however, how necessary it is for the churches to get to know each other better in order to understand the traditions and patterns of faith of other Christians and churches.

a) The Lima text has given us a great variety of suggestions for our worship life. We are glad to note that the convergence statement "Baptism,

Eucharist and Ministry" grew out of the worship service and regards the latter as the centre of Christian life.

b) Work with the Lima text provides an experience in ecumenical learning. Discussion of the Lima text led people to form groups in which "learning in community" took place, causing a change of consciousness. We learn that congregations and church members must surrender their provincial church self-satisfaction, overcome their own limitations and become open to ecumenical thought.

c) It is clear in all sections of the Lima text that worship and life, faith and action, sacraments and world responsibility belong together. We learn that worship services and prayer set free forces which prove themselves in practical action.

d) "The very fact that the Lima text confronts us, in a language from which we have become estranged, with the wealth of a forgotten Christian truth may possibly in itself be an aid for our spiritual life and witness. It could remind us that, although they may appear to be somewhat alien in our world, being at home in the language of the Bible and in the experiences and symbols of the church through the ages has repeatedly proved to be an integral part of the spiritual life which receives its strength from Christ" (EKD: "Gesichtspunkte . . .", p. 19).

*Question 4: What suggestions can your church make for the ongoing work of Faith and Order as it relates the material of this text on baptism, eucharist and ministry to its long-range research project "Towards the Common Expression of the Apostolic Faith Today"?*

A. As a first step in answering this question, the Westphalian general synod quotes the point of view of the EKD (EKD: "Gesichtspunkte . . .", p. 19):

1. We ask the Commission, after receipt of the requested answers, to send the churches a summary of them which makes clear:
   a) in which statements a consensus can be seen;
   b) where further convergence can be recognized on points on which the statements in the Lima text were still differing;
   c) concerning which statements there is evidently no agreement and what the opposing standpoints or reasons are.
2. The Commission for its part should provide suggestions on how the existing differences of opinion on the path to church fellowship can be overcome. We consider it important that the goal of the mutual recognition and the increasingly fuller fellowship of the churches not be lost from sight.
3. These convergence statements on baptism, eucharist and ministry as such have repeatedly demonstrated to us that they lack a basic statement on the common faith in which the churches have their roots. For this reason we wish to encourage the Commission to embark emphatically upon the new study on a common expression of the apostolic faith today and to include the churches in this work. In this context, the question must

also be clarified, under what conditions testimonies of faith in situations of concrete provocation can be formulated in such a way that they do not endanger the unity of the faith of the whole church (*status confessionis* and ethical heresy).

B. In detail, we would like further work to be done on the following questions in particular:

*1. Baptism:* Although the mutual recognition of baptism practised between churches is mentioned (§§6, 15), we feel there is insufficient emphasis on and explanation of the significance of this mutual recognition of baptism as harbinger of the unity which is already visible and as an important step towards mutual recognition as churches.

*2. Eucharist:* In our opinion, in this section the significance of proclamation is treated too lightly. Did not independent preaching services exist alongside communion services even in primitive Christianity? The formulation that the eucharist is "the central act of the Church's worship" (§1) raises the question of the significance of the sermon in the worship service. We request a study on the "epikletic" character of the whole action of the eucharist (§16) which would take into account our reservations (cf. II. d.6) and also the question of the significance of the sermon in the worship service. We suggest that the topic of the eucharist as meal of forgiveness also be given special attention.

*3. Ministry:* The New Testament testifies to different orders of ministries. Different orders of ministries can exist side by side in the church. Thus it is possible for different polities of ministry to be valid in the churches. It is not necessary for churches to accept a particular pattern of order, e.g. the threefold pattern of ministry, in order to achieve unity. We request an investigation of the extent to which a unified structure of ministry is necessary for the unity of the church. We request consideration of whether it might not be possible through joint deliberations on ministry to reach a similar convergence between churches with episcopal, presbyteral-synodal and congregational systems of government as has been reached in the Lima text in the statements concerning adult and infant baptism between churches of the corresponding traditions (B. 15, 16).

C. In our opinion, the ongoing work must take into consideration the fact that if the process of reception is to be comprehensive it must take place at different levels:
— at the level of scholarly theological work,
— at the level of the church governments,
— at the level of the local congregations, the church-related agencies and institutions and the various types of church-related groups.

Even though the three levels can be regarded separately, they do belong together in any comprehensive process of reception. Theological studies, the responsibility of governing the church and the living ecumenical fellowship of involved Christians and local congregations form a lively, if often very tense, whole. The "living ecumenical fellowship" in the local congregations deserves great respect. Christians of different churches and confessions experience community in prayer, in listening to God's word, in singing, in joint communion services and in joint responsibility for the world.

We hope that attention will be paid not only to the further clarification of traditional questions of doctrine and that the churches grow not only in the common expression of the apostolic faith, but that the manifold local expressions of living ecumenical fellowship, up to and including eucharistic hospitality, will be an object of theological reflection and interpretation.

D. Consequences for our own ongoing work drawn from the study of the Lima text:

1. The ecumenical committee and the liturgical committee will be commissioned to develop aids towards making the convergence text fruitful for the work of the local congregations and for worship services.

2. The standing theological committee and the liturgical committee will be commissioned to consider the question of a special act of blessing for children whose parents have decided to postpone their baptism for reasons of religious conviction.

3. The church board will be commissioned to ensure that the ideas from the Lima document for worship services be taken into account in the revision of our service book.

4. The church board will be commissioned to make the necessary preparations for incorporating the Leuenberg Agreement into our church constitution.

*Resolution No. 174 (1985) of the Westphalian General Synod*

The synod passed the following resolution with two abstentions:

The general synod accepts the response to the convergence declaration of the Faith and Order Commission of the World Council of Churches, "Baptism, Eucharist and Ministry", presented by the standing theological committee and the ecumenical committee in the version as revised by the theological conference committee II.

The church board is commissioned to forward this response to the Evangelical Church in Germany and the World Council of Churches.

The general synod encourages the local congregations to keep the conversation which has begun concerning the convergence declaration alive and to make use of the ideas provided in the declaration in their work.

In the name of synod, the Praeses expresses his thanks to the standing theological committee, the ecumenical committee and the theological conference committee II for their work on this response.

# UNITING CHURCH
# IN AUSTRALIA

The Uniting Church in Australia (UCA) rejoices, with the Faith and Order Commission of the World Council of Churches, in the presentation of the "Baptism, Eucharist and Ministry" document (BEM). We give thanks to God as a church, for this achievement and for renewed hope for the unity of the church of Christ kindled by the level of agreement shown in BEM.

In the UCA we developed our response to BEM out of a process of reflection across the church. BEM was widely promoted and study of the document encouraged in every kind of setting. Responses to the document were invited from across the country and these became the basis of a formal response. Academic theologians and lay and ordained members in parish congregations were contributors to this feedback. The commissions of our church responsible for ecumenical affairs and for doctrine, through a working group, prepared a single collated response reflecting opinions across the church. This was re-worked by the commissions for presentation to the national assembly, the council of the UCA with ultimate authority in matters of faith and doctrine.

We consider that the Faith and Order Commission wisely formulated the terms of response in a way designed to avoid dead-end statements that merely evaluate the text in terms of a particular church's current faith and practice. The present phrasing allows the churches to be challenged to think again about their own views, the reasons for which they are held and their continuing significance, and thus to contribute to an ongoing dialogue that anticipates that all the churches will go beyond otherwise entrenched positions.

Such a dialogue, however, will itself have to go behind and beyond the issue of baptism, eucharist and ministry to those of authority and ecclesiology, as the formula of anticipated response itself implies. Clearly the question of "the extent to which the faith of the church can be discerned in the text"

---

• 1,500,000 members, 3,200 congregations, 7 synods, 3,200 pastors.

must be taken as both historical and normative, i.e. about what the church should be confessing as well as what she has confessed, and that already points to the underlying issues of authority and ecclesiology which constantly surfaced in the Commission's discussions but which are not directly addressed in the document. Those issues arise because down through the ages there has been a variety of expressions of faith among those who claim to belong to the church and therefore to answer only the historical question, "is there a precedent somewhere in the church's history for this expression of faith?" would be of little value in pressing on to the ecumenical goal. But the normative question "what ought the church to believe?" already implies that some expressions of the faith of the church are unacceptable. Some people hold that the church can believe a wrong thing and be in error, others that one cannot believe the wrong thing and be the church. So the inter-relationship between the issues of authority and ecclesiology becomes apparent in the questions that emerge from the one the BEM document asks, viz. by what authority is the validity of the church's faith and practice to be tested? How is what genuinely belongs to the faith of the church to be determined?

Any response to the BEM document, therefore, needs to take account of the fact that while "theologians of such widely differing traditions" were able to "speak harmoniously about baptism, eucharist and ministry" (p. ix), the traditions from which they come are still far from harmonious in affirming that other traditions are genuinely part of the one holy, catholic and apostolic church. To reach agreement, therefore, on what is *meant* by baptism, eucharist and ministry is not yet to accept and *participate* in each other's baptism, eucharist and ministry, although the significance of agreement on meaning as a step towards such unity should not be underestimated.

## Baptism

GENERAL COMMENTS

The UCA can recognize, in general terms, the faith of the church throughout the ages in the BEM discussion of baptism. In many places in the document we find the understanding of Christian baptism which the Reformers expounded and which was carried forward in the reformed tradition of the church.

1. While recognizing that BEM does not set out to provide a complete theological account of baptism, eucharist and ministry, the UCA still finds somewhat artificial the way in which it considers these themes in isolation from the wider context of the means of grace.

We would insist, as heirs of the Reformation, that unless the sacraments are seen in that wider context they cannot be rightly interpreted.

The UCA would also maintain that, among the means of grace, the preaching of the word has its own peculiar place and efficacy, and that baptism and the eucharist should not be separated from it. This insistence on the inseparability of word and sacrament is, indeed, present in BEM, viz. in the section on the eucharist (§12), but in the section on baptism it is given less weight.

The explanation of the biblical understanding of baptism is presented there as something appropriate for inclusion in the baptismal service rather than as an essential element in it (§21).

2. The UCA also affirms that the sacraments derive whatever meaning they have from Christ and from what God has done, and continues to do, in him. Nothing happens *to* us in and through baptism that has not already happened for us *in* him, our representative. Nothing must be allowed to obscure the dependence of the sacraments upon him and upon God's action in him. We are therefore uneasy with some of the expressions used in the section on baptism, such as "Baptism . . . . unites" (§2), "Baptism makes Christians partakers of the mystery of Christ's death and resurrection" (§4), "Baptism initiates  . . ." (§7), and we note the significance of this for our liturgical forms.

We would prefer statements which spoke of God's action in baptism. The consistent use of the word "baptism" as the subject of the sentence in §7 has also led to the elimination of the personal language of "promise", which we consider ought to figure prominently in any statement on baptism. "Baptism is a gift of God" — indeed, but part of the gift is God's promise to bring about for those baptized all that baptism means and expresses. At the same time, we welcome the link made in this paragraph between baptism and the kingdom, an aspect of baptism which does not seem to have received adequate attention in our confessional documents.

DETAILED COMMENTS

1. While noting the statement that those baptized are pardoned, cleansed and sanctified by Christ, we look for a clearer affirmation that the sanctification effected in baptism means that believers are not only given "a new ethical orientation under the guidance of the Holy Spirit" but claimed by God as his own and drawn into his own life, in other words, regenerated (§4).

2. While accepting the statement in this paragraph that faith is necessary for the reception of the salvation embodied and set forth in baptism, we could wish for a clearer indication that faith is itself the gift of God, in that it is evoked in men and women by God through the word and sacraments of the gospel (§8).

3. At the same time, we miss a clear recognition of the point that, while baptism is efficacious, not all the baptized grow into the promised faith. The baptized person, whether baptized in infancy or adulthood, may reject the gift of life and stifle the voice of the Spirit. "What is given may become a judgment: what is grafted may wither: what is generated may never grow."[1]

---

[1] Church of Scotland, *Report of the Special Commission on Baptism*, 1961, p. 619.

If it should be objected that the last two paragraphs are difficult to hold together, we would reply that the New Testament is full of such antinomies.
4. We recognize the intention of this section to stress the common ground between those churches which baptize both believers and the children of believers and those which baptize believers only (§2).

However, we question the apparent implication that infant baptism is not to be recognized as the one baptism into Christ until the person baptized as an infant has himself or herself affirmed the confession of faith made by the parents and the congregation. If a baptism has been performed in obedience to the command of Christ and in dependence on his promise, it must be recognized as a valid baptism (§15).

Our own statements certainly affirm, in common with BEM, that baptism is an unrepeatable act (§13).

CONCLUSION

*Challenges to our teaching and practice*

Throughout our discussions we have tried to bear in mind that we are not simply being asked to measure BEM against our historic standards but to allow both our teaching and our practice to be challenged by it. There are several ways in which the practice of our church, if not its teaching, is thus challenged.

In particular, we find ourselves challenged to be more vigilant against the practice of indiscriminate baptism, against the willingness of some to comply with a request for rebaptism, and against any confusion of baptism with naming ceremonies (§16); to pay more serious attention to the nurture in faith of those baptized (§12, comm. p. 4); to consider how the celebration of baptism might be concentrated at particular festivals, viz. Easter, Pentecost and Epiphany, as in the early church (§17); and to devise more opportunities for the baptized to reaffirm their faith, at the eucharist, at Easter and at the baptism of others (§14, comm. c, p. 5).

**Eucharist**

GENERAL COMMENTS

In general terms, responses from within the Uniting Church indicate that the document clearly and emphatically expresses the faith of the church as understood and interpreted from the perspective of the traditions to which we belong. The Reformers were concerned, above all else, to exalt Christ and to affirm the uniqueness, finality and complete adequacy of what God has accomplished in him for our salvation. Since the sacraments derive their meaning from him alone, there can be no suggestion of separating the sacraments from Christ nor of repeating within the church what God has already done in Christ. Paragraph 8 of BEM, therefore, ensures that whatever else is said about the eucharist is understood within this all-important context: "What it was God's will to accomplish in the incarnation, life, death, resurrection and ascension of Christ, God does not repeat. These events are unique and can neither be repeated nor prolonged."

DETAILED COMMENTS

1. Grounding the meaning of the eucharist in the being and activity of the one God, Father, Son and Holy Spirit (BEM p.10) clearly expresses the faith of the church by linking its sacramental belief and practice to the normative Creeds (Apostles', Nicene and Chalcedonian), each of which emphasizes what is believed about the Trinity. Only by setting beliefs about the eucharist on this Trinitarian ground can the document deal with theological foundations of unity as well as with outward symptoms of division.

Nevertheless the order which the document then follows (thanksgiving to Father, *anamnesis* of Christ, invocation of Spirit) may obscure the centrality of Christ's death and resurrection for the celebration of the eucharist. That this is not intended is evident (§13), but a clear expression of the faith of the church through the ages would emphasize that the thanksgiving to the Father at the eucharist celebration focuses on the death and resurrection of Jesus Christ. This focus tends to be blurred in the BEM document when such references to the eucharist as the "benediction by which the Church expresses its thankfulness for all God's benefits" (§3); "the great sacrifice of praise by which the Church speaks on behalf of the whole creation (signifying) what the world is to become. ." (§4) are placed prior in order to the section on Christ.

2. The UCA would maintain with BEM that through the ages the church has rightly understood the sacrament of the Lord's supper not only as a sign but as a means of grace, and that in the eucharist Christ is truly present (§13).

As the commentary on this paragraph points out, however, there has been more than one way in which the real presence of Christ in the eucharist has been understood. "Many churches believe that by the words of Jesus and by the power of the Holy Spirit, the bread and wine of the eucharist become, in a real though mysterious manner, the body and blood of the risen Christ. . . Some other churches, while affirming a real presence of Christ at the eucharist, do not link that presence so definitely with the signs of bread and wine." While the liturgies of the Uniting Church reflect more clearly the second view, both are held in the UCA as a direct consequence of the theological traditions that were brought into union. We are therefore able to affirm that the text does accommodate the views of the Uniting Church, and can also give an affirmative answer to the question whether "the difference between the two views can be accommodated within the convergence formulated in the text" (p. 12), if that involved sentence means whether both views are allowed for in the text of §13. What is not so clear, and much more difficult, is whether this variety *should* be allowed for. Down through the ages and particularly since the Reformation the church has been bitterly divided on this issue, those holding one view refusing to discern in those holding the other "the faith of the Church through the ages". The UCA, along with other churches, is now challenged to affirm this diversity and not to unchurch those who take the other view of the real presence.

While the view of the UCA is clearly included in the section on the meaning of the eucharist, there is some question of balance between the two views in the section on the celebration of the eucharist. Further clarification is necessary, for example, of the justification for the reservation of the sacraments and the disposal of the elements. To say that the primary purpose for the former is for distribution among the sick and absent overlooks the fact that for many the purpose remains that of adoration. As well, the suggestion that "the best way of showing respect for the elements served in the eucharistic celebration is by their consumption" seems to rely on an interpretation of the presence of Christ in the eucharist on which the UCA would not insist.

The text then does allow for a varied interpretation of the real presence (§§13 and 15) and properly refuses to dissolve the mystery of the manner of his presence. There is, however, an underlying problem which the document does not address directly but which is bound to surface in any ecumenical discussion of the subject, namely the lack of universal agreement on what constitutes the apostolic faith. Consequently churches cannot settle the question of which views of real presence are valid by appealing to the authority of the apostolic faith since they do not agree on what constitutes that faith.

3. Apart from the provisos above, the UCA finds no reason for saying that the text runs contrary to what the church has held to. There are, however, some aspects of that faith, as witnessed to in the reformed tradition especially, which seem under-emphasized or omitted altogether.

For example, the section D on eucharist as communion of the faithful seems to neglect a major issue during and since the Reformation, viz., the nature of the sacrifice of thanksgiving and praise offered by the people of God. This has been replaced with reference to the search for appropriate relationships in social, economic and political life, which are certainly important but whose relation to the eucharist is only tenuously supported by reference to the apostolic faith. Much more strongly represented in that faith and not referred to explicitly at all in the text is the warning against eating and drinking unworthily which came to play such a large part in the theology reflected in the discipline of the church.

4. The section on the celebration of the eucharist challenges the practice of the UCA in a number of areas, especially:

i) Who receives? Paragraph 2 says "each baptized member. . . ." which implies that baptism is a sufficient condition for receiving the eucharist. The UCA has not come to this view officially, although recent studies of children and holy communion for the 1985 assembly represent this view and indicate that it is widely held.

ii) Who presides? It is the practice in most churches that only an ordained person may preside. While this is generally what happens in the UCA our regulations permit exceptions, and, while not seeing the difficulty as sufficient reason to change, we should recognize that this creates difficulties for other churches.

iii) How often? Paragraph 30 is cautious, but "frequent celebration" is advocated which presumably means more often than the common UCA practice of once a month.

5. The final paragraph ends properly on a note of hope, looking forward to the day when "Christ's divided people will be visibly reunited around the Lord's Table". Expression of the fullness of apostolic faith, however, calls for a penultimate paragraph that refers to the self-examination, repentance and forgiveness of those who are at odds before eucharistic sharing can take place. What is needed, therefore, goes beyond the "mutual understanding" between churches, to which BEM will undoubtedly contribute, to a genuine act of contrition for the hostility which so often underlies our dividedness.

## Ministry

### GENERAL COMMENTS

The response of the Uniting Church in Australia to the document in respect of "ministry" shows a strongly positive acceptance in general terms. In general, the Uniting Church recognizes in BEM the faith of the church throughout the ages, while identifying some areas for development and some issues in need of clarification. In §14 of the basis of union of our church there is recognition of "a period of reconsideration of traditional forms of the ministry" and a commitment to be open to the development of a renewed diaconate. In such a paragraph there is evidence that, as an ecumenically oriented church, we hope to remain open to God's possibilities for the church catholic in a discussion of ministry, such as BEM, especially in view of the hopes and intentions which are the context of the document. The document invites transition from talking theologically to discerning possibilities of mutual recognition. BEM most specifically addresses our church in the issue of ordering the ministry of the church and then in the issue of continuation of the church or apostolic succession.

### DETAILED COMMENTS

#### The calling of the whole people of God

There is strong affirmation in our church for these opening paragraphs of BEM on ministry. The section accords well with the basis of union of our church. There is, however, some opinion that from this beginning it is inappropriate that the subsequent discussion treats so fully the ordained ministry and so minimally the ministry of all members of Christ's church. Paragraph 6 calls us to recognize the specific issues of how the life and ministry of the church are to be ordered. Such a focus inevitably brings ordained ministry to the centre of discussion in a manner which is appropriate to the declared primary purpose of the document: "the agreed text purposely concentrates on those aspects of the theme (i.e. ministry) that have directly or indirectly related to the problems of mutual recognition leading to unity". Our church recognizes a commitment in BEM and will respond ecumenically to the question of the document: "How, according to the will of God and under the guidance of the Holy Spirit, is the life of the Church to be understood and ordered, so that the gospel may be spread and the community built up in love?" This question is a key invitation to the Uniting Church in the ministry section of BEM. In ongoing discussion of such a question, the UCA would want to search out and lift up the ministry of all members of Christ's body in community with one another seeking a creative balance in the ministry of the church inclusive of both lay and ordained.

The radical implications of the calling of the whole people of God are not spelled out sufficiently in the document, nor yet adequately lived out in the UCA. Where any person is refused participation in the ministry of the people of God because of sex, handicap, race or class, the radicality of God's calling of the whole of humanity is blunted.

We would make the further comment on this section, and indeed on the whole document, that the tension, so characteristic of the New Testament, between what is already true and what is yet to be is largely lacking. We read, to be sure, that baptism is a sign of the kingdom (§7); that the Holy Spirit, through the eucharist, gives a foretaste of the kingdom of God (§18); and that the church is called to proclaim and prefigure the kingdom of God (§4). Yet, over all, we find little to suggest that the life of the Christian, and of the church, is marked by hoping, longing, yearning, even groaning; and that we live in Christ away from Christ, constrained to cry, in the very celebration of his presence in the eucharist, "O Lord, come!"

In the same way, we miss the recognition, so fundamental to St Paul, that while the life of the church bears the imprint of the resurrection, the primary truth about its existence is that it is continually being given over to death for Jesus' sake.

*The church and the ordained ministry*

The document describes the ordained ministry as "constitutive of the life and witness of the Church" and "representatives of Jesus Christ to the community" (§11). The language of the document is in need of further interpretation in our church, particularly in light of §4 of our basis of union in which we recognize Christ as constitutive of the church:

The Uniting Church acknowledges that the Church is able to live and endure through the changes of history only because her Lord comes, addresses, and deals with men in and through the news of his completed work. Christ who is present when he is preached among men is the Word of God who acquits the guilty, who gives life to the dead and who brings into being what otherwise could not exist. Through human witness in word and action, and in the power of the Holy Spirit, Christ reaches out to command men's attention and awaken their faith; he calls them into the fellowship of his sufferings, to be the disciples of a crucified Lord; in his own strange way he constitutes, rules and renews them as his Church.

We are challenged by the document to be more considered in our affirmation of ordination and our understanding of the apostolic witness to Christ in the church. We recognize that, in the context of the document, "constitutive" and "representative(s)" are qualified: "responsible for pointing to (the Church's) fundamental dependence on Jesus Christ, and thereby provide, within a multiplicity of gifts, a focus of its unity". This is very close to our basis of union §14(a):

The Uniting Church, from inception, will seek the guidance of the Holy Spirit to recognise among her members men and women called of God to preach the Gospel, to lead the people in worship, to care for the flock, to share in government and to serve those in need in the world.

To this end:

(a) The Uniting Church recognises and accepts as ministers of the Word all who have held such office in any one of the uniting Churches, and who, being in good standing in one of those Churches at the time of union, adhere to the Basis of Union. This adherence and acceptance may take place at the time of union or at a later date. Since the Church lives by the power of the Word, she is assured that God, who has never left himself without witness to that Word, will, through Christ and in the power of the Holy Spirit, call and set apart members of the Church to be ministers of the Word. These will preach the Gospel, administer the sacraments and exercise pastoral care so that all may be equipped for their particular ministries, thus maintaining the apostolic witness to Christ in the Church. Such members will be called Ministers and their setting apart will be known as Ordination.

The Presbytery will ordain by prayer and the laying on of hands in the presence of a worshipping congregation. In this act of ordination the Church praises the ascended Christ for conferring gifts upon men. She recognises his call of the individual to be his minister; she prays for the enabling power of the Holy Spirit to equip him for that service. By the participation in the act of ordination of those already ordained, the Church bears witness to God's faithfulness and declares the hope by which she lives. In company with other Christians the Uniting Church will seek for a renewed understanding of the way in which the congregation participates in ordination and of the significance of ordination in the life of the Church.

We agree with the preservation in BEM of the proper distinction between the uniqueness of apostolic ministry as "witnesses to the resurrection of Christ" and the subsequent ministry of all others ordained.

We believe it is important that BEM should be more inclusive and integrative of the range of New Testament perspectives on ministry and not rely primarily on the Acts of the Apostles. There needs to be a fuller exposition of the diversity of patterns of ministry in the New Testament. There is general agreement with BEM, nonetheless, in respect of described functions of the ordained ministry and the relationship between lay and ordained (§§11–14).

Paragraphs 15 and 16 provoke a measure of uneasiness in our church. The commentary at §16 is perceived as an essential caution in the issue of ordination and authority. More could be said in BEM about the many gifts for ministry in the whole community of God's people especially in relation to the ordained being "bound to the faithful in inter-dependence and reciprocity".

In our church there are different ways of understanding priestly ministry. The Uniting Church in Australia would want to work ecumenically to develop our understanding and practice of priestly ministry in reference to the scriptures and confessional documents and BEM.

BEM calls attention to the ministry of men and women in the church. The Uniting Church acknowledges the principle of full participation of women in the life of the church and practises the ordination of women, while acknowledging that discrimination remains a discernible reality. We are challenged by the document to overcome this discrimination and, recognizing that most churches do not ordain women, to articulate in ecumenical discussion the theological grounds which underly our practice.

*The forms of the ordained ministry*

There is some hesitation in our church concerning the ordering of ministry in the traditional offices of bishop, presbyter and deacon. BEM develops the threefold pattern in a spirit of reform and therefore challenges churches presently ordered in this pattern and those who are not. The Uniting Church in Australia would also recognize that we are challenged in this church to discover a form of bishop-in-presbytery consonant with our present ordering. At union the traditions of our church accepted both presbyteral ordination and a corporate episkope in the form of a presbytery. Many presbyteries of our church have already discovered the desirability and need to appoint an officer to exercise pastoral care personally on behalf of the presbytery. A bishop-in-presbytery is a possible ordering of episkope in our church, especially recognizing the episcopal role as primarily pastoral. We must, in our church, recognize in BEM the commitment to reform: "the threefold pattern stands evidently in need of reform". Along with the kinds of reform indicated in the document our church is encouraged to discuss "whether the threefold pattern as developed does not have a powerful claim to be accepted".

In general terms the guiding principles for the exercise of the ordained ministry in the church outlined in §§25 and 26 are acceptable in virtue of our basis of union §§14, 15 and 16. The collegiality of ministers which BEM calls for was a significant element in our tradition, but it has been largely lost.

In terms of BEM, ordained ministers in the UCA can be understood as both bishop and presbyter within a local eucharistic community. We are prompted again by BEM to continue, with even greater care, the work of discovering afresh the ministry of an ordained diaconate. In the BEM description of a "deacon", however, we find nothing more than that which might be expected of any baptized lay member of our church.

Section III.D of the document provides an essential concluding perspective to the whole discussion of forms of the ordained ministry. Our church would affirm that the possibilities for ministry are never exhausted in ordained office alone. God, in the power and presence of the Holy Spirit, works where he wills in ministries of a special nature especially in the exercise of prophetic and reforming ministries. It is possible that this short section on the variety of charisms could more effectively follow §I.5. This may better set a context for the issues which are addressed in the following sections of the document.

## Succession in the apostolic tradition

As the UCA looks to the future, the need for further work on the authority of the ministry of the people of God is evident (§26). BEM offers the guiding principles that ordained ministry should be exercised in a personal, collegial and communal way. This raises questions about the way team ministries work — both teams of ordained ministers, and teams of elders, ordained clergy, and the whole congregations. It also raises questions about the nature of authority itself (§15). BEM says it is a gift for the edification of the church community. How is the Uniting Church to empower its whole community so that there will be the mutual sharing of gifts and service to the world? Many authoritarian styles of the ordained ministry lead to a passive laity, even though the UCA believes in the ministry of the whole people of God. Where the majority of clergy are male, and the majority of laity are female, old patterns of authoritarian leadership and passive acceptance are continuing and-encouraged. Further exploration of the model of authority we have in Christ, outlined in BEM (§16), is needed. As one aim of the BEM statements on ministry is to bring about a mutual recognition of ministries between the denominations, the UCA has further work to do within its life so that there will be mutual recognition of ministries of all its members — the question should also be faced as the Reformed Church in France has done, as to whether ordination is a hindrance to the working of the Spirit with the people of God.

The fundamental reformed understanding of the continuity of the church is acknowledged and lifted up for consideration, in BEM, alongside the historic episcopate (§§36–38). In conversation with other churches we are challenged to rediscover in an historic episcopate a helpful "sign" not a "guarantee", of the continuity and unity of the church. A reformed theology of apostolic succession cannot be overlooked or underestimated in such a conversation or rediscovery of the episcopate but is essential for a right understanding of apostolicity in the oikoumene of the one holy, catholic and apostolic church (basis of union, §4).

*Ordination*

The basis of union of our church is broadly consistent with the more developed theology of ordination offered in BEM §§39–40. In §§41–44 we are invited to assess our understanding of the sacramental nature of ordinations as an outcome of the sovereign activity of God and the confident invocation of the Holy Spirit by the church. This is in need of clarification in respect of a reformed theology of sacrament.

Paragraphs 45–50 beg the question of the ordination of women. The question could helpfully be included here in a positive context.

*Towards the mutual recognition of the ordained ministries*

The UCA responds enthusiastically to this section. The real calling of the document in respect of ministry lies in these paragraphs. We are invited to give an account of our Presbyteral ordination and the ways it stands in relation to the ministry of work and sacrament in continuity with apostolic times. We are invited also to give an account of our theological understanding of the continuity of the church and to take account of what BEM is saying. In all this we endeavour to explore liturgical means of celebrating mutual recognition of ordained ministries in the ecumenical community of the church.

**Conclusion**

The work of the Faith and Order Commission of the World Council of Churches, in presenting the churches with this discussion of ministry, is to be received with great joy and acknowledged in serious reflection and a commitment to greater unity of the church. We give thanks to God for the theological work of the Commission and for the activity of the Holy Spirit in the church which constrains us to seek new understanding and a larger appreciation of the ministry of the church. In the complex context of the modern world we recognize, with hope, the challenges in BEM to which we must seek to respond in fellowship with the whole church, so that the gospel of Christ will be clearly discernible in the reality of the church and its ministry.

# PROTESTANT METHODIST CHURCH IN THE PEOPLE'S REPUBLIC OF BENIN

The Protestant Methodist Church in the People's Republic of Benin accepts without reservation the Lima document on "Baptism, Eucharist and Ministry".

We accept it as the basis of our analyses and study towards the visible unity of the divided churches, although our church is aware of the difficulties it will encounter in order to come to a fundamental agreement with other churches on putting into practice the elements in this document.

Our general synod congratulates all those who have contributed to the study and drawing up of the reports contained in BEM, a text which will always be a milestone in the life of the WCC member churches and the Roman Catholic Church, because blessing it and putting it into practice will be the true sign of the unity we all seek and that the Lord alone can accomplish.

Harry Y. Henry
President

---

● 62,000 members, 370 parishes, 30 pastors.

# EVANGELICAL-METHODIST CHURCH: CENTRAL CONFERENCE IN THE GERMAN DEMOCRATIC REPUBLIC

## 1. General considerations

1.1. We welcome the World Council of Churches' "Baptism, Eucharist and Ministry" (BEM) as a document in support of churches' increasing awareness that they are to live together by commission of the church's Lord. It is suited for testing the current degree of agreement between individual churches and their ecumenical obligation in regard to baptism, the Lord's supper and ministry.

1.2. It is not the intent of BEM to bear the weight of a creed or of a fundamental statement addressing churches' questions about their identity as derived from the gospel. In the additive compilation and the comparison of various traditions alone we see only a possibility for churches of differing experiences and of historically developed convictions to become better acquainted with each other.

1.3. It seems to us that the Commission has complicated the process of reception of the document by linking this process to the larger question of the degree to which "the faith of the Church throughout the centuries" can be identified. The church's stature or its doctrine is not where its founding faith lies. It can lie only in holy scripture. The Reformation's insight *sola scriptura* leads us in the testing of the mission and the nature of the theology and the doctrine of individual churches as well as of the community of churches. When this hierarchy is disrupted, the form practised in each case and the understanding of baptism, the Lord's supper and ministry as preserved through tradition emerge as the church's master and as measure of its responsibility. Then it is forgotten that the church is *creatura verbi divini*. Then it is not surprising when, in countless presentations of the document, terminology freezes theological content. The theological meaning of this terminology is supported neither by exegesis nor by dogma, but only by the formula "faith of the Church through the centuries", and foreign matters can

---

● 30,000 members, 129 congregations, 140 ministers, 3 districts, 1 bishop.

then infuse its content. We regret this tendency, for throughout the document it leads to sacramentalism and consequently to the development of individual statements on baptism, the Lord's supper and ministry which fall short of the church's responsibility in the world and its missionary essence.

1.4. The tacit agreement in the conviction that the church's evolution has had normative power throughout the centuries goes against the conviction that Jesus Christ is Lord of the church and that through him it stands and falls. In him the unity of the church is presupposed; this unity is to be answered in the life of Christianity.

The unity of the church is a predominant theme discussed at the outset in the foreword to BEM and picked up repeatedly throughout the text, in a way that an ideology of unity seems to have developed. However, we emphasize that the gift of unity in Christ precedes.

With respect to the Lord's supper, for example, we think it necessary to refer to the Lord's table and his offerings as symbols of this given unity. We thus understand the Lord's supper as community given to us and the partaking of the whole body of Christ in God's salvation.

1.5. BEM uses terms like "sacrament", "sacramental sign", "sacramental community", "sacramental faith" or the term "sign" without accompanying explanations, thereby promoting the misunderstanding that traditions of liturgical customs hold greater value than the living word of Christ itself. However, we would prefer a stronger emphasis on the manifold presence of Christ in his community as witnessed in the gospel. Only from his presence can the necessary expression and character of faith, mission and ecclesiastical order be derived.

1.6. In many contexts the assertions of BEM prove to be ineffective for carrying out the tasks of evangelism and mission in the circumstances of the world in which we live. Modern-day persons' questions seem to have been disregarded. This is because the document speaks primarily from a historical perspective, and because its line of reasoning stems primarily from early Catholicism.

If we are in agreement that the age of Constantine is past, then we certainly do not do well to develop the concept of the church out of the age before Constantine and not out of the ecclesiology as expressed in the New Testament itself.

Neither "development" nor "continuity" of the church is a criterion for its service. We also see no hope in trying to reach an understanding along the line of the Orthodox or Anglican traditions. Such an understanding between Protestant and Catholic convictions does not appear to be possible. The return to the gospel alone is much more promising in light of the current world situation.

## 2. Baptism

### 2.1. *What do we agree with?*

2.1.1. We welcome the fact that the document describes the nature of baptism through fundamental reference to New Testament discussions of baptism (§§2–5).

2.1.2. We must stress that God's gift and our human response belong together. Therefore we are of the opinion that the nature of baptism is endangered when one of the two aspects is particularly emphasized (§8).

2.1.3. We place great importance on the repeated claim that baptism signifies unity among Christians (§§6 and 15). To us this is the essential argument against second baptism (§13).

2.1.4. We would like to underline strongly the importance of churches' obligation to examine the practice of indiscriminate baptism (§16).

2.1.5. Points 4, 5 and 10 emphasize the ethical implications of baptism, as well as its part in a Christian's process of growth. This meets with our unlimited approval and touches upon the Methodist concern with sanctification.

2.1.6. We welcome the call to incorporate the celebration of baptism in worship. This clearly expresses the baptismal vow of the person to be baptized (respectively of his/her parents) as well as the congregation's responsibility for the person being baptized. Both remain tasks to be continually taken into account long after the actual baptism (§23).

2.1.7. We feel called upon to seriously reflect on the pastoral-missionary aspect of baptism in the context of our social surroundings, and to recognize therein the inherent opportunity to proclaim the gospel.

### 2.2. *What do we disagree with?*

2.2.1. We reject statements which bring about an identification between baptism and Christian life (§7: "Baptism initiates the reality of the new life"). The sacrament of baptism has no legitimate effect from itself. The spirit of God gives life to the sacrament. What is decisive is one's personal encounter with Christ.

2.2.2. It appears to us that in BEM (§7) the Holy Ghost is placed subordinate to baptism and apparently conceived only in relation to it. We cannot agree with this, for this signifies the danger of over-emphasizing rites and signs which can serve only as references. The grace of God must not unawares become a possession of the church.

2.2.3. We cannot view the sanctification of life as bound to the fulfilment of baptism, as stated in BEM (§14b).

2.2.4. For us the right to take part in communion does not depend upon baptism. Instead, we see in the Lord's supper an invitation that is open to everyone, as well as an opportunity for mission.

## 3. Eucharist

### 3.1. What do we agree with?

3.1.1. The celebration of the eucharist is made legitimate through the command of Jesus (§1). We agree with the biblical foundation as stated in §1.

3.1.2. We stress the importance of the statements on the uniqueness in nature and time of the life and work of Christ.

3.1.3. The unity between proclamation of the word and the celebration of the Lord's supper is important to us.

3.1.4. We affirm the real presence of Christ in communion; its character, however, is the same as the character of his presence in the word.

3.1.5. We affirm the eucharistic communion (*communio*) with Christ and the members of his body that emerges from every celebration of the Lord's supper. This communion demonstrates the "oneness of sharers with Christ and with their fellow sharers in all times and places" (§19). It knows no church boundaries; it creates unlimited fellowship.

3.1.6. We view the Lord's supper as an invitation open to everyone and as an opportunity for mission. It demands and promotes reconciliation and community particularly within the family of God. Having been strengthened by the eucharist, the members of the body of Christ recognize their tasks in the world in which they live and thus try to carry out their duties responsibly in all aspects of their lives.

3.1.7. We would welcome greater frequency of celebration of the Lord's supper (§30).

### 3.2. What do we disagree with?

3.2.1. We regret that of all the customary terms for the Lord's supper, "eucharist" was chosen as the generic term. Without any given explanation for this choice *one* aspect of the Lord's supper is unduly emphasized. This means that emphasis is shifted from God's action in Christ to the celebrating congregation and its "activity" (praising God). We would prefer the term "the Lord's supper" (in German: *Mahl des Herrn, Herrenmahl,* or *Abendmahl*).

3.2.2. The incomparable position of the Lord's supper as formulated in its definition as "the central act of the Church's worship" (§1) and in the statement on the uniqueness of Christ's presence in the eucharist (§13) is unacceptable to us. We see no qualitative difference between celebration of the Lord's supper and the proclaimed word.

3.2.3. We can appreciate the liturgical diversity of the celebration of the Lord's supper (§27). What is of essence to us, however, are the words of consecration and the elements, although we remain open to the celebration's manifoldness, and practise it.

3.2.4. The understanding of the "eucharist as thanksgiving to the Father" (§§3–4) surpasses the meaning of the Lord's supper as it is established by

Christ. The same statement is to be made upon the increased *anamnesis* (§§5–11) and the idea of "an offering on behalf of the whole world" (§20). During the Lord's supper we are always the ones who receive, and never those who make offerings.

3.2.5. We think the discussion on the the distribution of functions within the Trinity is speculative and of little help (§14, second part).

3.2.6. To derive all Christian services from the Lord's supper seems an abridgment to us (§21, second para.). The saving power of Christ is manifold and free, it is not exclusively tied to the communion table (§21, first sentence).

3.2.7. Although the eucharist is characterized as God's gift, an autonomous power is attributed to it, of which it is said that healing powers go forth *solely* from this power to Christians (§26).

3.2.8. The accentuated function of the "minister of the eucharist" is linked to a concept of ministry that is unfounded on theological and biblical grounds (§29, second part; see also Ministry §14).

3.2.9. We reject the understanding "that Christ's presence in the consecrated elements also continues after the celebration" (§32).


## 4. Ministry

*4.1. What do we agree with?*

4.1.1. The ecumenical recognition that ministry is established in the priesthood of all believers and consequently in the priesthood of Christ has gained general acceptance (§§1–6, 12, 17). The responsibility before the people of God is also stated in this (§16).

4.1.2. The apostolic tradition manifests itself in the life of the church as a whole — not in particular rites only. Therefore churches of different structure and character can recognize in each other the continuity with the apostles and their proclamation (§34/35).

4.1.3. Every ministry in the church is established in Christ's ministry and is related to him. Above all it is proof that the church is dependent on Christ and his ministry (§§8 and 39).

4.1.4. The necessity of the *episkope* and the recognition of its manifoldness (as the basis of mutual recognition) is an ecumenical consensus that Methodists share wholeheartedly (§§23-24, 33). We recognize with gratitude that the different characteristics that have developed historically in the structure of our church have found their place and that they determine the practice of ministry (§26).

4.1.5. The description of ordination as action by God and the church (§40) corresponds to the Methodist understanding of the call and installation of pastors — especially with the emphasis on divine initiative (§42). Ordination is to be granted equally to women and men (§8). Therefore the ordination of women cannot be made an obstacle to preventing mutual recognition (§54).

*4.2. What do we disagree with?*

4.2.1. When only Christ and the totality of Christians are called "priests" in the New Testament, the "particular priestly service" of clergy cannot be adhered to at the same time. BEM identifies the problems and the fundamental divergence from the office of sacrificer (§17 Commentary), but it retains the concept.

4.2.2. The claim, too, that *one* clergy-person is head of the eucharistic congregation and that he/she has principal authorization to preside over the eucharist and carry it out (§§14 and ff.) contradicts this incorporation in the totality (cf. 3.2.8. of this response).

4.2.3. Although the apostolic tradition as a whole is emphasized (§35), the particular notion of succession is nonetheless established (§34 Commentary), and the call of the clergy is linked to episcopal succession (§36). Does the comment on Clement's tendency to concretize the apostolic tradition through succession (§36 Commentary) not apply even here? The question remains, in what sense is the apostolic succession a "sign" (§38)? The tendency to make it (succession) a means and goal of establishing unity is unmistakable in BEM (§53b). Thus old objections are fostered, as if the ecumenical movement viewed unity ultimately in a structure of unity, and not in the faith and discipleship of Christians.

4.2.4. The tendency to concretize is also shown in the "sacramental" understanding of ministry (§§41, 53) which endangers the strong personality of the tie to Christ (according to Reformation theology). This personality is also damaged when clergy take the place of Christ as his "representative" (§11 and repeatedly).

In this context we must express our astonishment at the fact that despite the intensive participation of Roman Catholic theologians in this comprehensive document, the Roman doctrine of papal primacy is not mentioned once.

4.2.5. BEM grants "threefold ministry", as developed in early Catholic times, an explicitly special status. It appears to be normative (§19), "although" (three times) objections are known and the need for reform is recognized (§24). We maintain that teaching and ruling (§§29–30) occurs with the participation of the whole congregation. Therefore lay persons share responsibility with ordained clergy at Methodist conferences.

## 5. Concluding remarks

We view our position on BEM as part of a dialogue that happily incorporates broad circles of the ecumenical community. We nonetheless encourage and call for a dialogue of equal intensity and within a similar framework that would address the missionary task of the church and its mission in the world.

# EVANGELICAL-METHODIST CHURCH: CENTRAL CONFERENCE IN THE FEDERAL REPUBLIC OF GERMANY AND WEST BERLIN

## 1. General considerations

1.1. The fact that representatives from so many different Christian churches could produce common statements on baptism, eucharist and ministry gives us cause to give thanks to God and to the people who took part in this process. We are aware that Methodist theologians also collaborated in this venture, and we affirm this endeavour. We hope that our response, even if it is critical, leads to further acquaintance, understanding and mutual agreement between churches and their statements of faith.

1.2. In the conversations that took place over several decades and developed into the BEM statements, apparently several confessional positions were brought closer together, relativized or traced back to an original concern. Sometimes, however, diverging positions were simply placed side by side. Controversial points were neutralized, concealed or completely silenced through variously explicit formulations. As a result, contradictory expositions were provoked. Thus the danger arises that statements feign more unity than actually exists. On the other hand, through ecumenical conversations seeking understanding of such statements, the possibility of reaching more agreement can also arise.

1.3. The distinction between the proper, enumerated main text and the appended commentary is questionable. According to the foreword (Lazareth/Nissiotis) only the main text contains reached agreement. But sometimes we find the points most important to us in the commentary, without which the main text would be too ambiguous and marked by unclear intentions.

1.4. We concur with the three statements to various degrees. We find the most agreement with the faith and praxis of our church in the document on baptism, less in the document on eucharist, whereas the document on ministry evokes from us the strongest criticism.

---

● 65,000 members, 260 congregations, 250 ministers, 8 districts, 1 bishop.

1.5. We welcome the goal of the BEM statements to encourage churches to decide on mutual recognition of their respective baptisms, celebrations of the eucharist and ministries.

1.6. The Evangelical-Methodist Church is a church that has its origins in a movement focusing on awakening and sanctification. It adopted some theological convictions, structures and forms of worship from older churches, particularly from the Anglican tradition; some (of these convictions, etc.) have emerged more recently via the example of the New Testament and out of necessities of praxis. The BEM statements challenge us to assess whether our theology and ecclesiastical praxis are sufficiently biblically based in all aspects, whether they consider the experiences of the church fathers, whether they are consistent and whether they are ecumenically open.

1.7. But the BEM statements must undergo a similar test as well. This holds true above all for its biblical foundation: indeed, numerous biblical concepts and references are mentioned. But at crucial points positions are substantiated by ecclesiastical tradition, especially that of the first centuries — one that has held its own against other traditions. We object to this. All historical formulations of the Christian faith are time-bound and all church history is also the history of error and sin. To be sure, we also believe that tradition, reason and experience determine the formulation of faith awareness. A more decisive criterion is, however, holy scripture alone.

1.8. The themes of the BEM statements are not pre-eminent in our theological tradition. Soteriology takes greater precedence. The fact that the subjective side of faith has practically not been taken into account, and that concepts important to us, such as "conversion", "rebirth" and "salvation" are formally mentioned at the most once renders these concepts an "objective", "institutional" and "sacramental" one-sidedness that is alien to us. When the individual person experiences no personal encounter with God, what prevails is mere "formal religion" (John Wesley), which causes humanity to miss the salvation in Christ.

1.9. All endeavours towards unity in the church must have the goal of promoting the church's ministry in the present. In the eyes of the "world", such a lengthy discussion about ministry and the church's acts of worship is a sign in and of itself of the blindness and backwardness of the church and of the self-importance and power struggles of its functionaries. This occurs all the more when the discussion is determined so much by formulations and ways of the past. We regret that the needs and hopes of people today are taken into account so little, and therefore we find little help in this document for our efforts to evangelize and to do missionary work.

1.10. We will not be answering directly the three questions posed to churches at the conclusion of the foreword to BEM. In the first place, the criterion mentioned in the first question, that is, whether we "can recognize in this text the faith of the Church through the ages" (1.7) is not a decisive one. Also, only agreement and further suggestions have been requested, whereas we would also like to comment on where we disagree. Therefore we join most other churches in the German-speaking area in presenting a threefold response to each of the three statements: where we agree with the text, where we meet challenges to assess ourselves and where we have critical objections to make.

## 2. Baptism

### 2.1. Agreement

2.1.1. We welcome the biblical foundation of the statements on baptism. The variety of images and descriptions of baptism in the New Testament prevent us from accentuating one particular aspect (§§ 1–7).

2.1.2. We too confess that Christian baptism is rooted in the ministry of Jesus of Nazareth and in his death and resurrection (§1).

2.1.3. The text's determination that baptism always encompasses the whole life of a person is important to us (§§4–10). This takes up the Methodist concern for salvation in that the life of the person baptized is described as a "life-long growth into Christ" (§9) which has ethical implications in all realms of life (§10).

2.1.4. We share the view that a "personal commitment is necessary for responsible membership in the body of Christ" (§8). Our church makes this clear through the special celebration of the reception of new members, which is understood as an act of the single reality of baptism. Both baptism and reception in the Christian church relate to each other as two sides of one and the same event. Reception into the church, linked with a confession before the whole congregation, is understood "as a personal response at a later moment in life" (§12). It is anticipated with the baptism of infants. So, too, confession, baptism and reception come together in the baptism of adults.

Therefore we explicitly stress the importance of the request that churches examine their practice of indiscriminate baptism when this is the sole basis for membership in the church (Baptism Commentary 21b).

2.1.5. The call to incorporate the celebration of baptism in public worship reflects our church's practice. The congregation's responsibility as witness to the baptismal act remains a task to be continually observed.

2.1.6. Since "the faithful participation in the life of the church . . . is essential for the full fruit of baptism" (§12, Commentary), the church is obliged to evangelize to those who have been baptized but do not yet or any longer live out their faith.

### 2.2. Self-assessment

2.2.1. Although the congregation is indeed reminded of their own respective baptism through participation in the baptismal service, appropriate ways of expressing one's personal renewal through baptismal vows should be sought.

2.2.2. We are not familiar with the signs of anointing, nor with chrismation. An explicit renunciation of evil is also lacking in our baptismal liturgy. The rediscovery of such actions from the early church could be taken into consideration in current liturgical studies and drafting of texts.

2.2.3. Since baptism ultimately attains its purpose through personal confession during reception, it is important to take basic instruction in reception more seriously.

## 2.3. Critical objections

2.3.1. We see a danger in over-emphasizing rites and signs. These can serve only as references. The giver and receiver of the promises dedicated during baptism is solely the crucified and risen Lord who ministers among us through his spirit. This also holds for the gift of the Holy Spirit.

2.3.2. We question whether it was always clearly established that the human person can be only one who receives in baptism. "The human response to this gift" (§8) is continually subordinated.

2.3.3. It is hard for us to see "the continuity between the old and the new creation" (§18 Commentary) in the use of water, and to acknowledge "a purification of creation". Here the symbolic dimension, which we do take seriously, is nonetheless exaggerated.

## 3. Eucharist

### 3.1. Agreement

3.1.1. We concur with the biblical foundation of the eucharist.

3.1.2. All aspects of the eucharist mentioned in §2 and developed in the rest of the text bear significance for us, even if to various degrees.

3.1.3. We stress the importance of the statement in §3 that the celebration of the eucharist always includes both word *and* sacrament, proclamation *and* celebration of the acts of God.

3.1.4. We affirm the understanding of the eucharist as an "anamnesis" — as a realization of the event and anticipation of the One to come (§7).

3.1.5. We welcome the clear statement maintaining that God's acts in Christ will not be repeated (§8).

3.1.6. It is important to us that the connection between the congregation's celebration of the meal and its participation in the world is made clear in several places throughout the text (§§10, 20, 24–26).

3.1.7. We completely share the passage on the real presence of Christ (§13). That faith is "required" is correct; however we do not view it as a prerequisite for taking part in the eucharist, for faith is bestowed upon many people through the meal.

3.1.8. The commentary on §13 describes two diverging positions in regard to the real presence of Christ in the eucharist. The Evangelical-Methodist Church stands more in agreement with the second position. In our opinion this divergence can be completely accommodated within the unity formulated in the text itself.

3.1.9. For us, too, the eucharist is a common meal. Paragraph 19 correctly emphasizes that the community is more fully manifested in the eucharist than when it simply gathers at any given time.

3.1.10. Children's participation in the eucharist (Commentary to §19) is being increasingly supported in the Evangelical-Methodist Church. Congregations should consider "organizing their eucharist services in such a way that children are able to take part in them".

3.1.11. Leadership of the eucharist service is reserved for ordained clergy in our church as well. This is a matter of pastoral responsibility and of order, not one of a particular understanding of ministry ("representative of Christ").

3.1.12. The doctrinal conversation taking place between the United Evangelical Lutheran Church and the Evangelical-Methodist Church of the Federal Republic of Germany and West Berlin can serve as an example of efforts among individual churches "to attain a greater measure of eucharistic communion" (§33).

*3.2. Self-assessment*

In many places, BEM goes beyond our theological understanding, above all, beyond our practice. We see ourselves taking the following into consideration:

3.2.1. Thanksgiving and praise (§§ 3 and 4) are neglected in our eucharist celebration. In one of the three eucharist liturgies (B) this element is almost completely lacking or touches only on subjective experience ("You have made your faithfulness and mercy known to us again through your holy meal").

3.2.2. Our eucharist celebrations lay primary emphasis on remembrance. But it has not been made sufficiently clear that what is meant is *anamnesis* as the *realization* of the holy event in the crucifixion, resurrection and coming of Christ.

3.2.3. Our eucharist liturgies do not articulate clearly that "the whole action of the eucharist . . . depends upon the work of the Holy Spirit" (§16). The eucharist celebration requires the *epiklesis*.

3.2.4. Our "social principles" make clear that the gospel of God's love to all people demands our mission for justice and peace. The celebration of the meal also implies a "constant challenge in the search for appropriate relationships in social, economic and political life" (§20). This association must be made clear in our celebration of the eucharist, especially when the "dignity" of the celebration is wrongly called into question. In connection with this we could link up with a formulation from the Anglican-Methodist tradition: "You, who sincerely repent of your sins, who want to live in love and harmony with your fellow humankind, and are determined to lead a new life according to God's commandments and to travel in His holy ways: Come here in faith . . ."

3.2.5. According to the Methodist constitution, the following: "The eucharist immediately shows us the future in Jesus Christ: It is a joyful indication of the returning Lord, and the festive joy that God's children anticipate in the splendour of the Father."

BEM speaks beyond this to the promised "final renewal of creation, . . . whose signs are present in the world. . . . The eucharist is the feast at which the Church gives thanks to God for these signs and joyfully celebrates and anticipates the coming of the Kingdom in Christ" (§22). Except for in the words of institution, this element of hope has been expressed in our eucharist liturgy through only *one* prayer: "Secure us in joyful hope for your day, and let us one day be guests at the table of mercy in your kingdom." There is no celebration of the coming kingdom of God, nor of its anticipation in the Evangelical-Methodist liturgy.

3.2.6. The relative infrequency of the celebration of the eucharist makes the Lord's supper seem like a "peripheral act" in our church's life of worship. The Evangelical-Methodist rules of liturgy state: "The frequency of the celebration of the eucharist is determined according to the needs of the congregation. However, the eucharist is not to be celebrated less than four times a year . . ." (KO 410).

BEM states: "As the eucharist celebrates the resurrection of Christ, it is appropriate that it should take place at least once (!) every Sunday" (§31).

Starting from the basis of very different grounds, minimum and maximum positions stand in contrast to each other. The eucharist should be celebrated more often in the Evangelical-Methodist Church.


*3.3. Critical objections*

3.3.1. We regret that of all the customary terms for the Lord's supper, "eucharist" was chosen as the generic term. Without any given explanation for this choice *one* aspect of the Lord's supper is unduly emphasized. This means that emphasis is shifted from God's action in Christ to the celebrating congregation and its "activity" (praising God). We would prefer the terms "communion" or the "Lord's supper".

3.3.2. We cannot totally concur with the sentence in §1: "Its celebration continues as the central act of the Church's worship". Here a (sacramental) concept of worship predominates, which we cannot accept. Our view is that a service in which the word is preached is of no less value than one in which holy communion is celebrated. The Lord is not any more "present" in the feast of the eucharist than in prayer or in the proclamation of his word.

3.3.3. According to §2, " . . . each baptized member of the body of Christ receives in the eucharist the assurance of the forgiveness of sins . . . and the pledge of eternal life". For us the invitation to the eucharist holds for everyone who seeks the grace of God and "are conscious of the meaning of this sacrament" (KO 409). Therefore we believe that baptism is not a prerequisite or condition for taking part in the eucharist.

3.3.4. The Lord's supper is characterized as "the great sacrifice of praise by which the Church speaks on behalf of the whole creation" (§4). The substantiation that follows seems speculative to us. But above all we cannot go along with the idea of sacrifice expressed in this (see "offering," mentioned twice).

3.3.5. "In the memorial of the eucharist . . . the Church offers its intercession in communion with Christ, our great High Priest" (§8). The understanding of the feast *as* intercession for all people is not theologically conclusive to us. Therefore a leap to the Catholic idea of propitiatory sacrifice, presented as a possibility in Commentary 8, is unthinkable.

3.3.6. We cannot speak of the eucharist *as* invocation of the Holy Spirit (as in the heading to Section C), but we can speak of celebrating it *during invocation* of the Spirit.

3.3.7. In §20, (similarly in §4), the Lord's supper is characterized as a "representative act of thanksgiving and offering on behalf of the whole world". This formulation seems exaggerated and biblically unfounded. We hold a similar opinion of the "global" statements in §23.

3.3.8. The first sentence of §24 ("Reconciled in the eucharist, . . .") appears as if salvation is from the eucharist, which is only a sign and expression of the reconciliation *"in Christ"*.

We view §26 similarly: It is not the eucharist but *Christ* who is God's gift, which "brings into the present age a new reality", which transforms people and makes them his witnesses. The eucharist is an agent of grace through which the exalted Christ is communicated.

## 4. Ministry

### 4.1. Agreement

4.1.1. We heartily agree when God's gift to us is described first, and from this our mission follows, indeed, as a call to *all* Christians (§§1–6). We emphasize that "the churches need to work from the perspective of the calling of the whole people of God" (§6) if they intend to overcome differences based on tradition in the structure and valuation of their ministries. The Evangelical-Methodist Church tries to realize this in obliging all of its members right from the start to share in their cooperation and gifts in the service of their local congregation.

4.1.2. Ordained ministry stems from the ministries to all Christians, which again, in our view, originates in the ministry of Jesus Christ. We welcome the statements on the inter-relatedness of ordained and lay persons (§12) and the description of the minister's authority as service to the congregation (§16). This includes the ministry of "episkope". In our churches too, persons have been continually called from the congregation to full-time, lifelong ministry in which they are ordained after theological training.

4.1.3. It is good that the historical development of all ordained ministries is pointed out (Commentary to §11). Indeed, it seems to us that the disparities between the church's ministries have more to do with regulations that have increased throughout history, that is, are time-bound, and have less to do with the absolute truth of faith.

4.1.4. "The ordained ministry should be exercised in a personal, collegial and communal way" (§26); accordingly, the structure of an ideal church should contain elements of the episcopal, presbyteral and congregational systems of government (Commentary to §26). At first this may look like the quadrants of a circle. We have determined that the order of the Evangelical-Methodist Church realizes all of these elements (episcopate, committee structure, regional autonomy).

4.1.5. "The primary manifestation of apostolic succession is to be found in the apostolic tradition of the Church as a whole" (§35). We verify that we recognize in principle the apostolic character of the churches contributing to BEM — apart from their respective constitutions. (This is also how we view §§34 and 37.)

4.1.6. We essentially agree with the description of ordination (§49–50). The reciprocity between God's action (the personal call) and that of the community (commission by the church, §40) corresponds to our views. The Evangelical-Methodist Church ordains women to spiritual office; the United Methodist Church, to which we belong, has also installed women in the office of bishop.

## 4.2. Self-assessment

4.2.1. The Evangelical-Methodist Church has no formulated ordination doctrine in creeds. Perhaps it is necessary to portray ministries in the local communities, where members exhibit cooperation and share responsibility, as theologically consolidated. The call to and ordination in full-time, spiritual ministry can then be more clearly viewed as a particular instance of ministry, to which Christ calls everyone.

4.2.2. The threefold form of ordained ministry exists throughout the United Methodist Church, but not in the German Evangelical-Methodist Church. Here threefold ministry is combined in one ordination. This is impetus for us to reflect once more upon the meaning and arrangement of this threefold form. We ask ourselves whether this form can help to give expression to things other than theological ministries in the church. Currently we are considering the position of those who have no (complete) theological training, but who practise full-time ministry in certain areas of the church (work with children and youth, diaconate, missions work). In addition we are considering the ordination of lay preachers.

## 4.3. Critical objections

4.3.1. The visions and ministries of lay persons, as described in §§1–6, are not further developed in the text that follows. Rather, the congregation appears as a passive object of ordained ministry's activity (§§11, 12, 14). Apparently the reality of the large, so-called popular churches has become the criterion for theological opinion. We oppose this. The communities of the New Testament as well as those of our churches are more autonomous and active.

4.3.2. We cannot totally agree with the assertion that "ordained ministers are representatives of Jesus Christ to the community" (§11). Rather, anyone who speaks to and acts in the congregation on his behalf, including those who are not ordained, represents Jesus Christ. Ministry receives its authority in the end only from the word of God (*ministerium verbi*). The congregation shares the responsibility of ensuring that this authority is in agreement with the gospel.

4.3.3. Ministry in the church is described as "a focus of [the church's] unity [which] is constitutive for the life and witness of the Church" (§8). Indeed, this is desired, but is simply historically false. The truth of the matter is that it is exactly the ordained clergy who have brought about the splits in the Christian church. It is also true that through the ages clergy have separated themselves more and more from the laity and have incapacitated them — with disastrous consequences for the unity, witness and service of the church.

4.3.4. All special ministerial assignments are characteristics of *one* ministry, that of the proclamation of Jesus Christ. The introduction of a threefold pattern of ministry (§19ff.) has historically led to the perversion of the structure of ministry within ordained ministry to a hierarchical structure of dominance. This danger is always present. The New Testament explicitly addresses the equality of different services and visions of God's people, and does not give priority to the office of leadership, rather to the vision of love. In light of the variety of ministries in the New Testament and in church history, the tendency must be to prevent setting up a hierarchically structured ministry as a model or prerequisite for the unity of the church.

4.3.5. The ministry of preaching and teaching is carried out in the Evangelical-Methodist Church by the synods. At the regional level the synods consist primarily of lay persons, at the cross-regional level, of proportionate numbers of lay and ordained persons. Therefore we cannot concur with the function ascribed to bishops (§29) and the presbytery (§30). We question whether the authors did not have a compositional structure in mind that was too hierarchically-episcopal, and whether structures just as qualified were not disregarded. We also wonder whether the times we live in don't require completely different ecclesiastical structures than the structures of a particular time in the history of the early church.

4.3.6. We reject the use of the term "priest" for ordained clergy (§17). This term depicts one who sacrifices and is a mediator of salvation. Therefore, to us it obscures the unique and saving sacrifice, Jesus Christ, and for this reason is not used in the New Testament to designate ordained ministry (see Commentary to §17). Although the problems of later traditions are actually acknowledged here, they (the problems) are placed above the New Testament (!) — a significant valuation that we categorically reject.

4.3.7. The uninterrupted succession of the episcopate throughout the ages is only a sign or "an expression of the . . . continuity of the Church" (§35). It is not readily apparent that the adoption of this sign is required for mutual recognition (§53b). Isn't this sign thus made into a necessary, even fundamental element for the apostolic character of the church? If this is indeed the case, (see 4.1.5.), the sign could, on the contrary, be relinquished.

4.3.8. In our estimation, ordination essentially consists of call and intercession; it is not automatic confirment of the Spirit (§39 sounds this way), or the conveyance of a particular quality. Frequently visions are received prior to ordination, thus it ensues from recognized and unrecognized gifts. The term "sacramental" (§§41 and 43) and the almost magical explanation of ordination does not seem appropriate to us.

4.3.9. The statement that many churches ordain women, whereas some do not, each for whatever reasons (§18 with Commentary) is not satisfactory, nor is it an expression of convergence. For us the recognition of ordained women as valid clergy serves as a decisive test as to whether there is a mutual recognition of ministries.

4.3.10. In 1965, the Roman Catholic Church gave a new presentation of its doctrine of ordained ministry in the Constitution *Lumen gentium* of the Second Vatican Council. We regret that its fundamental doctrines of papacy, of Mary as the mother of the church, of requisite celibacy of ordained clergy and of their central function in mass were all left unexamined or simply alluded to. Thus this is merely an apparent convergence, at least in regard to this great Christian confessional church.

4.3.11. "The unity that we seek" should be "expressed" and "sought" (§22) through a structure of ordained ministries that is as uniform as possible. Our goal is an "order of life of a reunified Church" (Commentary to §26). We think that this objective of wanting to attain unity through uniform structures is wrong. What is necessary is a unity in faith and in spirit, a unity that arises from proclamation of the word of God and from imitation of Jesus Christ. Then churches can be of more unified service to the world, even if they maintain different structures and traditions. The good and necessary goal of a mutual recognition should not be burdened, made more difficult or hindered by tendencies towards uniformity.

# UNITED FREE CHURCH OF SCOTLAND

The United Free Church of Scotland, while finding much to disagree with, receives with interest the document, "Baptism, Eucharist and Ministry". We still find it easier to identify the church's faith, down through the ages, with the historic expression of the Apostles' and Nicene Creeds, rather than baptism, eucharist and ministry.

For us, the significance of the document lies in the interest it has aroused in Christendom, and the lively discussion on three central issues of the church's life, doctrine and witness. We accept that the Lima document contains many diverse views, and sometimes attempts to forge these together. We consider that the document will enjoy more than "passing interest", and will become a reference point for future discussion on the doctrine, organisation and structure of the church of Jesus Christ, in her many branches.

We consider that some of the views expressed in "Baptism, Eucharist and Ministry" will not find ready acceptance in our congregations. However, we share the hope that all branches of the church of Jesus Christ will continue to grow towards one another in love, so that we may witness together for the cause of our One Lord and Saviour, Jesus Christ.

*Adopted by the General Assembly in 1985*

---

• 11,750 members, 5 presbyteries, 83 congregations, 72 ministers, 5 unordained missionaries.

# BURMA BAPTIST CONVENTION

**Foreword**

The Executive Committee of the *Burma Baptist Convention* convened a special consultation on BEM from 21 to 22 August 1986. The consultation was assigned to formulate a draft response which is expected to reflect a general attitude of all member Baptist churches towards that historic document. After two full days of intensive study and discussion the consultation was able to put up a draft to the Executive Committee. This draft was finally approved by the Executive Committee at its regular meeting held 26–28 August 1986. What follows therefore can be regarded as the official response of the Executive Committee of the Burma Baptist Convention to the Lima document on "Baptism, Eucharist and Ministry".

Being Baptists, the Executive Committee is well aware that this response is its own. It cannot yet be interpreted as the response of every single Baptist member church of the Convention. The Committee therefore sends this response to all members with the hope that it will be received, studied and finally approved by all members at one of our biennial conventions.

At the same time the Committee informs all members that it will be sending this response, as its official response, to the Geneva secretariat of the WCC Commission on Faith and Order.

**Preamble**

The Burma Baptist Convention, being a member of the World Council of Churches, has been invited to give its own response to the Lima document on "Baptism, Eucharist and Ministry". We are grateful to God for this opportunity, and we respond in faith — the faith that has guided us through almost two centuries of our life and mission in Burma. Before we respond to

---

● 398,005 members, 2,917 congregations, 143 ordained pastors, 914 workers and evangelists.

the three ecclesial events, we present the following introduction to convey our attitude, and perhaps our overall "response", towards BEM.

## Introduction

1. First and foremost we respond with a spirit of thanksgiving. We are grateful to God for the advent of BEM. Surely it is not by might nor human power that this historic "ecumenical milestone" has been reached. We express our thanks also to all who have committed themselves to this unforgettable ecumenical task and laboured to bring this document into being.

2. We do not feel that we are responding to a "foreign" document. Even though delegates from Burma were not present at Accra or Lima, we do not feel that the text is alien. Because in the first place even though we are Burmese, we are at the same time members together in the one family of God on earth. And in the second place we can regard the document as our own, because we share the belief mentioned on page viii of the preface that "the witness of local churches itself is an important factor for the coming into being of this ecumenical achievement".

3. The third point is our motive for responding to BEM. We do not respond simply because it is expected of us. We respond because of our commitment to unity and the ongoing mission of the whole church in the whole world. BEM is not just a domestic concern among the separated churches. It is intrinsically related to the life that we are to offer for the whole world.

4. We try our best to respond from an ecumenical perspective. We do recognize the theological convergence that has been achieved after years of preparation. Hence we will not deliberately raise new issues which might split up that convergence or stand in the way of achieving mutual recognition and unity.

5. At the same time since we are not asked simply to give an unreflective assent, but to "respond" to it, we must be responsible enough to point out certain facts which need to be either added to, or deleted from the text, or at least in some places to be reformulated. We know that we have been called upon to respond to the text especially in the light of what is being asked on page x of the preface. But we feel we have to respond with our suggestions also; and we do this in full awareness of the points mentioned in the last paragraph of page ix of the preface. Hence we hope that our suggestions will not be looked upon as being exclusively "Baptist" in character.

6. Several Baptist churches as well as some Baptist seminaries have already begun their studies and discussions on BEM. Prominent Baptist pastors have already initiated co-celebration of the eucharist together with ordained ministers of other confessions at some national ecumenical meetings. In a sense therefore, we can say that "a process of reception" has already begun among the Baptists in Burma.

7. Finally we would like to offer our prayers for the continuing reception of BEM. May God grant us penitence, humility and wisdom to learn from each other, and work together so that God's will may be done on earth, as it is done in heaven.

**Baptism**

1. We note that the text admits differences in terminology with regard to "Ministry" (p. 21, Ministry §7), and also in a certain manner with respect to "Eucharist" (p. 10, Eucharist I §1). But there is no mention of differences in terminology regarding "Baptism". This is significant. "Baptism" has no other substitutes like "the act of immersion" or "the laying on of hands", etc. Tracing the etymological meaning of baptism need not be a cause for further division.

2. We observe also that §11 and §12 precede §13. Thirteen does not and cannot stand by itself. It is a direct consequence of the expositions expressed from §§1 to 10, and especially from the expositions revealed by §11 and §12. Hence §13 should begin with the word "therefore". This is not simply an editorial amendment. Baptism is an unrepeatable act because of the "meaning", "faith", and "practice", given to it by the preceding passages. Some have even suggested adding another word to §13. That word is "normally". They want to see §13 beginning with: "Therefore, normally, baptism is an unrepeatable act, etc.". Reasons given for this second addition are profoundly practical and existential. There still *are* many cases in Burma where new members, coming from other churches (Christian groups) which do not yet belong to the worldwide ecumenical movement, themselves request to be given a second baptism. The case here is therefore not just a matter of "baptismal practice". It has to do with a deep and personal faith of each believer.

3. We may need another additional sentence or at least a commentary for §16. As it stands, the text calls on those believer Baptists who seem not to have expressed more visibly "the fact that children are placed under the protection of God's grace, *to express that fact more visibly*". It also calls on those who practise infant baptism and who seem not to have taken more seriously their responsibility for the nurture of baptized children, "*to take that responsibility more seriously*".

There is nothing to be said against these two calls. But at the same time the text must recognize that there *are* believer Baptists *who have expressed that fact visibly*, and also that there *are* those who practise infant baptism, *who have taken their responsibility for continual nurture seriously*. Paragraph 16 therefore should either have the following additional sentence, or at least include it as a commentary to §16:

"One way of overcoming their differences is for churches *also to perceive how* those who practise believer's baptism are already making manifest their belief that all, including infants, are constantly under God's grace and care;

and also *on the other hand to perceive that* many churches which practise infant baptism do in fact take their responsibility for continual nurture of all their members, including infants, seriously".[1]

4. Regarding §18 a question still remains: Why are Baptists called "Baptists" and not "immersionists"? Is it only because of their understanding of the "practice" of baptism? Has it also to do with their understanding of the "meaning" of baptism? Or are Baptists "Baptists" *both* because of their understanding of the practice as well as the meaning of baptism? For the Baptists in Burma, Burmese words for "Baptist" and baptism are nearly identical. For some Baptists in Burma Baptists are "Baptists" because they baptize! The truth, of course, is that Baptists are "Baptists" not only because of their particular baptismal practice (which is also performed by other confessions), but also and primarily because of their other doctrines. Hence we have responded in §1 of this section that tracing the etymological meaning of baptism need not be a cause for further division.

5. The Lima text states that baptism is related not only to a momentary experience, but to a life-long growth into Christ (p. 4, §9). Paragraphs 5, 10 and 12 also interpret baptism as a process[2] which can begin from infancy and continue as a life-long growth into Christ. Baptism is also understood both as God's gift and our response in faith and commitment to that gift. Personal faith (of the baptized) as well as the faith of both the parents and the church have also been taken into account (§§1, 8, 11, and 12). We therefore perceive that a convergence has taken place. With such understanding of baptism *mutual recognition of baptism has become a possibility.*

**Eucharist**

1. Burma Baptists do not use the word "eucharist" for that ordinance signifying the last meal of our Lord. As mentioned in the text (§1) we use the terms "the Lord's supper" or "the holy communion". We will *not*, of course, insist that the term "eucharist" be exchanged for another term. Incidentally, the Burmese word for eucharist is not "eucharist". It means "a blessed feast", and, surprisingly, this Burmese term is being used commonly by Baptists as well as by several other eucharistic congregations of Burma.

2. But we suggest that the last sentence of the second paragraph under §1, on page 10, be modified as follows: "It has also been called by other names, for example, the Lord's Supper, etc., . . ." As the text stands it seems as if the term "eucharist" is original, whereas others like "the Lord's supper", etc. came to be *acquired* later on in the course of history. Granted that other names are historically later than "eucharist", that should not be a ground for making the term *seem* more "original" than the others.

---

[1] Such mutual perception is already a living reality for many churches in Burma.
[2] "Process" is not a term directly used by the Lima text.

3. We note that §§5, 6 and 7 interpret *anamnesis* to mean more than what some Baptist churches understand by "Do this in remembrance of me." Here also a further commentary may be required. We cannot *seem* to belittle the eucharistic celebrations of those, who, so far, have never understood their celebrations in the light of *anamnesis* as expounded by the text. Are those which do not understand *anamnesis* in that particular sense to be treated as invalid? We cannot but admit that years of discipleship and witness by those churches stand as an unfailing testimony to the genuineness of their celebrations.

4. We observe also that the meaning of *anamnesis* and the words "the real presence of Christ" as mentioned in §§6, 13, and 14 must be interpreted *in conjunction with* the last four sentences of §8. Christians who do not accept transubstantiation shall not be called upon or even expected to require "a new faith" in order to discern the body and the blood of Christ" at the celebration of the eucharist. In short we note that all portions under "eucharist", when taken organically, call neither for a belief, nor an unbelief, in the doctrine of transubstantiation.

We note also that line 20 of §2 should not be cut off or abbreviated in any way. If we put a full stop after "liturgical meal", the meaning will be different. Similarly, if we drop the word "liturgical", the meaning will be substantially changed.

5. We are very glad to note that the text contains very significant portions under "eucharist" D and E. Because of the need for exposition in A, B, and C, these portions under D and E have to come last in chronology. But we take note that they are equally as important as those under A, B, and C. In certain living contexts they become even more salvific than our comprehension of the eucharist theology.

6. Paragraph 31 is problematic. All eucharist celebrations may be celebrations of the resurrection of Jesus Christ; but the converse need not always be the case. One cannot say that all celebrations of the resurrection of Christ are or must necessarily be eucharistic celebrations. The word "appropriate" in §31 may not be appropriate. Thirty-one should be rewritten to mean simply that — every Christian should be encouraged to receive communion frequently.

7. We note also the distinction between "Christ's presence at the eucharist" and that of "Christ's presence in the consecrated elements of the eucharist". We take it that the text also recognizes this distinction. In other words Christ's real presence at the eucharist should not be equated or identified *exclusively* with his presence in the consecrated elements of the celebration.

## Ministry

1. We note that the text relates the role of the apostles to that of the church as a whole, as well as to the later role of the ordained ministers. We note also

how the text recognizes "the difference between the apostles and the ordained ministry, whose ministries are founded on (the ministry of the Apostles)" (§10).

2. We note also how the text affirms that the authority of the ordained minister is rooted in Jesus Christ who has received it from the Father.

3. We observe also how the text recognizes that the word "priest" is not universal (§7), and that Jesus Christ is the unique priest (§17). We note also how the text states that in a certain sense ordained ministers may appropriately be called "priests" (§17).

4. We are glad to note that the text takes into account the ministries of both men and women in the church (§18). We note also that §18 simply states the differences among churches regarding the admission of women to ordained ministry, without laying down an imperative as to what ought to be the case. Hence we have to admit that as far as this vital issue is concerned, no theological convergence has yet taken place.

5. We note how the text states that the New Testament does not describe a single pattern of ministry (§19), which might serve as a blueprint or continuing norm for all future ministry in the church. But we take note also that the New Testament not only does not describe; it also does not prescribe, or lay down an imperative pattern for all future ministry.

6. The text proposes however that "the threefold ministry of bishop, presbyter and deacon may serve today as an expression of the unity we seek and also as a means for achieving it" (§22). We, as Baptists of Burma, will study that proposal. At the same time we have to point out that the threefold pattern should not be used as a pre-condition for the sake of mutual recognition.

7. The question of "apostolic succession" has been replaced by that of "succession in the apostolic tradition". At the same time the document also continues to speak of "succession in the apostolic ministry". But all portions from §§34 to 38 as well as Commentary §36, together present a balanced position between those who practise succession through the episcopate and those who do not.

8. Paragraph 50 again seems to evade the question of women's ordination. Lima has not been able to state that churches which refuse to consider candidates for the ordained ministry on the ground of handicap or because they belong, for example (note these words — "for example"), to one particular race or sociological group, *or sex*, should re-evaluate their practices. The call here is "to re-evaluate". We must all be humble enough to re-evaluate our positions regarding sex discrimination in relation to ordained ministry.

9. As mentioned earlier, because of our commitment to unity, we welcome the steps suggested by the text for bringing about mutual recognition of the ordained ministry.

**Conclusion**

1. BEM is important. It is a matter of our "faith" as well as our "order". But we must treat it as more than a matter of faith and order. It is targeted towards unity and mission. That is why we in Burma have taken it to heart. There are crucial problems facing humanity today. If our response is to have any validity, it must be life-giving. In other words we fully endorse what is expressed in the last paragraph on page viii of the preface.

2. Our response in some way reflects the extent to which we in Burma recognize the faith of the church through the ages. Baptists in Burma have been ready since the end of the Second World War to enter into dialogue with other confessions for the sake of mutual recognition and unity. Several Baptist churches have already invited ordained ministers from other confessions to co-celebrate the eucharist together with their own Baptist pastors. They have expressed their willingness to keep on extending such invitations even though the invitations so far have never been mutual.

3. Much more can be said of BEM. But, as mentioned earlier, it is for the sake of overcoming the problems of mutual recognition leading to unity, that we, the Baptist churches of Burma are ready to receive this text with the suggestions stated above. We hope and pray that other churches also respond positively and join hands to move on together in unity, beyond the call of BEM, towards even more vital areas of Christian witness, commitment and action that is sorely needed in the world today.

October 1986                                            Executive Committee

# UNION OF EVANGELICAL FREE CHURCHES IN THE GDR (BAPTISTS)

## Preliminary observations

We see within the explanations of this document the remarkable attempt to make an inquiry not directly into the consensus of the churches, but rather into the convergence of their respective views. In this way the undertaking seeks to cope with the divisions of church history and to aid in bringing together different understandings of the unity of Christians. It is understandable in view of the intended goal of the document that its language should strive more towards a general and equivocal style rather than towards a strict dogmatism. Yet it does so, in our view, at the expense of the clarity and perspicuity of its statements.

We perceive in the question directed to us concerning the degree to which we are able to recognize in this text "the faith of the Church through the centuries", a relativizing of the principle which is decisive for us, namely, that we acknowledge only the holy scripture as the norm for faith, life and teaching. Different confessional traditions surface in the document, i.e. the faith of the church(es) as it has "developed" through the centuries, and in our opinion this limits the possibility of clear definition of the "original source", the "tradition of the gospel", and the "apostolic faith". For only the gospel itself can be normative.

To the question concerning the consequences of the document for our relations and dialogues with other churches, we reply that we understand and receive the Lima text as an impetus for dialogue making possible concrete and mutual clarification and correction. For us, however, the unity in theological insight does not precede the unity in the Spirit which is effected by Christ and which creates brotherhood. The priority of ecclesiological themes over the basic question of salvation in Christ, as is peculiar to these texts, bestows upon these themes a weight of their own which does not properly belong to them.

---

● 20,031 members, 217 churches.

In the following discussion, we seek to represent more precisely the response of our free church (which does not belong to the WCC) to this ecumenical document. In this way, we hope to be able to make a contribution to the dialogue between the churches. The statement developed as follows: appointed theologians prepared texts on the respective themes, the Ecumenical Committee of our Union reviewed these texts, and the Executive Committee (*Bundesleitung*) approved them. The texts were prepared against the background of the faith and practice of our congregations, and the language of the respective authors was preserved; the presentation, however, reflects the basic positions of the congregations of our Union.

## Baptism

*1. The concept of baptism*

The conclusion of §2 of the document reads: "The images [for baptism] are many but the reality is one." For the first half of this statement, the document brings forth sufficient evidence, but for the latter half it remains wanting. In the various interpretations of baptism such as "receiving salvation", "representation of salvation", "sign of the new life", "sign of the kingdom", "cleansing of the creation", "washing of the body", "cleansing of the heart", "rite of commitment", "gift of God", "death and burial", "consolation", "sacrament", "initiation", "human response", there is simply no common denominator to be found. Also lacking is an awareness of the exegetical problems involved, as though there were but one recognized exegesis in the world through which all baptismal practices could be brought into agreement. Only with the discussion of "re-baptism" (without registering the arguments of those concerned) does one read: "must be avoided", "will want to refrain", and "recognition should be expressed" (§§13, 13 Commentary, 15).

With regard to the interchangeable use of the terms "infant baptism" and the "baptism of children", we consider the expression "infant baptism" as the more precise of the two.[1] It clarifies the distinction from our own view, according to which baptism is received by those — adults, young people, and children — whose faith has been awakened by the gospel.

Baptism upon personal profession of faith is for us not merely "the most clearly attested pattern in the New Testament" (§11), but rather the only practice documented in the New Testament. By way of contrast, infant baptism, whose date of origin is contested, may be clearly documented only a hundred years after the close of the New Testament.[2]

---

[1] Translator's note: the German text of "Baptism, Eucharist and Ministry" refers to both *Säuglinstaufe* and *Kindertaufe* while the English text uses the term "infant baptism" for both.

[2] Tertullian, *De baptismo* 18, 5; between 200 and 207.

Inherent to the concept of infant baptism is the understanding that the parents of the baptized infant are church members. The document, however, requires that the circle of privileged children be drawn even tighter. Infant baptism should no longer be "practised in an apparently indiscriminate way" (§21 Commentary, cf. §16), but evidently only when the parents are professing and committed Christians. That would apply, in view of the millions of members of state churches, to only a small percentage of all parents. If this qualification is now recommended "in order to overcome differences" "between believer baptists and those who practise infant baptism" (§16), then it is based on a complete misunderstanding. Because the proposal moves infant baptism still further away from the character of grace. Baptism may be understood as an event of grace only when it is also an event of faith, without any active or passive merits.

Paragraph 12 states: "When an infant is baptized, the personal response will be offered at a later moment in life." It is intended here apparently, as it is later stated, that "a personal confession is expected later". The role of the parents and the obligation of the local church are at least supposed to be directed to that end. For the document, the expected confession of faith plays a thoroughly indispensable role (according to §12 Commentary, the "personal faith" of the recipient is "essential for the full fruit of baptism"). According to §15, even the recognition of the baptism of other churches is connected to this fact that the confession of the church, or more precisely, the parents and the godparents, is "affirmed later by personal faith and commitment".

Infant baptism is followed by personal faith only in some cases, and years, perhaps even decades, pass before these baptized people become believers. Our question: What about the many cases of baptized unbelievers? A further question: Which concept of faith stands behind §12 Commentary, where we read of "the faith which the child shares with its parents"? According to the scripture, faith is accessible only through the gospel and is a creation of the word itself (Rom. 10:17; Gal. 10:14). Where nothing is heard, there is nothing to believe.

Do these remarks and questions directed towards the churches which practise infant baptism make our complaints perhaps a little more understandable?

## 2. The sequence of faith and baptism

The document goes into this question under the subtitle "Baptismal Practice" (Section IV), for it sees within this "variety of forms", within the two "equivalent alternatives", two "patterns" of the one New Testament baptism which has "developed" in the course of history (§§11–13). Whether baptism follows faith or faith follows baptism makes no difference. In this regard we must raise the question whether a different sequence does not also lead to different theological implications of the respective practices.

Paragraph 14, whose context clearly includes the practice of infant baptism, states that: "Baptism in its full meaning signifies and effects both", namely "participation in Christ's death and resurrection" and "the receiving of the Holy Spirit", this *nota bene* also for infants, without such a candidate for baptism having heard the gospel, without believing in it and without confessing Jesus. In contrast, the matter is quite different with believer's baptism.   We ask: Don't these two baptisms entail two completely different teachings on becoming a Christian, being a Christian, on the Holy Spirit, the reception of the Spirit and on the church? Is infant baptism only *another* practice and yet the same, or not rather *another* baptism than the *one* baptism of Ephesians 4:5? In the question of baptism, is it really variety that dominates among us or does not rather something irreconcilable fall apart? The document does not face the seriousness of this question.

*3. Baptism and exegesis*

Section II of the document, "The Meaning of Baptism", operates unfortunately without explicit references to New Testament passages on baptism, so that a picture emerges of a churchly rite which is everything, gives everything, and accomplishes everything, (a total of approximately 50 definitions and metaphors of baptism is offered). Exegetical soberness calls for far greater caution in the use of implicit biblical references to baptism. Is, for example, the baptism "by the Spirit" (1 Cor. 12:13) or the washing of regeneration "by the Holy Spirit" (Tit. 3:5) or the washing "by the Spirit" (1 Cor. 6:11) not contrary to the usual wording and thus something different from the baptism with water? Should we understand being "born again" through water (John 3:5) as being fulfilled in the baptism with water, an interpretation clearly contrary to the context which speaks only of the work of the Spirit? Likewise, can we really equate the "pure water" of Hebrews 10:22 with baptism? Are not figurative expressions like "water", "washing", and "being given to drink" (*Tränken*), to name but a few, anchored in the Old Testament promise of the Spirit; are they not employed also by the New Testament in a pneumatological sense?

Certainly the sacramental interpretation of such passages has a long tradition, such that it is rarely discussed any longer as a genuine problem. But when something has become so obvious, then it is time for a new inquiry.

*4. The work of the Spirit in baptism*

"The Holy Spirit is at work in the lives of people before, in and after their baptism" (§5). Indeed, the baptismal candidate does not come to baptism in the New Testament without the Spirit. The rite does not initiate the spiritual life. By the same token, additional work of the Spirit is also promised for the time following baptism. But what does the Holy Spirit effect in baptism itself? Surely not what he effected before baptism, neither what is promised for later.

It would be a step forward in our theological discussion if we could grasp the unique work of the Spirit in baptism.

Baptism is "a pledge made to God from a good conscience, through the resurrection of Jesus Christ" (1 Pet. 3:2) made in the context of a public questioning. It is the confession, coming from the heart: "Jesus is Lord" (Rom. 10:9; cf. 1 Tim. 6:12). According to several passages it is connected with a basic calling upon the name of the Lord. As a burial it documents that one has died with Christ (Rom. 6:4). What is always involved is the transition into another category, the change of the inner, the private and the individual into the public, juridical and communal. In baptism one commits oneself publicly and in a binding manner to the gospel, to the proclamation of which one has responded in faith. However, this public submission under the lordship of the Crucified in baptism is precisely a breakthrough of the Holy Spirit (1 Cor. 12:3). In this sense the congregation celebrates in its baptismal service a very specific victory of the Holy Spirit in its midst and in this world.

### Eucharist

*1. The eucharist concept*

For our free church, the terms "supper", "Lord's supper" and "breaking of bread", which are tied to biblical tradition, stand in the foreground. Usage of the term "eucharist" is not common, although an old, legitimate tradition of thanksgiving to God, who, in Christ, offered himself for us sinners, stands behind it.

We agree with the document's statement (§1) that the eucharist is a gift from the Lord; for it has been instituted by Christ. We see the eucharist anticipated in the passover feast commemorating the liberation of Israel from the land of bondage and in the covenant meal at Mount Sinai. It is the meal of the new covenant. At the same time it is an anticipation of the "marriage feast of the lamb" (§1).

Jesus Christ gave the eucharist to his disciples as a memorial of his death and resurrection. As a result we place particular worth on the irreplicability (*Nichtwiederholbarkeit*) of the once-and-for-all event of the sacrifice of Christ. We appreciate the attempt of the document to let the different understandings of the eucharist flow together into a common view of the New Testament *anamnesis* of Christ. Christ's sacrifice on the cross, accomplished once and for all, is for us a present and at the same time an anticipated reality in the *anamnesis* of the eucharist (§§6–8). With §9 we see in the *anamnesis* of Christ "the basis and source of all Christian prayer". The self-sacrifice of our high priest Christ makes it possible that justified sinners offer their lives as living and holy sacrifices to Christ (§10). This sacrifice of our lives must consist in bearing witness in the world, by word and deed, to reconciliation with God in Christ.

Fellowship with Christ present in the eucharist signifies at the same time fellowship with those participating and with the whole church (§19). Nevertheless, personal relationship with Christ, and not nominal church membership, is the prerequisite for participation in the eucharist. With the document we affirm the consequences for society, social service, economics, and politics emerging from the eucharistic fellowship (§§20–26).

In distinction to the elements of the eucharistic celebration (§27), which may be arranged differently and may differ in importance, our celebrations of the supper are marked by distinctly simple liturgy, usually including: hymns of praise, adoration, proclamation of the word of God, Christ's words of institution, thanksgiving for bread and cup, breaking of bread, eating and drinking in communion with Christ and every member of the church, concluding praise, benediction and commissioning. Not customary are: act of repentance and declaration of pardon, creed, a comprehensive thanksgiving derived from the Jewish tradition of the *berakah*, the invocation of the Holy Spirit on the community and the elements of bread and wine. While we cling to the New Testament data, we should ask ourselves how we can enrich our liturgy. We agree with the opinion that the eucharist should be celebrated frequently (§§30–31).

We cannot follow the opinion that the presence of Christ in the consecrated elements continues after the celebration. For us, the main emphasis falls upon the celebration itself and the consumption of the elements when they are distributed. However, we are open to the suggestions made in §32.

## 2. The term sacrament

The term "sacrament" is foreign to our free church. For us the term is associated too closely with a magical, mechanical action in which we see a contradiction to the New Testament.

We do not share the conviction, which in §2 is based on Matthew 26:28 and John 6:51–58, that every baptized member of the body of Christ receives in the eucharist the assurance of the forgiveness of sins and the pledge of eternal life. According to our understanding, the assurance of the forgiveness of sins is a pneumatic event through the agency of the risen Lord Jesus Christ, who has offered himself for the sins of the world. Bread and cup are but the signs of his sacrificed life. John 6:47 belongs unquestionably to John 6:51–58. Here it is without question *faith* in Jesus Christ, and not participation in the eucharist, which is the condition for eternal life.

In contrast to §13, we cannot envision a special real presence of Christ in the elements of the eucharist. We affirm the real presence of Christ, but we conceive of it in a pneumatic way. Christ is present for us in the eucharist in the same way in which he is present in the worship service of proclamation or where two or three are gathered in his name. The *is* of the words of institution does not want to be understood as a "transubstantiation" (in the hour of institution Jesus is still seated bodily in the midst of his disciples and his blood has not yet been shed; consequently, he cannot mean to say that the bread is his body and the cup is his blood). The *is* is only a device of translation and has no place in Jesus' own saying. In the words of the institution of the eucharist, the copula-forms have quite obviously a figurative sense. Therefore, it is not the substance of bread and wine, but rather the act of the breaking of the bread and the offering of wine which is the saving sign standing in correlation to the saving surrender of the body and blood of Christ.

Since in our free church the eucharist is viewed strongly under the Christological aspect, the Trinitarian conception of the eucharist in the document is foreign to it, especially the invocation of the Holy Spirit upon the elements of bread and wine (§14). We find no New Testament evidence for this.

### 3. The practice of the supper

We see no basis for the suggestion that the eucharist should only be celebrated under the presidency of an ordained minister (§29). Taking seriously the priesthood of all believers, we are convinced that according to Acts 2:46 the eucharist is properly celebrated where believers in Christ share among themselves bread and cup in the name of Jesus Christ, independent of office and ordination.

While, as has been shown, there are many convergencies between the faith tradition of our free church and the eucharist document, we cannot, as has also been shown, agree to the present text as a whole. We are, however, open for a continuation of the dialogue concerning questions related to the eucharist. For our part we are willing to offer eucharistic fellowship to all guests who stand in a living relationship to the Lord Jesus Christ.

### Ministry

#### 1. The establishment of goals

The document mirrors a "'kairos' of the ecumenical movement" (according to the preface, p. x) along the way towards the final goal postulated by the authors: "to realize" the "visible unity of the church" (preface, pp. vii–viii). The statement of purpose of the WCC (preface, p. vii) speaks, on the other hand, not of the "unity of the church", that is to say, also of the ministry, but of the "fellowship of the churches". Furthermore, the document mentions phenomena which stand in contradiction to this long-range goal, without treating the tension. "In the New Testament there appears rather a variety of forms which existed at different places and times" (§19). The hope, or the claim, that a greater unity is possible today than existed in the time of the NT is stated without support; the "nevertheless" (§22) is not sufficient. Finally, "today" a "multitude of experiments in new forms of ministry" is noted

(§50). Our question: Do we not deny all of these experiments their situation-conditioned legitimacy if we oppose them with a uniform model?

We note the mention of an immediate goal, the relationship of which to the long-range goal is not specified, which may stand substantially nearer to the concept of "the fellowship of the churches" which occurs in the document (§1), namely, "mutual recognition of the ordained ministries" (§§51–55). This concept involves a question which has been posed repeatedly in ecumenical worship services. The churches have tried to give answers to related issues in their interdenominational dialogues. The term "recognition" needs to be defined more closely since it is used in the document with another meaning, as well (§§12, 40, 44f.) and since the sense which it has in §37 (which seems useful to us as a goal) will hardly satisfy the authors. Did they have common worship services in mind? or exchange of pulpits? Are we to recognize official acts of other churches, or should officers of another church be allowed to perform them in our churches? Are transfers to be accepted? Should the authority of one official extend to other churches? Does recognition lead automatically to church union (§55)? It is noteworthy that in practice many small steps have already been taken, without waiting upon theological clarification. On the other hand, the document is far ahead of practice in its statement of long-range goals.

## 2. The proposed solution

Paragraph 1 of the document, "The Calling of the Whole People of God" carries an appropriate title and offers a good presentation of the New Testament data. Contrariwise, in the preface, the "people of God" are juxtaposed to "the churches" (§§18f.), indeed the laity are juxtaposed to the ordained (§12). Even if "the Holy Spirit" bestows gifts "on any member of the body of Christ" (§7a, cf. §32), or if "the church as a whole can be described as a priesthood" (§17), or if indeed ordination can be held to be "an act of the whole community" (§41), so is, nevertheless, this NT concept of "the calling of the people of God" (§6) repeatedly shoved aside. For it is not this calling in accordance with the NT which forms the comprehensive common denominator in the document; rather, it is the tradition of the "threefold ministry of bishop, presbyter, and deacon" (§22), which "may serve today as an expression of the unity we seek and also as a means for achieving it".

Bishop, presbyter and deacon are NT terms, but they are not set one above or under the other or arranged according to rank so that the NT could back up a threefold office.

From the threefold pattern the document "raises questions for all the churches". The "episcopal, presbyterial and congregational systems" are seen only as "ways", "aspects" or "dimensions" (§26 and commentary) of the ordained office and each church is advised to develop more fully that aspect which it has neglected. Churches which have maintained the threefold pattern are an exception; they "will need to ask how [their] potential can be fully developed for the most effective witness of the Church in this world" (§25). Our question: Are precisely those churches, which are in closest proximity to the New Testament practice of the priesthood of all believers, to be asked to undergo the most comprehensive restructuring, thereby distancing themselves from the New Testament, in favour of an old, partly modified and discarded tradition?

*3. Ordination*

The ordained ministry is pictured in the document as "the visible focus of the deep and all-embracing communion between Christ and the members of his body" (§14; cf. §§8, 13, 21 Commentary). Thus it has its dignity. Apostolic succession is argued at length (§§34ff.), but only with quotations from apostolic fathers (§36 Commentary); the special place of the apostles is overdrawn. How the unity of episcopal churches could have been broken (§38) is not explained. It is even acknowledged that "churches which have not retained the form of the historic episcopate" have preserved "a continuity in apostolic faith, worship and mission" (§37). Nevertheless ("on the contrary", §38), they are to accept episcopal succession (§37). Our question: does the document not present the office here as a rather vague foundation of unity?

Moreover, the ministry is endowed with authority: the community needs ordained ministers (§12), the church needs "this ministry of unity in some form in order to be the Church of God" (§23). As an independent fellowship, which recognizes no canon-law authorities, we can identify with §16, at any rate we would strike the terms "ordained ministers" and "authority" from this passage also and emphasize rather the idea of "service". In our eyes the office, in itself, carries no authority, and cannot, therefore, establish or guarantee unity.

Finally ordination is lifted up as a sacrament (of the consecration of the priest, §§7d, 17; cf. §43b). This is strange because earlier mention was made of sacraments (by the way, this term also would need to be clarified) as if only baptism and the Lord's supper were meant. If we cannot find a sacramental character in baptism and the Lord's supper, the demand for a sacramental ordination seems totally unacceptable to us.

# BAPTIST UNION OF SWEDEN

## Foreword

The Baptist Union of Sweden, although not a member of the World Council of Churches, has always followed with great interest the work of the Faith and Order Commission of the WCC. When the Lima document on "Baptism, Eucharist, Ministry" appeared, it seemed therefore natural that the Baptist Union of Sweden should formulate a response to this document. This response has been worked out by a committee of five persons and has been approved by the executive board of the Union.

## Baptism

INTRODUCTORY NOTES

A study of many years within the frame of the Faith and Order work has led to a common understanding of baptism in many respects, especially regarding the meaning and importance of baptism. After all, different churches with various traditions can say the same things about baptism. The difficulties have been evident when it comes to the point of putting the common view into practice. As no church wants to practise "re-baptism" or have its baptismal practice looked upon as such, there will be problems in connection with the mutual recognition of baptism. New points of view must be considered in order to avoid the question ending up in a blind alley. With the present varied practices in different churches it is hardly possible to come to a united standpoint. The question is if the Lima text initiates a new start.

THE INSTITUTION AND MEANING OF BAPTISM, §§1–7

In accordance with the above we can agree with what is said here. Yet the indicated difficulty emerges in the last sentence in §6: "Therefore, our one

---

● 20,924 members, 370 churches.

baptism into Christ constitutes a call to the churches to overcome their divisions and visibly manifest their fellowship." Can we in earnest talk about "our one baptism" as long as baptismal practice in a decisive way divides us? In the subsequent commentary the importance of the practice is clear. But sure enough it is also emphasized that baptism is not the only dividing factor.

BAPTISM AND FAITH, §§8–10
Here baptism is said to be both God's gift and our human response. Likewise the necessity of faith for the reception of the salvation embodied and set forth in baptism is accentuated. It is further pointed out that personal commitment is necessary for responsible membership in the body of Christ. But various baptismal practices indicate different consequences of this common understanding.

BAPTISMAL PRACTICE, §§11–16

*A. Baptism of believers and infants*
The list that is presented here is not complete, at any rate not for Swedish conditions. There are churches in which the individual is at liberty to decide not only the form of baptism but also if he should be baptized at all. The Society of Friends and the Salvation Army, for example, do not practise any baptism. In these cases there is a deliberate repudiation of sacramental administration. There are, however, cases when the importance of baptism is strongly asserted but baptism is not considered to be necessary for membership in the church in question.

This raises the question: should a church be looked upon as a church if not all or even any of its members are baptized or if the sacraments are neither taken into account nor administered? Anyway, churches which are reluctant to recognize infant baptism have been prepared to answer this question in the affirmative. An answer like this can be regarded as deviation from what is said in for instance §6: "Through baptism, Christians are brought into union with Christ, with each other and with the Church of every time and place." We are, however, obliged to observe that there is an inconsistency between doctrine and practice when the necessity of baptism is strongly stressed at the same time as membership without baptism is accepted and justified. Nor is a personal response later on necessary for membership. This is best exemplified in our country by the Church of Sweden with its state church idea and increasing number of unchristened members. This naturally creates difficulties in ecumenical relations and discussions when the church and the importance of sacraments for the church are to be defined. In such circumstances it is difficult to take seriously the accusation that we Baptists deny sacramental integrity when baptizing someone who is a member of another church.

In §12 it is said that baptism always takes place in a community of faith. When someone who is a believer is baptized he confesses his faith in connection with the baptism. When an infant is baptized, it is taken for granted that a personal response will be given at a later moment in life.

One question remains unanswered. Does baptism have any effect without this response? The very stress of the fact that no baptism can be repeated or made undone possibly implies an answer in the affirmative. A supplementary question ought to be asked: Can such a kind of baptism—as long as this personal response is not given—be said to have another meaning than the blessing of children has in churches where baptism of believers is practised?

When it is said in the commentary to §12 that "both forms of baptism require a similar and responsible attitude towards Christian nurture", it should be pointed out that anyone who has been blessed as a child and consequently is not baptized, is to be regarded as a catechumen, in the proper sense of the word, whose instruction is a preparation for baptism and life as baptized. We hesitate to put someone in the situation to have a claim "laid upon" him as long as there is no possibility of response. On the other hand there is the possibility as well as the obligation to express "that children are placed under the protection of God's grace" (§16) in an act that goes back to Jesus' action. Here we want to comply with the request "to express more visibly that fact". The place and theological foundation of the blessing of children has probably not been given enough attention in this connection but should be the subject of a close study, which hopefully could give a new basis of the question of mutual acceptance of baptismal practices. Further aspects on blessing of children and its meaning are dealt with in the supplement.

In §13 with commentary it is said that any practice which might be interpreted as "re-baptism" must be avoided. We can agree with this wording. But it makes the question whether re-baptism is practised dependent on who interprets. It is doubtful whether baptism of believers with its consequences should be looked upon as a denial of the sacramental integrity of other churches. The churches that baptize believers only do not seem to find it most difficult to recognize the ministries of other churches. Moreover, it is the recognition of other churches and their members as members of the body of Christ that is the reason why open communion and sometimes even open membership are practised in our churches. We mean that unity in Christ can be manifested in spite of different baptismal practices.

### B. Baptism–chrismation–confirmation

We agree that "Christian baptism is in water and the Holy Spirit", §14. We cannot see that baptism has to be completed by another act of sacramental character in order to receive the Holy Spirit or share in the eucharist. That would imply to diminish the meaning of baptism and not take its consequences seriously.

We maintain that the imposition of hands, in the baptismal rite itself or in a special ceremony afterwards is not associated with the giving of the Holy Spirit but an act of blessing with intercession for the baptized person, a consecration to membership and personal commitment in the Christian church.

### C. Towards mutual recognition of baptism

Questions in connection with these items have already been touched upon and will be discussed in the supplement concerning blessing of children. However, we want to emphasize that a terminology should be used that is not depreciating or insulting. This would to a great extent contribute to an increasing mutual understanding of our convictions. We Baptists must admit that we have often used the expression "sprinkling" to demonstrate repudiation of the practice of churches baptizing infants. This is naturally perceived as offensive and we should show respect for the conviction of these churches by using the word "infant baptism" when baptism of infants is referred to. In the same way we Baptists find it insulting when our baptismal practice is described as "re-baptism" and we want others to show respect for our conviction by avoiding referring to our baptism in this way. When we want to accentuate our practice as a contrast to infant baptism we speak about believers' baptism. The matter in concern — to handle the question of how to look upon one another's baptism — will benefit from a mutual respect which also manifests itself in our choice of words.

THE CELEBRATION OF BAPTISM, §§17–23

Paragraph 17 describes what is necessary about the celebration of baptism.

For a person who practises immersion it is natural to say "baptize in water" especially since that is what was said in §14: "The Christian baptism is in water and the Holy Spirit."

Naturally enough the rich contents of baptism benefits from a form that fully does justice to it, §18. That is e.g. the reason why we baptize by immersion. We find that immersion does not only express participation in Christ's death, burial and resurrection but also other factors as e.g. when the purification that baptism aims at is described by "washing", Acts 22:16, "a body washed in pure water", Hebrews 10:22, or as "the washing of regeneration and renewal in the Holy Spirit", Titus 3:5, or when it is said: "Baptized into union with him you all put on Christ as a garment", Galatians 3:27 (quotations from *New English Bible*.) Other instances are given in the commentary to this item of the text.

Regarding what is said in §19 we refer to what we have commented on §§13 and 14 above.

One baptismal rite may differ from the other by being more or less comprehensive, §20. Such differences should not impede Christian unity.

Several elements of the baptismal ritual here enumerated are, in accordance with what was said in item 18 above, included in the very baptismal rite. Moreover, we believe that over-explicit explanations can "rationalize away" the inherent symbolic force of the rite. But we do recognize elements here enumerated which should be included, e.g. the proclamation of the scriptures referring to baptism, the creed and the *epiklesis*. See further §14 above.

Paragraph 21 accords with what was said about the proclamation of the scriptures referring to baptism in the preceding paragraph.

What is said in §22 applies to us as well.

We would like to emphasize that baptism is intimately connected with the corporate life and worship of the church, §23.

SUPPLEMENT ON BLESSING OF CHILDREN

*Excursus about the blessing of children*

Since the middle of the 1930s the blessing of children has been increasingly practised in the Swedish Baptist churches. There are some examples already from the 1860s as well as from the beginning of the twentieth century. The impulses seem to have come from abroad, mainly from the United States and England. Nowadays most newborn children are involved in such a practice. From the handbook of 1954 and onwards there is an agenda for the performance of the act which is followed by most pastors.

The blessing of children has a threefold content: a thanksgiving to the Lord of Life for the newborn child, an act of prayer for parents and child in which the parents also are given the opportunity to accept their Christian calling as parents and eventually an opportunity for the church to accept its responsibility for the newborn child. The act as a whole is a marking of the place of the child in the church family and points towards the day when the young man/woman presumably accepts the Christian faith and the fellowship of the church where he/she has grown up.

So performed and understood the blessing of children is an expression of the Baptist understanding of the children growing up in the church. The Baptists do not adhere to the teaching of inherited sin in the sense that the children already from birth should live under the judgment of sin. They live under the atonement of Christ and also in the protection of the faith of their parents and the church fellowship. For this no special performance is required but the blessing of children is an expression and a reminder of this situation of life. For Baptists the baptism belongs together with a personal conversion and the acceptance of faith which occur later in life.

The tendency is that the blessing of children is increasingly practised also in denominations which so far mainly have been practising infant baptism. Internationally the blessing of children is also used as a complement to baptism in situations where one wants an act of blessing in another geographic environment than parents' church or for instance with adoption.

We recommend churches that baptize children, and especially those in which uncertainty about infant baptism has arisen, to seriously consider the question of blessing of children.

Of course there are important possibilities to understand infant baptism and blessing of children as related expressions for several momentous parts of the Christian understanding of the children. Even the blessing of children "stresses the corporate faith" (see note to §12) and the participation of the child in the fruits of the parents' faith. The blessing of children underlines the being of man as a continuation of a divine act of creation. Many important biblical thoughts and sayings which often are related to the baptism of children can very well be used also for the blessing of children. For Baptists it is possible to look at infant baptism as a form of blessing of children and there are examples that priests and pastors who practise infant baptism look upon it in the same way. In the new order of baptism of the Swedish Lutheran Church there is also a special moment of blessing:

1. Against this background it is possible for a Baptist to acknowledge that infant baptism "embodies God's own initiative in Christ and expresses a response of faith made within the believing community" (B12, commentary).

2. The line of difference between "belonging" and "membership" can possibly prepare for a new understanding. Both opinions of baptism therefore count a form of relation between the church and the child.

3. So understood infant baptism can be looked upon as an alternative to the blessing of children, but the consequence is not that Baptists feel themselves prevented from baptizing people who in this manner have been blessed in the form of infant baptism.

Churches where infant baptism, and especially those where hesitation about the rise of infant baptism is at stake, should consider the possibility of offering parents blessing of children as an alternative to infant baptism. The more the blessing of children gains ground the more the need for a common study of the relation of the two acts to each other increases.


**Eucharist**

INTRODUCTORY NOTES

The document gives a good summary of the meaning of the eucharist. As points of special value may be mentioned:

— that the relation to the Triune God is stated in such a clear and comprehensive way;

— that the old crucial question of *how* Christ is presented in the eucharist is answered in such a wise and cautious way;

— that the fellowship of believers is so clearly underlined;

— that the eschatological perspective is given due attention.

COMMENTARIES

A. *A tendency towards sacramentalism*

There is, it seems to us, a tendency towards sacramentalism in this document. Eager to clarify the meaning of the eucharist, the document gives to this sacrament such a comprehensive function and such a unique position that other elements of Christian worship and Christian experience are eclipsed, such as prayer, Bible study, praise, service and fellowship. All these elements are, to be sure, present in the eucharist but only in part. They can and must function also outside the eucharist.

Examples: "Its celebration continues as the central act of the Church's worship", §1. "The eucharist is essentially the sacrament of the gift which God makes to us in Christ through the power of the Holy Spirit", §2. "The eucharist is *the* great sacrifice of praise by which the Church speaks on behalf of the whole creation", §4. "It is a representative act of thanksgiving and offering on behalf of the whole world", §20. "Through the eucharist the all-renewing grace of God penetrates and restores human personality and dignity", §20.

It seems as if the text tries to make the eucharist an all-embracing and all-empowering sacrament, which gets a unique position as centre and resource for Christian life. This tendency is also there in the paragraph about the celebration of the eucharist. This liturgy is very elaborate in comparison with what the NT tells us about the Lord's supper.

In accordance with this tendency to give the eucharist such a unique position, the document encourages us to celebrate the eucharist frequently, §30, 31. If the eucharist is the only way — or almost so — in which Christian life is nurtured, it is, of course, necessary to celebrate it very often. On the other side, if as in Baptist tradition other resources are considered as being of equal value, the question of how often the eucharist should be celebrated is still important but not in the crucial way that the Lima document indicates.

B. *Eucharist and baptism*

Eucharist and baptism are well kept together in the Lima document. The text presupposes that the participants in the eucharist are baptized, §2, commentary to §19. This is, no doubt, the New Testament order: first the breakthrough of the new life in baptism, then the food for this life in the eucharist. But if less importance is attached to the sacraments and more to faith, it may be possible to support the practice in most Baptist churches in Sweden to invite all believers to the Lord's table, whether they are baptized or not.

C. *Eucharist and forgiveness of sin*

The Lima document agrees with the general conception that "each baptized member of the body of Christ receives in the eucharist the assurance of the forgiveness of sins", §2. On the other hand, it supports the practice of many churches to place very early in the eucharistic liturgy an "act of repentance" and a "declaration of pardon", §27.

There seems to be a lack of consistency here. In the NT we hear little or nothing about repentance in connection with the eucharist. What we do hear is that they were "breaking bread in private houses" and "shared their meals with unaffected joy", Acts 2:46 NEB. To be sure, Paul speaks about an individual self-examination before partaking of the eucharistic gifts. He seems, however, to be warning against a thoughtless and secularized eating. Something like a collective confession of sin and a collective declaration of pardon is, as far as we can see, unknown in the churches in NT time.

Even believers may and should feel the need of pardon of their sins. But according to the eucharist theology quoted above, this pardon is given in the eucharist itself. It seems, consequently, to be a strange liturgic custom to declare the pardon of sins already in the beginning of the service, when this pardon is given in the celebration of the eucharist as such.

It appears that the question of forgiveness of sin in connection with the eucharist needs a great deal of theological reflection. In the NT time, the eucharist seems to have been primarily the joyful fellowship between the risen Lord and his followers.

### D. The invocation of the Holy Spirit

The *epiklesis* is a conception that has attracted fairly little attention in Protestant traditions, including the Baptist tradition. It is, however, as far as we understand, a very important conception. The Lima text gives a good interpretation of the *epiklesis* and, in connection with that of the *real presence* of Christ in the eucharist, §14 and 15 with commentaries.

Very important is the statement that in the early liturgies "the invocation of the Spirit was made both on the community and on the elements of bread and wine", §14 with commentary. This should be the norm for the churches also today.

### Ministry

INTRODUCTORY NOTES

The Lima text on ministry is by the Swedish Baptists understood as a valuable document that gives good material for their own theological thinking on the matters. This is said although the document in itself reveals a great deal of "high church thinking", which is unfamiliar to Baptists in general. The roles of the bishops, their authorities and even their necessity for the essence and the unity of the church are items where Baptists look for further clarification and definitions before they can give their total consent.

The latter part of the Lima text on ministry (IV–VI), is concluded by a chapter that indicates that the churches are on the way towards the mutual recognition of the ordained ministries. The pre-requisites of attaining that end are at least given. The document calls for a far-reaching willingness for action from the churches, which can be seen as an acknowledgment of the dedication to a purpose that has marked the work of the commission.

THE CALLING OF THE WHOLE PEOPLE OF GOD, §§1–6 ·

We would not suggest that there are any controversial statements under this headline. On the contrary, we joyfully agree when it is said about the calling that it is a calling to the whole people of God and that "the Holy Spirit unites in a single body those who follow Jesus Christ and sends them as witnesses into the world", §1. We agree that in this sense all the members of the church are called to discover their gifts and to use them for the building up of the church and for the service of the world, §5.

Differences in understanding appear when we turn to the questions of church order and organization, and, in particular, to those questions that are related to the ordained ministry.

THE CHURCH AND THE ORDAINED MINISTRY, §§7–18

Ministry is constitutive for the church. Christ came to serve. Persons "who are publicly and continually responsible" for pointing to the church's fundamental dependence on Jesus Christ thereby provide a focus of its unity within the multiplicity of gifts, §8. For the unity of the church it is also necessary that the ministers are recognized as such by the church. This applies to all the different ministries. Some special ministries are recognized in a special act of ordination, the ordained ministry. However, the form of that special act of ordination, the comprehensiveness of the education that precedes it, or the partnership in any kind of hierarchy, that it leads to, cannot be something constitutive for the church.

The "unique and unrepeatable" role of the apostles, §10, as witnesses to the resurrection of Christ means to us that no bearers of specific authority and responsibility in the church today rightly can claim to be invested by a special apostolic authority that goes further than the apostolic authority which is given to the church as a whole. We would say that the apostolic authority given to the church as a whole is the solid basis on which all authority, which is conferred to different members in their ministry, rests. So understood, the ordained ministry exerts its authority *in* the church and never over or against it. Particular forms of the ordained ministry are relevant to different historical and practical circumstances and cannot in themselves belong to the essential and constitutive elements of the church.

In the Baptist churches it is the most common practice that an ordained minister presides at the Lord's table, §14. However, there are exceptions from that rule if "ordained" means "trained and ordained". On the base of the priesthood of all believers the local church is free to appoint somebody among its members who has gained the confidence of the congregation to fulfill that service. Usually such a person has functioned as lay pastor of the church. "Ordination" in this case means nothing more or less than that the church occasionally has commissioned a trusted member to perform a certain task.

Interdependence and reciprocity between those ordained and the faithful in the church is expressed in a brilliant manner in the Lima text, and we agree, §§15, 16. The danger that ordained ministers should become dependent on common opinions of the community, as expressed in the commentary to §16, is a danger that has to be overcome by a church that is ready to look for guidance from the Holy Spirit knowing that Christ alone is the head of the church.

As is confirmed in the commentary to §17 the terms "priesthood" and "priest" in the New Testament are used only referring to the priesthood of Jesus Christ and to the priesthood of all baptized. It seems strange to state that the term "priest" *appropriately* should be used referring to ordained ministers. It might be convenient with regard to tradition but hardly appropriate with regard to the New Testament.

The admission of women to the ordained ministry, §18, has been practised for many years by the Baptist Union of Sweden. There has been no serious opposition against that practice. Recently a woman pastor was unanimously elected as the general secretary of the Union. This title is secular, but the person who holds it is in function equal to a bishop in episcopalian churches. As we understand the meaning of Galatians 3:28 there is no difference in kind between the ministry which can be provided by women and the ministry which can be provided by men in the church. We would suggest that the bringing in of women into the ordained ministry has enriched our experiences of the unity of men and women in Christ and also brought with it a deeper understanding of the essence of the Christian message.

THE FORMS OF THE ORDAINED MINISTRY, §§19–33

The traditional threefold pattern is pictured as pre-eminent and important.

Churches maintaining the threefold pattern are asked how its potential can be fully developed, and those churches which do not have the same pattern are asked whether it "does not have a powerful claim to be accepted by them", §25.

We are faced with this powerful challenge *although*:

1) the Lima text itself points to the fact that "the New Testament does not describe a single pattern of ministry which might serve as a blueprint or continuing norm for all future ministry in the church", §19;

2) referring to a pattern of bishops, presbyters and deacons we are referring to a pattern that is neither uniformly understood nor beyond dispute (Clement of Rome, vindicating the status of the bishop, says that the apostles knew through our Lord Jesus Christ that disputes would arise concerning the name of bishop);

3) the Lima text points to the following facts:

3.1. the pattern to be seen has gone through "considerable changes", §19;

3.2. "the Spirit has many times led the church to adapt its ministries to contextual needs", §22;

3.3. "the threefold pattern stands evidently in need of reform", §24;

3.4. "there have been times when the truth of the Gospel could only be preserved through prophetic and charismatic leaders", §33.

With all those reservations taken into consideration it is doubtful if the threefold ministry of bishop, presbyter and deacon is so important for "the unity we seek and also a means for achieving it", §22.

How is the "ministry of *episkope*" to be understood as the "ministry of unity"? According to our understanding the role of the ministry of *episkopé* within the unity of a threefold ministry is in the setting of the local church, corresponding to what is said about the earliest instances, where threefold ministry is mentioned; the reference is to the local eucharistic community, §20. We think that such an understanding would be helpful in the search for a mutual recognition among the churches concerning their ordained ministers.

The primary and close attachment of the threefold ministry, including the ministry of *episkopé*, to the local church is a reason for us as a non-episcopalian church not to choose the title of bishop for those who serve several local churches in their regional or nationwide functions.

The role of the elders (presbyters) should be as colleagues and deputies of the pastor.

We do think that the restoration of the ministry of deacons is an important concern in many churches. A revitalization of the primary meaning of the ministry of deacons (service) is needed.

SUCCESSION IN THE APOSTOLIC TRADITION, §§34–38

*A. Apostolic tradition in the church*

The Baptist Union of Sweden accepts the basic view of the section on the apostolic tradition of the church, §34, but is, at the same time, of the opinion that this tradition many times has been broken. This can also be expressed by stating that the apostolic tradition has survived outside the formal succession of the apostolic ministry. An unbroken succession of apostolic ministry is, according to our opinion, no better guarantee for a living apostolic tradition than other forms of leadership in the church. It is also to be noted that mostly only the episcopate has been considered of importance in maintaining the apostolic tradition, while other parts of the threefold ministry have not been given the same importance. We also want to question the reason for giving a very high regard to the formal ordination, while the way of fulfilling the ministry has not been crucial in determining if there is an unbroken apostolic tradition or not.

From this point of view it is well-advised that the document recommends a distinction between the apostolic tradition of the church and the succession of the apostolic ministry. It also needs to be said that the basic principle of *ecclesia semper reformanda* (the continuous reformation of the church) is of vital importance for Protestant theology. As we see it, the course of reformation goes on, independent of the succession of apostolic ministry.

*B. Succession of the apostolic ministry*

Summarizing we note that the fact that the Baptists do not share the very deep appreciation of the succession of the apostolic ministry, that characterizes most of the Christian church, does not mean that we disregard the values that such a succession is said to protect. However, we cannot see that the apostolic succession under all circumstances emphasizes and preserves the apostolic tradition. On the contrary, that succession has not infrequently counteracted and persecuted those who have tried to stand up for essential parts of this tradition. Therefore, it is not possible for us to see an unbroken apostolic succession as an essential part of the Christian church.

We appreciate the balanced and considerate way of arguing that is predominant throughout the section. However, once again it is necessary to point out that, according to our understanding, essential parts of the apostolic tradition to a great degree have been preserved by churches and movements that by churches with pretensions to apostolic succession have been identified as heretical, §35.

The Lima text seems to admit that the episcopal succession is only one of the possible ways through which the apostolic tradition of the church was expressed during the first centuries. It is, however, also evident that the document considers this factor to be the most important without comparison. We cannot agree to such a judgment, §36.

We gladly note and emphasize the recognition of the form of ordination in churches that have not preserved the historic episcopate, §37.

Remembering the considerable restrictions already expressed, we are, nevertheless, ready to recognize the value of the episcopal succession for those churches where it exists. Recognizing those churches as a part of the body of Christ in the world, we can see that the values that the succession of the apostolic ministry emphasizes, are significant to us as well. These values are, however, not so essential that we because of them are ready to change the constitution of our Union, §38.

ORDINATION, §§39–50

*A. The meaning of ordination*

The Baptist Union of Sweden accepts ordination for specific ministries in the Christian church as an act of fundamental nature. We have noted that the English version of the text has the word "ministry" where the Swedish text has "ämbete", the equivalence of which would be "office". As Baptists we use the Swedish word "tjänst", which is equivalent to "ministry". By that expression we want to emphasize that the ordination does not separate some individuals from the rest of God's people and that many of the tasks that the ordained fulfill can be done also by those who are not ordained. By the ordination the comprehensive ministry of the pastor is recognized.

The meaning of the text in the commentary, §39, we find very vague. To us recognition and respect to episcopal ordination has the sense that is indicated under §38, and presupposes that the word "bishop" has the meaning, indicated in §37.

We want to mention that in Swedish we do not use the word "ordination" but "avskiljning", that means "set aside for special tasks". The reason for this way of expression is exactly the meaning or interpretation of the Latin terms *ordo* and *ordinare*, referred to in the commentary, §40.

### B. The act of ordination

We agree that it is important that all forms of ordination are combined with a worship service. We concur with the description of the act, except the definition of the ordination as a "sacramental sign", that does not make sense to us. The ordination among the Baptists emphasizes the promise of professional secrecy, regarding what is revealed in confessions and other forms of pastoral care, §§41–44.

### C. The conditions for ordination

We share the view presented in this section. To us it is natural to accept candidates for ordination without regard to race, social group, gender or handicap. Because of the congregational character of the Baptist church much of what is being said in this chapter is more relevant to the local church than to the Union, §§45–50.

TOWARDS A MUTUAL ACKNOWLEDGMENT OF THE ORDAINED MINISTRIES, §§51–55

We share the opinion that it may be necessary for the churches to re-examine their view and their praxis concerning the ordained ministry. It seems even more important that the churches re-examine their understanding for the opinions and praxis of other churches and try to understand the problems from the total point of view of the churches, §51.

It is not possible for us to give the question of apostolic succession priority before other important questions. What is said in §38 is still valid.

We share the opinion that the laying on of hands and prayer for the descending of the Holy Spirit should be part of the ordination, §52.

It is not possible for us to separate the bishoply succession as being more important than other parts concerning the continuity from the church of the apostles.

Baptists should, however, be aware of the high value that this circumstance has in many churches, §53. As to the churches that do not ordain women we are hopeful that they will be able to respect other churches' ordination of women and also when it is needed cooperate with them, §54.

We consider it valuable if this double acknowledgment of the ministry within different churches could be expressed by regular participation of representatives for other churches in the ordination services. This would underline the thought that the ordination is not for a special church but the church of Jesus Christ, §55.

# RELIGIOUS SOCIETY OF FRIENDS (QUAKERS) IN GREAT BRITAIN

**Preface**

In preparing our response to the Lima text we have been mindful of the question which, as Friends, we are enjoined regularly to ask of ourselves: "Is your distinctive Quaker witness characterized by humility and a willingness to learn from others?"

We offer our response not as travellers who have arrived at the end of a spiritual journey but as seekers still on a path. Throughout the exercise, we have been glad to learn from other churches. Yet we joyfully reaffirm, from the depths of our experience, insights which the Religious Society of Friends has found and tested over three centuries.

We hope that we may share these insights; we pray that we may build on them, growing spiritually, as humble learners in the school of Christ.

**Introduction**

1. This response is made by London Yearly Meeting of the Religious Society of Friends (Quakers). London Yearly Meeting is defined as "the final constitutional authority of the Religious Society of Friends in Great Britain" (*Church Government* section 789[1]). It comprises some 18,000 members, a very small body in relation to many of the other bodies making responses to the World Council of Churches. There are some 200,000 Quakers worldwide and upwards of fifty Yearly Meetings. In the Religious Society of Friends these Yearly Meetings are autonomous bodies. This is relevant to some of our convictions on the nature of the church, to be considered later.

2. London Yearly Meeting is not a member of the World Council of Churches (WCC), having in 1939 and 1940 declined an invitation from the

---

• 18,000 members, 450 meetings for worship in Great Britain, excluding Northern Ireland.

[1] *Christian Faith and Practice* (last revised 1959) and *Church Government* (last revised 1967, reprinted with amendments 1980) together form the "Book of Christian Discipline of London Yearly Meeting of the Religious Society of Friends".

provisional committee. London Yearly Meeting is, however, an associate member of the British Council of Churches (BCC) and has been, nationally and locally, associated with the ecumenical movement over the last 75 years.

3. In preparing this response (which has been approved by London Yearly Meeting in session) we have relied on background work by our Committee on Christian Relationships. That committee prepared a short guide to help Friends to get to grips with the Lima text (for its language is not that of our everyday use); and in preparing the first drafts of this response the committee had the benefit of the reports of some meetings for church affairs, many study groups held in local meetings, and the observations of a number of individual Friends.

4. While, therefore, the issues raised have not been officially referred to our Monthly Meetings, we have in London Yearly Meeting attempted to "feel the Society's pulse". Insofar as this response comes from Yearly Meeting in session it is official and represents "the highest appropriate level of authority". Insofar as the text is based on comments from a wide variety of groups within the Yearly Meeting's membership we believe that we are "speaking with authority". But the use of words like "authority" and even "response" and "reception" raise questions to which we must now turn.

### Authority and decision-making in Quaker experience

5. Early Friends as a whole shared the vision of George Fox (1624–1691) of a "gospel order" in which, under the guidance of the Holy Spirit, the insights of individual Friends could be tested by the gathered group. It is true that some early Friends were affected by Ranterism, but it was the general Quaker experience, re-echoed throughout our history, that the "bold personal adventure [must be] tempered by humility in the face of individual fallibility and by the necessity for sharing experience with others" (*Christian Faith and Practice*, section 146).

6. We see our meetings for church affairs not as business meetings preceded by a period of worship, but as "meetings for worship for business". Ideally, the sacred and the secular are interwoven into one piece. Believing that all our business is brought before God for guidance we deprecate all that may foster a party spirit or confrontation. We therefore seek for a spirit of unity in all our decision-making.

7. In our experience a discipline of expectant waiting under the directing spirit of God is necessary in the search for this unity. This process may on occasion be a protracted one. We wish to make clear that when we speak of unity we do not necessarily mean unanimity, but a clearly recognized "sense of the meeting". Nor do we mean consensus, which, however humanly desirable, is but a measure of human agreement. The will of God may (uncomfortably) be what nobody in the meeting wants. However far short we may fall at times in practice, it is our considered experience that the discipline of open-minded seeking makes the practice of voting an irrelevance. We

therefore welcome the Lima text's emphasis on the guidance of the Holy Spirit.

8. The precise order of meetings for church affairs, and the functions of such meetings, have varied from time to time. In Great Britain there were traditionally local congregational meetings (Preparative Meetings), area Monthly Meetings, county Quarterly Meetings, and a national Yearly Meeting. Though the county Quarterly Meetings were modified in area and from 1967 gave way to regional General Meetings, the structure of widening groups both geographically and experientially has meant not only that individual insights can be tested by the group but that the different insights of different groups can be tested against one another.

9. The Quaker experience has always been that as insights are shared with geographically widening groups they tend to gather in weight and momentum. Our concept of the nature of the church is, therefore, neither a congregational one, nor one of authoritarian government from above. So that all things may be done decently and in order it may be necessary to entrust a particular administrative responsibility to this body or to that. London Yearly Meeting alone may revise the *Book of Christian Discipline.* and it seeks the Holy Spirit's guidance in so doing. But this does not mean that it pretends to greater access to the Holy Spirit's guidance than its 370 Preparative Meetings.

10. Early Friends, conscious of the headship of Christ, did not vest authority in an individual. At every level of our meetings for church affairs, however, there is appointed a clerk whose task it is to present business to the meeting, to listen attentively to the exercise and frame a minute which will then be read to the meeting, amended as necessary, and adopted. The clerk will properly remind Friends of precedents, but it is not her or his task to guide the meeting (save as it may feel the need of a guiding hand). The clerk serves for a limited time and is the servant of the meeting. "The power of God is the authority of all your men's and women's meetings," wrote George Fox. This authority becomes a real one, and commands allegiance, as the power of God in individual disciples recognizes and answers to the power of God in the gathered meeting.

11. *Church Government* contains such advice and regulations as experience has shown to be helpful to meetings for church affairs. As an appendix to this response to BEM we include sections 711–722 of chapter 17, "General counsel on church affairs".

12. In 1945 London Yearly Meeting forwarded to the continuation committee of the World Conference on Faith and Order a document on "The Nature of the Church According to the Witness of the Society of Friends". We conclude this section by quoting a few sentences from it. "Our characteristic stress, being both mystical and practical, is concerned with the spiritual conditions of the actual moment. We do not lay special stress upon the authority of tradition, though we with others have regard to our past. We

look rather to the living presence of the Spirit of God. This presence is known both as the individual is illumined by the light of Christ, and as the community is made aware of the same ever-present Holy Spirit."

## Our understanding of Christian unity

13. There remains another subject which needs to be touched upon before we turn to the three texts in the Lima document. Some of the comments we have received have expressed anxiety lest BEM should be but one more step to equate "visible unity" with "organic unity". We see (and welcome) BEM as a further step by which Christian communions may come to know and understand one another better and to appreciate the richness in the variety of insights which are thus brought to our common life in God. Lest there be any misunderstanding, however, we think it right to place upon record our Yearly Meeting's views on the nature of Christian unity.

14. London Yearly Meeting was represented at the 1910 World Missionary Conference. From 1914 it has been active in the Faith and Order movement, and was represented at Lausanne (1927) and Edinburgh (1937); and, after the formation of the WCC, Lund (1952) and Montreal (1963), Friends have been involved, though perhaps less actively, in the Life and Work movement. A substantial number of Friends promoted the first meeting of the World Alliance for Promoting International Friendship through the Churches (1914).

15. In February 1916 a joint sub-committee of the Archbishops of Canterbury and York's Committee and a Free Churches' commission issued a statement entitled *Towards Christian Unity*. Our Yearly Meeting's Commission on Faith and Order found that statement unsatisfactory "since it implied that unity was to be sought along the lines of agreement in doctrine and practice, while the essential basis of Christian experience and the Christian spirit and way of life were insufficiently emphasised". It therefore submitted to Yearly Meeting 1917 a document expressing Friends' views, entitled *The True Basis of Christian Unity* (*LYM Proc* 1917 pp. 151–9 for report and text). This document states a position which this Yearly Meeting has consistently maintained ever since.

16. We quote one extract from this document: "It is not in the life itself, but in the attempt to formulate its implications and to fix it by uniform religious practices, that divisions arise. We do not in the least deprecate the attempt, which must be made since man is a rational being, to formulate intellectually the ideas which are implicit in religious experience. . . But it should always be recognised that all such attempts are provisional, and can never be assumed to possess the finality of ultimate truth. There must always be room for development and progress and Christian thought and enquiry should never be fettered by theory. Statements of doctrine, therefore, however venerable, can never in themselves be regarded as a satisfactory basis of union" (*LYM Proc* 1917 pp. 158–9).

17. The 1917 statement had been revised and reissued in 1927 and 1937 in connection with the Faith and Order conferences in those years. In August 1964 London Yearly Meeting drew up a briefer statement, *The Basis of Christian Unity* (*LYM Proc* 1964 pp. 213–4). Arising from discussion following the statement *Visible Unity: Ten Propositions*, issued by the Churches Unity Commission in 1976, our Committee on Christian Relationships concluded that it would be timely to set forth once more Friends' beliefs on the nature of Christian unity, doing so in the context of a succinct but substantial statement of Friends' involvement in the ecumenical movement. It therefore published in 1979 *Unity in the Spirit: Quakers and the Ecumenical Pilgrimage*. Drawing on a variety of expressions of experience from the seventeenth century onwards, the committee thus expressed Yearly Meeting's position: "It is only natural that within the great household of God there should be different families doing things differently, developing different family traditions, each perhaps enriching the life of the whole by their particular insights and emphases. There is neither scandal nor sin in this."

## The text: preliminary considerations

18. In the corporate life of our Religious Society, as in our worship and our own lives, we try to work under the guidance of God. We have to discern the promptings of love and truth in our hearts, and to recognize and respond to God's leadings.

19. Our worship, our practical work and our social lives express the paradox of the homeliness of grace. We worship in total dependence on God's Spirit for inspiration, and with a full awareness of the many ways in which our inadequacy, our self-centredness, and our habits of mind can hinder the movement of the Spirit.

20. We may seem at times to take God for granted. But we know the beyond in our midst; we rely on grace, on God's free, sustaining, creative and lively action as we rely on the air we breathe and the ground we walk on.

21. In our experience, God works with those who are true to their deepest nature. Those whom Jesus called friends cooperate with him knowing how he works, and we know the depths of the pattern of love, truth, faithfulness, death and resurrection which he exemplified. We are aware of the life and power of the Spirit of God, maintaining us as a society and as local worshipping communities. We welcome the stress in the Lima text on the work of the Spirit, and know in our meetings the Spirit's less spectacular fruits and gifts.

22. Alongside Friends' stress on the primacy of God's action, we set great store by the centrality of ordinary experience. We agree with the witness of the universal church that mystical experiences are attested by the moral quality of people's lives. The whole of our everyday experience is the stuff of our religious awareness: it is here that God is best known to us.

23. However valid and vital outward sacraments are for others, they are not, in our experience, necessary for the operation of God's grace. We believe we hold this witness in trust for the whole church.

24. We are not generally drawn to speculative theology. We try as individuals and as a body to be faithful to the truth we have discovered. We prefer not to crystallize our understanding of the truth; our corporate experience is a growing and living tradition.

25. We understand the Bible as a record arising from similar struggles to comprehend God's ways with people. The same Spirit which inspired the writers of the Bible is the Spirit which gives us understanding of it: it is this which is important to us rather than the literal words of scripture. Hence, while quotations from the Bible may illuminate a truth for us, we would not use them to prove a truth. We welcome the work of scholars in deepening our understanding of the Bible. May we offer the comment that occasionally the Lima text shows too little critical discrimination in the evidential use of scripture?

26. We respond to the Lima text in Christian language, but many Quakers would prefer less specifically Christian terminology. We worship, live and work together in unity, however, valuing the variety of expressions of truth which each individual brings.

**Baptism**

27. We know the power of God's Spirit at work in the lives of people within the community of our meetings. These people may have been drawn into the community by a sudden convincement, a long period of seeking, or have grown up within it from childhood. We also know that we are engaged in a life-long growth into faith, and experience a continuing irruption of grace into our lives which demands and sustains a commitment to a life of discipleship. We recognize this power at work in people of all ages, races and creeds: transforming power which can issue in lives of joy, humility and service. Where these experiences are reflected in the statements of BEM we rejoice at this measure of our unity and are challenged to search for more.

28. The Quaker conviction is that the operation of the Spirit outruns all our expectations. We acknowledge that the grace of God is experienced by many through the outward rite of baptism, but no ritual, however carefully prepared for, can be guaranteed to lead to growth in the Spirit. A true spiritual experience must be accompanied by the visible transformation of the outward life. Our understanding of baptism is that it is not a single act of initiation but a continuing growth in the Holy Spirit and a commitment which must continually be renewed. It is this process which draws us into a fellowship with those who acknowledge the same power at work in their lives, those whom Christ is calling to be his body on earth.

29. It is out of this understanding that we have historically rejected water-baptism, seeing no necessary connection between this single event in a

person's life and the experience of transformation by the Spirit. We cannot see that this rite should be used as the only way of becoming a member of the body of Christ. Nor do we find the use of water-baptism to be an inescapable inference from the New Testament's account of Jesus' life and practice. On the contrary, scripture does not persuade us that baptism as initiation is any more important than circumcision as initiation, since either clouds the issue that neither the correctness of opinion nor religious observance, but only the undeserved grace of God, enables us to walk in faith and be active in love.

30. Part of the meaning of baptism is a proclamation of becoming a member of the church. Entry into membership of the Religious Society of Friends is a public acknowledgment of a growing unity with a community of people whose worship and service reflect, however imperfectly, their perception of discipleship and their recognition of the work of the Holy Spirit in the world. This unity is grounded in the experience of being "gathered" in the love of God in the silent expectancy of our meetings for worship and in a willingness to surrender ourselves to a corporate seeking for the will of God in such measure as we can comprehend it.

31. We too feel the tensions which divide the wider church over the place of infants and young children within the congregation. We know also that there are those whose membership of the Society may be little more than a formality, while many of the most faithful participants in our meetings do not seek formal membership.

32. Our witness to the unfettered operation of the Spirit must involve a humble confession of our own failings; yet we must testify to the fact that lives which display the fruits of the Spirit have been nurtured within the Society of Friends.

## Eucharist

33. We are impressed by the breadth of insight shown in this section into the nature of corporate worship. Many of the aspects noted here are in accord with our own aspirations and experience of Quaker worship. We welcome the interpretation of the eucharist as the gift of God, granting communion between the human and the divine, renewing the members of the worshipping body and binding them together. We too see our worship as a thanksgiving and celebration of the work of God in all creation and for all people, and a recognition of the cost of love and commitment. Particularly also, we welcome the forthright statement of the implications of worship, its implicit call to reconciliation and service in our daily lives and its challenge to us to work for justice in all areas of life; our worship focuses our hope for the fulfilment of God's purpose. Thus although our practice appears very different, we recognize many of the spiritual aspirations expressed in the symbolism of the eucharist.

34. In Quaker worship neither the elements of bread and wine nor any eucharistic liturgy is used. Our liturgy is one of silence and waiting on God

for the words that may come, to any one of us, from the depths of that waiting together. We recognize that the words and symbolic actions of the eucharist are experienced by very many Christians as a most powerful means of grace, a grace which shines forth clearly in their lives. Nevertheless, it is our experience that the grace of God is not restricted to any particular form of eucharistic liturgy; the reality of God's presence may be known in worship that retains none of the traditional elements that are central to the life of many churches.

35. In 1928, at a time when parliament and the religious life of our nation were rent with strife on the nature of the Real Presence, London Yearly Meeting wrestled to understand its own experience and expressed it in these words: "In silence, without rite or symbol, we have known the Spirit of Christ so convincingly present in our quiet meetings that his grace dispels our faithlessness, our unwillingness, our fears, and sets our hearts aflame with the joy of adoration. We have thus felt the power of the Spirit renewing and recreating our love and friendship for all our fellows. This is our eucharist and our communion" (*Christian Faith and Practice*, extract 241).

36. We would assert that the validity of worship lies not in its form but in its power, and a form of worship sincerely dependent on God, but not necessarily including the words and actions usually recognized as eucharistic, may equally serve as a channel for this power and grace. We interpret the words and actions of Jesus near the end of his life as an invitation to recall and re-enact the self-giving nature of God's love at every meal and every meeting with others, and to allow our own lives to be broken open and poured out for the life of the world.

37. We realize that others will have reservations about our open and unstructured form of worship. Absence of form and of structure no more guarantee depth and spirituality of worship than do their presence. Our bold experiment in worship is not always the embodiment of the claims we make for it; nor does it always embody those realities of which eucharistic worship can be a profound symbolic expression, realities which should provide sharpness of focus and nourishment. When we are faithful it does.

38. We fear that separating a particular sacrament and making it a focal point in worship can obscure the sacramental validity of the rest of creation and human life. We fear too the dangers of over-familiarity, of perfunctory or passive repetition of the act and of imagining the act to have power of itself. Admission to the eucharist only of those whose status is considered satisfactory by the church can exclude many sincere seekers after God and for this reason we find it difficult to see conformity to this practice as the true basis of unity in the life and spirit of Christ. The Lima text offers no reassurance on this point. Further, through its failure to acknowledge the experience of those Christian groups which express their commitment in ways other than through a eucharistic form of worship, the Lima text makes us profoundly uneasy.

39. We would wish to unite with all Christians and also with those of other faiths who work for reconciliation and healing in a broken world. Our membership includes those who, whilst ill at ease with orthodox formulations of Christian belief and doctrine, are nevertheless counted among those who do the will of God. As Friends we wish to recognize the divine gifts in those who call God by other names or see their commitment to truth in very different ways from those expressed in the Lima document.

**Ministry**

40. We respond with warmth and delight to the opening paragraphs which describe the calling of the whole people of God. We know "the liberating and renewing power of the Holy Spirit" and the call, as members of the body of Christ, to faithful mission and service. The priesthood of all believers is a foundation of our understanding of the church.

41. We turn, then, to the question in §6: "How, according to the will of God and under the guidance of the Holy Spirit, is the life of the church to be understood and ordered, so that the gospel may be spread and the community built up in love?" We note that the text seeks a "common answer" to this question. We doubt, not only whether a common answer is possible, but whether it is desirable in the many situations and cultures in which churches find themselves.

42. The text (E29) speaks of Christ as the one who gathers, teaches and nourishes. He is the shepherd, the prophet and the priest. The task of exercising these functions in the world belongs to the whole community of God. We cannot accept those aspects of §11 and §13 which claim these tasks for the ordained ministry. Our own experience leads us to affirm that the church can be so ordered that the guidance of the Holy Spirit can be known and followed without the need for a separated clergy.

43. Paragraphs 9, 10 and 11 make the assumptions that the twelve are the apostles and that the apostles are the authority for ordained leadership. We cannot make these simple equations. Beside the apostles there were many other witnesses of the life, death and resurrection of Jesus, including the faithful women who witnessed all these events. We see in the New Testament churches a variety of structures and leadership roles as the church grew and changed. This gives scriptural support for many present day patterns and for continuing experimentation and flexibility. Our own founders claimed that our church order was "gospel-order" and "primitive Christianity revived". However, apostolicity for the church is not the restoration of ancient systems, even if these could be discovered. It is, rather, to live in the Spirit in which the apostles lived. This Spirit, which was poured out at Pentecost on all the church, young and old, women and men, continues in our experience to call and empower all members of the church in a variety of ministries.

44. The Spirit has led us from our foundation to recognize the equality of women and men in the people of God. Early Friends taught that the

redemptive activity of Christ restored men and women to their position before the fall, as equal help-meets both made in the image of God. Though we have not been immune from influences in our surrounding culture, we have sought to practise this equality in our structures. We know that the Spirit gives as wide and diverse gifts to women as to men and acts as effectively through women as through men. In our mind, a church which does not fully recognize and encourage the gifts and ministries of all its people is imperfectly realizing the body of Christ.

45. To be without an ordained clergy is not to be without either leadership or ministry. The gifts of the Spirit to us include both. For us, calls to particular ministries are usually for a limited period of time, and these gifts pertain to the task rather than the person. In one lifetime a person may be called to a number of ministries, each with its own charism.

46. We identify in our structure *elders* with a responsibility for the spiritual life of the meetings; *overseers* with a responsibility for pastoral care within meetings; and *clerks* who serve administrative needs. At one time we recorded as *ministers* those whose vocal contribution to worship was particularly acceptable. This practice, however, was abandoned after a decision of the Yearly Meeting in 1924.

47. We now recognize a variety of ministries. In our worship these include those who speak under the guidance of the Spirit, and those who receive and uphold the work of the Spirit in silence and prayer. We also recognize as ministry service on our many committees, hospitality and childcare, the care of finance and premises, and many other tasks. We value those whose ministry is not in an appointed task but is in teaching, counselling, listening, prayer, enabling the service of others, or other service in the meeting or the world.

48. The purpose of all our ministry is to lead us and other people into closer communion with God and to enable us to carry out those tasks which the Spirit lays upon us.

49. Throughout our history we have rejoiced in the ministry we have received through "concerns" formed by the Spirit in the hearts of individual Friends. These concerns may have been for personal service or for the furtherance of some particular insight. Such concerns need to be brought before a meeting for church affairs so that they may be tested by the meeting as a whole. This may ultimately be seen as a leading of the Spirit to which the meeting must be corporately obedient. The discerning of such leading and the subordination to it of individual opinion is a ministry to which we are all called.

50. Like all the church, we have a high calling — to be the body of Christ, to live empowered by the Spirit, to do the will of God. We admit our weaknesses in carrying this out. With our structure we risk failures in understanding and transmitting our tradition, and failures in pastoral care. We do not always adequately support one another. When we appoint people

to carry out tasks for us, there is a danger in approaching this in too secular a way, failing to see its significance as an "ordination" — an occasion when we can and must pray for them to receive the necessary gifts and strength from the Spirit. Paragraph 40 is a help to us on this.

51. We recognize that the different circumstances and traditions of parts of the church have led to different forms of organization. We respect those who have forms different from our own for we acknowledge that what is important in the formal structure is whether it allows people to know and respond to the call of God. However, when we see the emphasis in the text on an ordained, threefold ministry, it arouses in us a number of fears.

Firstly, we believe that without an adequate development of the ministry of the laity there will continue to be an unbalanced relationship between clergy and community which will encourage the people to depend too much on ordained leadership.

Secondly, we are disturbed at the linking of ordination with authority, for this can legitimize authoritarian leadership and limit the exercise of spiritual authority. We agree with the statement in §16 that authority in the church can only be authentic as it conforms to the model of Christ.

Thirdly, we fear the emphasis on a threefold ordained ministry as an "expression of the unity we seek and also a means of achieving it". Such a ministry manifestly is not a focus of unity and has not achieved unity. We regret that the text does not take more seriously the first three clauses of §22 which recognize New Testament diversity, the Spirit-led adaptation of ministries to context, and the gifts of the Spirit with which many forms of ministry have been blessed.

52. What, then, is the focus for Christian unity? It must be Jesus, who calls us not into structures but into discipleship and to follow him in his way. Can we not know that we are one in him when we are faithful to his calling and when we exercise towards one another that greatest gift of love? Can we not rejoice in our diversity, welcoming the opportunities to learn from each other? Can we not seek a recognition of each other's ministries as the work of the same Spirit? That Spirit can, if we are ready to adventure, lead us into ways we have not known before.

## The four World Council of Churches questions

53. We now turn to the four specific issues in the preface to the Lima text. It will be appreciated from all that has been said that the words in which the questions are couched and, indeed, some of the assumptions behind them are foreign to Friends' usage, and our response in consequence may seem, though it is not intended, to be negative.

*The extent to which we recognize in the text the faith of the church through the ages*

54. We recognize the witness to the grace of God in Jesus, to "the liberating and renewing power of the Holy Spirit" (§3), and to the new life

experienced in the church as it seeks to follow Jesus in the power of that Spirit. But we also find that witness obscured by an emphasis throughout the text on the sacramental *form* in which the faith is expressed and nurtured. There has never been one form of faith or one form of church at any time "through the ages", even in apostolic times. Nor do we believe that it is necessary or desirable to seek unity at that level, since, as the text itself says (§1), "the Holy Spirit unites in a single body those who follow Jesus Christ", and keeps them "in the truth" (§3).

*The Society of Friends and "its relations and dialogues with other churches"*

55. We greatly value relations and dialogue with other churches, and want to remain open to whatever we can learn from them. But we acknowledge that churches which accept the Lima text's presentation of baptism, eucharist and ministry as essential elements of a truly Christian faith must find it difficult to recognize the Religious Society of Friends as a genuinely Christian body. Indeed, the text's use of the expression "the eucharistic community" as a designation of the local Christian church implies that Quakers, along with members of the Salvation Army, are not a part of the local Christian community. This saddens us. The designation carries the further suggestion that the most efficacious aspect of the churches' witness in the world is their sacramental belief and practice. We do not see any justification for this view in the New Testament or in the history of the church.

56. We have been thankful in the past for the recognition by other churches of our particular insights. At the 1927 Lausanne Faith and Order conference the second draft of the statement on sacraments was amended to take account of Quaker views, including the now memorable words, commended by Bishop Gore: ". . . in the gifts of his grace God is not limited by his own sacraments". The final statement included also the words: "Others again, while attaching high value to the sacramental principle, do not make use of the outward signs of the sacraments, but hold that all spiritual benefits are given through immediate contact with God through his Spirit" (Proceedings, pp. 430, 472-3). The Montreal Conference (1963) recorded that "we gladly acknowledge that some who do not observe these rites share in the spiritual experience of life in Christ" (Report, p. 72). We hope that Lima will not prove a backward step from Montreal and Lausanne.

57. What then can we contribute to ongoing ecumenical dialogues about valid sacraments and authentic orders of ministry? Perhaps little more than our testimony to such fruits of the Spirit as may still be evident among us. Over more than 300 years we have witnessed to a redemptive religious experience. Though this has been without baptism, eucharist or ministry in the traditional senses, it has been a consequence of personal and repentant response and corporate worship in the context of silent, receptive waiting upon God.

*The Society's "worship, educational, ethical and spiritual life and witness"*

58.  We are in full accord with the Lima text's emphasis on worship as a source of spiritual vitality, practical Christian living and convincing Christian witness. We also accept the value of scripture in Christian education, although we have to admit that all too often we do not make enough use of it. And we recognize that discipleship of Jesus carries ethical implications not only in personal life but "in all realms of life" (B10), which indeed is why, throughout our history, we have been concerned with peace, justice and social questions. Nevertheless, we must ask ourselves again, with other Christians, whether we still pay attention to "the will of God in all realms of life". We have strong reservations about the language in which this is expressed in the text: it seems to be too academic to be of great use in religious education, and too inward looking to stimulate concern for the wider world.

*"Towards the common expression of the apostolic faith today"*

59.  In our discussion of the text throughout the Society there was a strong feeling that we should reaffirm those convictions which we have tried to make clear throughout the document. We believe we have been entrusted with these insights as our offering to the common life of the whole church.

We recognize the central place which baptism, eucharist and ordained ministry continue to have in most historical forms of Christianity, and also their efficacy as means of spiritual grace for most Christians. We can see that other churches may find greater unity if they can draw more closely together in their understanding of their sacraments and sacerdotal orders. But for us this could never be the basis of Christian unity. Our emphasis will always be on unity as a fellowship of the Spirit in which diversity becomes creative, and, in which, with the Holy Spirit's help, we learn to love one another.

Approved by London Yearly Meeting
Exeter, 1–8 August 1986
Roger B. Sturge, Clerk

**APPENDIX**

(See footnote to paragraph 1 and also paragraph 11)

One of the most impressive things about the initial establishment of the monthly meetings in 1667–9 was the spirit of divine exhilaration in which Fox travelled the country — despite the fact that after nearly three years' imprisonment in Lancaster and Scarborough he was so stiff and swollen-jointed that he could scarce mount a horse. He saw no administrative set-up, no series of business meetings, but an "order of the gospel, which is not of man, nor by man, but sent from Christ the heavenly man, above all the orders of men in the fall, and it will be when they are all gone, for the power of God the everlasting gospel lasts for ever". There have been sombre periods in the Society's history since then as well as joyous ones: there have been periods when the organization has seemed to cramp new life instead of fostering it. A Christian community needs organization if it is to maintain an effective life, but it must be free from authoritarian domination. Jesus said: "In the world, kings lord it over their subjects; and those in authority are called their country's 'benefactors'. Not so with you: on the contrary, the highest among you must bear himself like the youngest, the chief of you like a servant." Only as we have learned this in experience will our decisions reflect the vision and compassion of Christ.

Our meetings for church affairs are held in the spirit of worship. This does not mean that laughter and a sense of humour should be absent from them. It does mean that at all times there should be an inward recollection: out of this will spring a right dignity, flexible and free from pomp and formality. We meet together for common worship, for the pastoral care of our membership, for needful administration, for unhurried deliberation on matters of common concern, for testing personal concerns that are brought before us, and to get to know one another better in things that are eternal as in things that are temporal.

If we sometimes think things are wrong with our meetings for church affairs, it would help us to look at the situation in perspective if we could realize how many troubles arise not from the system, but from our human imperfections and the variety of our temperaments and viewpoints. These meetings are in fact occasions not merely for transacting with proper efficiency the affairs of the church but also opportunities when we can learn to bear and forbear, to practise to one another that love which suffereth long and is kind. Christianity is not only a faith but a community and in our meetings for church affairs we learn what membership of that community involves.

Our method of conducting our meetings for church affairs is an experience which has been tested over three hundred years. In days of hot contest and bitter controversy, the early Friends, knit together by the glorious experience of the Holy Spirit's guidance in all their affairs, came into the simple understanding of how their corporate decisions should be made. Decisions arrived at after subtle lobbying and clever debate were not for them. They had discovered that there were deeper satisfactions and greater certainties in finding their way ahead in love and understanding and in the conscious presence of God.

The purpose of our meetings for church affairs is to seek together the way of truth — the will of God in the matters before us, holding that every activity of life is subject to his will. It is necessary for the proper conduct of our business meetings that we should assemble in a worshipping spirit, asking that we may be used by God in our day. The time of worship which precedes our consideration of the business in hand should be no mere formality but a time for collectedness of spirit. The silence which concludes our assembly may be used to give thanks for the divine leading.

The right conduct of our meetings for church affairs depends upon all coming to them in an active, seeking spirit, not with minds already made up on a particular course of action, determined to push this through at all costs. But open minds are not empty minds, nor uncritically receptive: the service of the meeting calls for knowledge of facts, often painstakingly acquired, and the ability to estimate their relevance and importance. This demands that we shall be ready to listen to others carefully, without antagonism if they express opinions which are unpleasing to us, but trying always to discern the truth in what they have to offer. It calls, above all, for spiritual sensitivity. If our meetings fail, the failure may well be in those who are ill-prepared to use the method rather than the inadequacy of the method itself.

It is always to be recognized that, coming together with a variety of temperaments, of background, education and experience, we shall have differing contributions to make to any deliberation. It is no part of Friends' concern for truth that any should be expected to water down a strong conviction or be silent merely for the sake of easy agreement. Nevertheless, we are called to honour our testimony that to every one is given a measure of the light, and that it is in the sharing of knowledge, experience and concern that the way towards unity will be found. There is need for understanding loyalty by the meeting as a whole when, after all sides of a subject have been considered, a minute is accepted as representing the judgment of the meeting.

Not all who attend a meeting for church affairs will necessarily speak: those who are silent can help to develop the sense of the meeting if they listen in a spirit of worship.

It is sometimes assumed that unity can be found only by the submission of a minority to the decision of a majority. This is not so but neither should it be assumed that positive steps cannot be taken without unanimity. A minority should not seek to dominate by imposing a veto on action which the general body of Friends feels to be right. Throughout our history as a Society we have found that through the continuing search to know the will of God, a different and a deeper unity is opened to us.

Out of this deeper unity a new way is often discovered which none present had alone perceived and which transcends the differences of the opinions expressed. This is an experience of creative insight, leading to a sense of the meeting which a clerk is often led in a remarkable way to record. Those who have shared this experience will not doubt its reality and the certainty it brings of the immediate rightness of the way for the meeting to take.

The meeting places upon its clerk a responsibility for spiritual discernment so that he may watch the growth of the meeting towards unity and judge the right time to submit the minute, which in its first form may serve to clear the mind of the meeting about the issues which really need its decision. In a gathering held "in the life" there comes to the clerk a clear and unmistakable certainty about the moment to submit the minute. This may be a high peak of experience in a meeting for church affairs and for the most part we have to wrestle with far more humdrum down-to-earth business. It must always be remembered that the final decision as to whether the minute represents the sense of the meeting is the responsibility of the meeting itself, not of the clerk. Friends should realize that a decision which is the only one for a particular meeting at a particular time may not be the one which is ultimately seen to be right. There have been many occasions in our Society when a Friend, though maintaining his personal convictions, has seen clearly that they were not in harmony with the sense of the meeting and has with loyal grace expressed his deference to it. Out of just such a situation, after time for further reflection, an understanding of the Friend's insight has been reached at a later date and has been ultimately accepted by the Society.

# THE SALVATION ARMY

## Introduction

The Salvation Army willingly responds to the invitation to comment upon the Lima document despite the fact that the Army's traditional approach to the subjects dealt with differs significantly from the hypothesis on which the present study rests.

Salvationists regard with great respect the worship patterns of denominations which include sacramental observances, and in most parts of the world find The Salvation Army's non-sacramental stance no barrier to the enjoyment of rich Christian fellowship even when that stance is not fully understood. It is, therefore, a matter of regret and concern that the sincerely held views of non-sacramentalist Christians are ignored in this document. We feel it our duty, then, to respond not in a spirit of confrontation or denial, but of witness born out of our experience of the work of grace in our midst for more than one hundred years.

The Salvation Army finds no difficulty in maintaining its association with the World Council of Churches on the terms of the Council's own definition:

> A fellowship of churches which confess the Lord Jesus Christ as God and Saviour according to the Scriptures and therefore seek to fulfill together their common calling to the glory of the One God, Father, Son and Holy Spirit.

This accords with the Army's emphasis on Jesus Christ as Lord and only Saviour, on personal salvation, inner sanctification and outward holiness, as evidenced in its written documents and the lives and service of its people.

It was disconcerting to find a new emphasis emerging when in 1975 the functions and purposes section of the WCC Constitution was revised to give increased prominence to the World Council's role in encouraging church unity. Two phrases, "visible unity" and "eucharistic fellowship", were

---

• World membership approx. 1,500,000, works in 89 countries, 14,540 corps (churches), 16,724 officers (ministers).

introduced. This appeared to narrow the interpretation of unity implied by the basic membership statement and to seek for the first time to dictate the form of worship the churches should adopt.

In their reading of the Lima text Salvation Army leaders are again sensitized to the apparent change of emphasis which tends to reduce the original recognition of the church as the body of Christ, united in him irrespective of worship practices, to a group of baptized people who observe the sacrament of the Lord's supper. We aver that the continued existence of The Salvation Army and the Society of Friends renders such a definition invalid.

Differences in our approach may be partly understood in the light of our historical background: the composition of the early-day Army—an amalgam of Christians of differing denominations and sacramental traditions and new converts, unwelcome in the churches of that day and including many for whom the fermented wine presented problems. To these features must be added female ministry which quickly became an important aspect of Army life and worship. In the face of these problem-stimulating factors the Army's founders were compelled to seek the guidance of the Holy Spirit in their interpretation of New Testament teaching on the sacraments of baptism and the eucharist and on the ministry. Gradually but positively there emerged that conviction which salvationists cherish to this day, that the Holy Spirit was confirming this new expression of Christian faith and practice as a part of the body of Christ, his church, with a distinctive witness and purpose, which included the non-observance of the traditional sacraments on theological as well as practical grounds.

In our opinion this witness enriches rather than diminishes the universality of the Christian message, declaring that the Holy Spirit is not bound to time-honoured ways, nor does he necessarily conform to set patterns, but is free to and does give himself to God's people even outside the traditional means of grace. This, we believe, is sound New Testament teaching. Against this background we see in the Lima text a grave danger of limiting that message and causing further polarization by concentrating as it seems to do on the basic hypothesis that baptism and the eucharist are essential to the interpretation of the apostolic faith. We feel that even many churches which observe the sacraments would hesitate to make that claim. The apparent elevation of apostolic tradition to the level of apostolic faith confuses the vital issues and weakens the message and witness.

We foresee the danger of over-emphasis on sacramentalism creating a problem similar to that faced by Paul in the young church in Galatia (Gal. 4 and 5). We take encouragement from Dr Philip Potter who, in *Life in all its Fullness* quoted in *International Review of Mission*, wrote:

> He or she who hears the voice of Christ can only answer with the voice of his or her own culture, not somebody else's . . . The freedom to be different, and yet in that difference to be part of the freedom which Christ

has brought us. The other element is the freedom of the unity (not uniformity) of his people.[1]

Dr Potter continues in a further paragraph with expressions which could likewise have come from a salvationist's pen:

> What Paul was fighting for (in his concern for the church in Galatia) was the true unity of the Church: on the basis of Christ's death and resurrection for us, and on the one condition of our faith in him we have a unity. . . all are one in Christ Jesus (Gal. 3:28). Freedom in Christ is the one condition for the true unity of God's people in this diversity.

To date The Salvation Army has been happy to accept assurances given by WCC leaders over many years and repeated in recent dialogues between leaders of the World Council and the Army, that the terms of the 1950 Toronto Statement hold good, namely that "no church. . . is required to give up its self-understanding or to subscribe to one understanding of the Church". On this basis in 1981 The Salvation Army's leadership deemed it appropriate to remain in active fellowship with the World Council of Churches although requesting a change in relationship.

It is hoped, therefore, that the amendment of the functions and purposes statement, and the development of the emphasis on sacramental unity inherent in the Lima text, does not presage a change in the original inclusive membership standard of the constitution within which Christians of so many churches, each with its distinctive and enriching features, find happy and fruitful unity in diversity. In our opinion to move further in that direction would not only intensify the sense of isolation felt by many Christians and churches sharing our viewpoint, but would again highlight difference in interpretation which a significant number of Christians would consider unessential to personal salvation and the church's real role in mission and the proclamation of the gospel.

A former international leader of The Salvation Army, General Frederick Coutts, summed up the Army's position in this way:

> Our non-observance of sacraments is not due to any theological carelessness, a kind of slap-happy evangelism, which thinks it to be of no consequence whether these have any place in our corporate life or not. This is a matter of utmost consequence. . . .

Indicative of the serious approach of The Salvation Army to the study of "Baptism, Eucharist and Ministry" is the fact that in all five continents study groups composed of theologically and experientially qualified salvationists, ordained and lay, have independently considered the terms and implications of the Lima text. This response, given under the hand of General Jarl

---

[1]July 1983, p. 319.

Note: Scripture quotations are from RSV except where otherwise stated.

Wahlström, present international leader, therefore represents the thoughtful and prayerful transworld presentation by that part of the church of Christ called The Salvation Army of another valid approach to the gift and appropriation of divine grace.

## 1. Preface

Reflecting on the opening section of the Lima text salvationist reviewers are troubled by the apparent inference that we start divided and must see how we can achieve unity. The basis of The Salvation Army's cordial relationships with other denominations is its belief that we are already "one in Christ Jesus". The task facing the church is to see how this can be realized and made visible in relationships between and within the churches.

We believe there is a serious imbalance in the witness of the church whenever the face we present to the world reflects only matters which tend to factionalize. It is in the vital issues of the faith committed to us by Christ himself and proclaimed by the apostles, that the church has the only viable basis of unity.

It is therefore our contention that the Lima emphasis on matters which still divide beclouds the real issue and challenge of the gospel and its message to a world which sees little relevance to its needs in church debates on forms of worship.

We do, however, see the penultimate sentence of paragraph 2 (p. vii) as indicating an area in which, on the basis of our common faith, the unity of the church should and can most effectively be made visible — Christian witness and service.

We also endorse references in paragraph 3 (p. vii) to church unity being "God's gift" and support the aim of the Commission (paragraph 4, p. viii) "to proclaim the oneness of the Church of Jesus Christ. . . expressed in. . . *common life in Christ"*. The underlining is ours, pointing to our firm belief that to make any act of worship, however sacred and meaningful, the basis of unity, creates the risk of losing the emphasis on life together in Christ.

With this in mind we consider the term "grow *into* unity" (paragraph 8, p. viii) dilutes the more positive expression of paragraph 3 (p. vii): "manifesting more visibly God's gift of unity". The growing process applies more particularly to personal relationships between Christians and Christian communities already able to enjoy God's gift of unity in Christ.

We welcome the allusion in the same paragraph (8, p. viii) to the present debate seen in relation to "the true meaning of the Church" and to "human community". The Salvation Army urges that "mission" remains paramount in all ecumenical discussions and that the spiritual and social implications of the gospel in relation to the "human community" be fully realized.

Referring to "consensus rooted in the communion built on Jesus Christ and the witness of the apostles" (paragraph 2, p. ix), the general tenor of the text leads us to read this as referring to the apostolic tradition. We again express our doubts about elevating to near-scriptural authority any tradition, however rooted in the history of the church, interpreted differently by different readers of the same history.

With due deference to the scholars and scholarship involved in the Lima text, the document appears as a "high church" pronouncement which comes close to advocating a "baptismal regeneration" and a "eucharistic sanctification", with sacramental language seeming to take precedence over biblical terminology. Thus "the Body of Christ" or "the fellowship of believers" becomes "eucharistic community" worshipping in "eucharistic fellowship".

With "one faith" and "one fellowship" we agree wholeheartedly. These belong to the essence of life in Christ. "Eucharistic fellowship", we claim, is of a different order.

Words of General Frederick Coutts may again be used to echo salvationist sentiments:

> The words of Jesus as quoted in John 17:21 — "That they may all be one", have nothing to do with what are called schemes for organic union. This is not a prayer for unity of organisation, nor can the "oneness" to which the phrase refers be brought about by administrative changes. The words refer to a spiritual unity as is manifest in the oneness of the Father, Son and Holy Spirit.

We concur that "the churches have much in common in their understanding of the faith" (paragraph 4, p. ix) and again strongly advocate that much more be made of this fact. The unifying force in the Christian church has always been and is today fidelity to the cardinal doctrines concerning Christ and salvation — the atonement, repentance, justification by faith, adoption into God's family by regeneration, the infilling of the Spirit — strong biblical doctrines not dependent on any sacramental rite.

In our view it would be a tragedy for the Christian church if the "hostilities" referred to in paragraph 4 (p. ix) were accentuated by the introduction into this document of judgmental, exclusive elements, counterproductive in a search for common ground.

As noted in our introductory statement salvationists around the world embarked on their review of "Baptism, Eucharist and Ministry" with deep respect for the integrity of those churches whose observances differ from our own. We therefore share the satisfaction expressed in paragraph 5 (p. ix) regarding "significant theological convergence" discerned by Faith and Order in the work of the Commission, representing, it is claimed, "virtually all" confessions. Our hope would be that this theological convergence will result in renewed and more effective mission and evangelism.

We are, nevertheless, compelled to reiterate our painful awareness of the fact that the integrity of the *non*-sacramentalist approach to the apostolic faith, as distinct from the apostolic tradition, has been ignored. Even the "reformed" or "non-conformist" view seems to find little acknowledgment in the Lima thesis.

Confronted with the text, salvationists in many lands have felt challenged to a fresh examination of their own theological position vis-à-vis baptism, eucharist and ministry. The resultant consensus reflected in this response indicates a confirmed belief in the soundness of that position in relation to our divine institution as a movement with a particular commission and vocation.

It is not without importance to us that with our name, The *Salvation* Army, God gave us deep convictions born of the Spirit through the holy scriptures. We have therefore been led to insistence on the very essentials of the faith, the inescapable elements of salvation:

1. *The need for regeneration* by the power of the Holy Spirit, through repentance towards God and faith in our Lord Jesus Christ. We firmly reject the idea that any work or rite can accomplish what God has promised in response to faith.

2. *The call to sanctification*, the life of holiness, the inseparable consequence of salvation, an experience created and maintained only by obedient trust in the Saviour indwelling the believer by his Spirit.

3. *The grace of ministry and service*, open to all believers. All Christ's followers are called to be evangelists and have a responsibility for the care of his flock. Some have privilege of a calling to full-time service in the church.

The Salvation Army's response is therefore in the nature of an explanation, an apologia, and above all a witness to the experience granted by the Holy Spirit to many salvationists of succeeding generations and differing nationalities. Having clearly stated our position, our faith and our fears in our introduction and in these comments on the preface, we will not commit to this response the line by line critique of the Lima text produced by our numerous study groups. The following pages record only selected comments illustrating the basic principles either of divergence or harmony stated in the preamble. In conclusion we shall endeavour to answer the four questions posed by the compilers of the document to which we shall add appendices presenting statements of the salvationist's faith and order, supplemented by other supportive material.

## 2. Baptism

### I. THE INSTITUTION OF BAPTISM

1. Assuming (as later §17 supports) that water baptism is referred to throughout this section of the document, we observe that historically baptism was a common initiation feature in both Jewish and pagan religions. It would be natural, therefore, for John, heralding the coming of Christ's kingdom, to adopt the customary mode of initiation. We note the assertion of those in whose form of worship today baptism plays a key role, that "Christian baptism is rooted in the ministry of Jesus of Nazareth, in his death

and resurrection", and indicates to the believer "incorporation" also into Christ's death and resurrection.

Salvationists consider the experience rather than the symbol as "the gift of God" and are impressed by John's prophetic testimony that water baptism would be superseded by Jesus who would baptize with the Holy Spirit (Mark 1:8). We refer also to Mark 10:38 and our Lord's question: "are you able. . . to be baptized with the baptism with which I am baptized?", reminding us that "incorporation" into Christ is a costly business, involving sacrificial commitment.

We do not find any single, uniform or fully developed concept of water baptism in the New Testament, which possibly accounts for the lack of a unified view of baptismal practice acceptable to all.

Although not critical of fellow-Christians whose views differ from ours, the salvationist position on baptism is based on the belief that the only distinctive and utterly unique Christian baptism is baptism with the Holy Spirit. That cannot be duplicated by any other religion — it is peculiarly Christ's: "He shall baptize you with the Holy Spirit."

II. The meaning of baptism

2. At various points in the text baptism is acknowledged as a "*sign*" of new life, as "*images*" expressed by the "*symbolic*" use of water. But the text also becomes distinctly categorical: "Baptism *is* participation. . .", "a washing away of sin". . . . "a new birth". . . "a renewal by the Spirit".

Believing that it is the sacrificial death of Jesus which, together with baptism in the Spirit, effects the new birth, we salvationists must record our witness that all the experiences described in §§ 1 to 10, said to be implicit in or effected by water baptism, are our privilege also without the rite described.

*A. Participation in Christ's death and resurrection*

3. With Christians who observe the sacrament of baptism with deep spiritual understanding, salvationists have a true fellowship in spirit. We find it difficult, however, to follow the thought that "solidarity with sinners. . . ", immersion "in the liberating death of Christ" and the radical works of grace here described, can be attributed to the rite itself, as implied by the opening words: "Baptism means. . . ".

Our name, The *Salvation* Army, indicates our emphasis on the redeeming work of Jesus Christ, and we are uneasy about any suggestion that the agent of liberation from sins is any other than salvation itself, as proclaimed in the New Testament.

*B. Conversion, pardoning and cleansing*

4. The Salvation Army has always been concerned that outward acts should not overshadow the need for inner personal experience and we see

with satisfaction the statement that: "baptism. . . implies confession of sin and conversion of heart".

Analogous to the call of John the Baptist for public repentance for the forgiveness of sins (Mark 1:4) is the Army's invitation to seekers to kneel at a mercy seat (Ex. 25:21,22), thus emphasizing the need for a personal response to Christ in humility and penitence. Care is taken to deny any special virtue or power in the mercy seat itself, which makes us sensitive to the claim that "those baptized *are* pardoned, cleansed and sanctified by Christ".

The inclusion of "sanctification" in the meaning of baptism is of special interest in that The Salvation Army, like some other churches, holds a distinct doctrine of sanctification as a work of the Holy Spirit creating holiness of character (cf. Luke 1:74,75; Eph. 4:22–24). The tenth tenet of the Army's doctrines quotes 1 Thessalonians 5:23.

We are therefore gratified to read the summing up of the growth of the spiritual life included in §9 on p. 4, which corresponds to our belief that conversion is only the beginning of a "life-long growth *in* (rather than into) Christ", and of our interpretation of sanctification as the commencement of the Holy Spirit's work of transforming us into Christlikeness.

This emphasis on sanctification and holiness is basic to The Salvation Army's stance and its continuing non-observance of the rites of baptism and eucharist. However beautiful and helpful these visible symbols may be as a means of grace to so many of our Christian brethren, salvationists bear testimony to their firm belief in and experience of the personally mediated redeeming grace of God in Christ without their use.

## C. *The gift of the Spirit*
5. We find the phrase: "God bestows upon all baptized persons the annointing and promise of the Holy Spirit. . ." theologically imprecise and inaccurate. The impression given is that the gift of the Spirit is theirs through baptism, whereas God's gift is a response to the faith of the believer which in our experience does not require participation in a symbolic rite.

Salvationists are encouraged by the New Testament record that the empowerment of the apostles at Pentecost was not related to any act of theirs save obedience, faith and prayer. Cornelius and his household were evidently first baptized with the Holy Spirit and later went through the ceremony of water baptism as a sign of their acceptance of and into the Christian faith.

## D. *Incorporation into the body of Christ*
6. We can accept that to those who observe the sacrament baptism signifies reception into the body of Christ, but feel the argument for baptism as a unifying feature of church life is undermined by *commentary 6.*

We prefer to declare that union with each other is by virtue of our union with Christ, which seems a more positive and powerful emphasis on unity and a more authentic basis for witness to a world that sees the Christian's life and character, but is oblivious of the way we worship in our churches.

*E. The sign of the kingdom*

7. We do not deny that baptism can be a "sign of the Kingdom of God" in a secondary sense, but baptism is here invested with the power to produce new life and give "participation in the community of the Holy Spirit". 1 Corinthians 1: 30 expresses the salvationist's belief that: "He (God) is the source of your life *in Christ Jesus*". This provides the "dynamic" to "the gifts of faith, hope and love" whether or not the "sign" is there.

III. BAPTISM AND FAITH

8. "The necessity of faith for the reception of salvation" and "personal commitment. . . necessary for responsible membership in the Body of Christ" fully accord with The Salvation Army's understanding and teaching.

We see our own "swearing-in" procedure or a symbolic act such as baptism, as a "human response" to what God offers as a gift.

9. We are impressed with the fact that 2 Corinthians 3 credits the Holy Spirit with effecting all the experiences to which it refers, and "where the Spirit of the Lord is, there is freedom" (v. 17).

On this basis salvationists humbly but confidently witness that it is the indwelling Spirit of Christ which makes us and marks us his own, gives us life, leads us into sonship with God, gives us an inward witness, deals with the problems of human nature and facilitates our prayer life. Not only "those baptized" but all Christians irrespective of their form of worship "are called upon to reflect the glory of the Lord as they are transformed by the power of the Holy Spirit, into his likeness, with ever increasing splendour" (v. 18). Reference to the Articles of War signed by would-be salvation soldiers reveals an equal understanding of the "new relationship" expected of "the baptized".

10. We are bound to say that the liturgical interpretations contained in this paragraph are hurtful to some believers. Not all believers are baptized as the text implies, but all may enter into the privileges described. Paul is quite explicit: "If you confess with your lips that Jesus is Lord and believe in your heart that God raised him from the dead, you will be saved" (Rom. 10:9). We believe the experience is immediate and mediated directly to the heart of the believer. Again, Galatians 3 is about faith (v. 26) not ritual, Christian behaviour not baptismal practice.

Salvationists, who believe that the weight of emphasis in the New Testament is on faith in and union with Christ, are surprised to find Ephesians 2:5,6,8 quoted under the heading: "The Meaning of Baptism" (§3). Read on its own merits the meaning of Ephesians 2 hinges on verse 8: "By grace you have been saved through faith; and this is not your own doing (not by your own actions), it is the gift of God." We understand the apostle's teaching to mean that Christian unity is to be secured by Christ's reconciling work through the cross, and the unifying presence of the Holy Spirit in the lives of those so reconciled.

## IV. BAPTISMAL PRACTICE

### A. *Baptism of believers and infants*

11. The effort to find consensus between baptism of believers and that of infants was noted with interest especially by salvationists in some countries where a strong state church influences the thinking of a majority of Christians.

It does seem certain, however, that many Christians, including salvationists, will not be able to reconcile the manifold interpretations of baptismal practice as outlined in the Lima text and by which faith is said to be initiated and sustained. It could be said that the Acts of the Apostles does record a diversity of form and pattern: baptism prior to receipt of the Spirit; Spirit prior to baptism; Spirit without baptism; baptism followed by laying on of hands. But the "one (common) baptism" is by the Spirit.

In this situation we find ourselves on sure ground in recognizing the freedom of God to meet faith when and as he pleases, for, as Jesus told Nicodemus: "The wind blows where it wills. . . so it is with every one who is born of the Spirit." (J. B. Phillips: "Nor can you tell how a man is born. . . by the Spirit".)

Further, we believe Paul's emphasis was that "real circumcision is a matter of the heart, spiritual and not literal" (Rom. 2:29), as having replaced the ritual act of the old Israel and on "a new covenant in the Spirit".

The Salvation Army, in common with some other churches, responds to the example of Jesus who himself was dedicated in the Temple, and called young children to him, blessing them by laying his hands on them.

As in infant baptism, The Salvation Army dedication ceremony takes place within congregational worship and is a commitment by the parents and the local congregation to bring up the child in the nurture and admonition of the Lord.

12. We are left with a big question regarding the implication here that the child shares the faith of the parents and actually becomes a Christian by being baptized. This, to quote Kierkegaard, "savours of salvation by proxy; whereas the church of the New Testament is entered by a personal profession of faith".

The encouragement of family worship and the family altar for prayer and Bible study are implicit in the Army dedication service, in the hope that the child will thus share its parents' faith with growing perception. Salvationists declare their firm belief in the ability of a child of even tender years of understanding to accept Jesus Christ as Saviour, friend and guide, then, after instruction, to be accepted as junior soldiers in the Salvation Army.

In The Salvation Army the "swearing-in" ceremony for over-fourteen-year-olds desiring to become soldiers in the Army, marks acceptance as a member of the visible church — for the believer, a public confession of Christ as Lord and Saviour; for the church, a sign that the believer is received and welcomed into Christian fellowship. The salvationist so received would attest to the same sense of incorporation into the family of God and the life and service of Jesus Christ, with the beginnings of the inner working of the Holy Spirit, as does his baptized believer brother. Like that of baptism, this ceremony is always "celebrated and developed in the setting of the Christian community".

13. The meaning of the statement that "baptism is an unrepeatable act" is not quite clear. If it guards against the presumption of one church that the baptism administered in another church is invalid, we agree. We take it also that the possibility of the baptized falling from grace, ignoring his baptismal vows, is taken into account, and that a means of grace and restoration to the Christian fellowship is open.

### B. Baptism, chrismation, confirmation

14. Salvation Army teaching emphasizes the inter-relationship of Christ's death and resurrection, the gift of the Holy Spirit at Pentecost and the life of the believer in resurrection power both now and for eternity. That baptism "signifies" all this may be true, but that it "effects" a spiritual experience can only be the result of the personal faith of the one baptized. We make passing reference here to the Jerusalem Council and to the recognition that the Gentiles had their hearts cleansed and received the Holy Spirit by faith and not by ceremony (Acts 15:8-11).

Regarding the "sign of the gift of the Holy Spirit" we must again witness to the freedom of the Holy Spirit to act without visible means. We look for the "sign" or "seal" of the Spirit in the life of the recipient — with Paul we see "fruit unto holiness" (AV), "sanctification" (Rom. 6:22) as the "sign", when "God put(s) his stamp of ownership on you by giving you the Holy Spirit" (Eph. 1:13).

In *commentary 14* one might have expected a more detailed reference to the place, purpose and content of confirmation, referred to only in passing. The importance of adequate preparation for church membership, including assurance of personal salvation, cannot be overstated. The Salvation Army has similar courses for young people.

### C. Towards mutual recognition of baptism

15. From time to time transfers take place between The Salvation Army and churches. Usually an official note is provided and honoured by the recipient church. If adult baptism is practised as a witness to faith and sign of reception into that particular part of the church of Christ, the transferee may well wish to share in this. This does not negate the reality of his acceptance of

Christ and his salvation or of his entry into the kingdom and church of Christ within The Salvation Army.

Transferees from churches are welcomed into fellowship in The Salvation Army if they sincerely feel that is God's leading in their lives. Usually they also bring some form of introduction from their former place of worship and if they wish to accept the additional disciplines of salvationism, they may be "sworn-in" as Salvation Army soldiers, their declaration of faith being regarded only as a reaffirmation of spiritual vows already made.

16. From the foregoing may be deduced the salvationist's conviction that the worship and practices to which he is accustomed incorporate all the spiritual elements claimed by sister churches, and take cognisance of the needs of both infants and older believers. But Jesus himself remains the unifying factor within his church—Jesus is Lord!

V. THE CELEBRATION OF BAPTISM

18. The symbolic nature of the ceremonies is now clearly stated—the emphasis on "the symbolic dimension of water" which can "vividly express the reality" puts many other statements in the text in proper perspective.

*Commentary 18* provides helpful explanatory information.

19/23. As non-participants in the practice of water baptism it is not our place to comment further, save to express surprise that in the Lima text the only reference to "baptism of the Holy Spirit without water" appears in the last sub-paragraph of the baptism section (commentary 21c) with a remark regarding "some African churches". This further and crucial lack of recognition of sincere Christians in many parts of the world who, like salvationists, preach and witness to the power of the Holy Spirit at work in the life of the believer irrespective of visible forms, is sadly disappointing.

We reiterate our belief that experience teaches that the outward act is not of supreme importance, but the experience is vital to the Christian's character and witness.

## 3. Eucharist

The salvationist declares his own experience of the mediation of divine grace without symbol or sacrament. As already stated, The Salvation Army maintains its belief in the scriptural doctrine of spiritual cleansing, motivation and empowering by the Holy Spirit, which we define as sanctification or the life of holiness.

Some Christian friends are generous enough to suggest that The Salvation Army's non-eucharistic witness acts as a reminder of the essential spirituality of the Christian experience and we likewise acknowledge the challenge and spiritual enrichment derived from study of this section of the Lima text, meaningful as it is to so many of our fellow Christians.

For information and as a reference point in understanding some of our salvationist views, we include as an appendix a statement of the Doctrines of

The Salvation Army.[2] These are vitally concerned with the spiritual realities symbolized by the practices under review in the Lima text, and the way by which these realities can become part of personal experience.

### I. THE INSTITUTION OF THE EUCHARIST

1. With the historical background we agree, but stop short of investing the last supper with the significance here claimed for it. For instance, we find our own attitude to the practice of the eucharist strengthened by implication through the omission of the "words of institution" from some manuscripts of the gospels, and by the fact that John's gospel, written to present Jesus as the source of eternal life (20:30), preserves what in the Bible is a five-chapter-long record of the vitally significant words of Jesus during and after the meal, without any reference to an "institution".

The synoptic gospels do present us with a picture of the last supper as a "liturgical means employing symbolic words and actions". (It is perhaps appropriate here to observe that the "forgotten sacrament", the foot-washing, seems only to rate symbolic status!) But the gospels also clearly indicate the sharing of a common meal — they dipped bread in the same dish. . . all drank from the cup — a token of unity and fellowship.

A thought expressed by Dr J. H. Jowett commends itself:

The day is marked with glory when our daily bread becomes a sacrament,

which is echoed in a Salvation Army statement on the sacraments:

Every meal is sacramental to those who partake with remembrance of him who provides for both material and spiritual needs.

This supports the old Christian custom of saying "grace before meal", which includes thanksgiving as Jesus is remembered and a sense of his presence hallows the meal, unites the partakers in fellowship and reminds them that strength received is to be used for the cause of Christ. The salvationist feels this simple act of worship is an indication of the extension of spiritual communion to the totality of life as taught by our Lord in the whole of his discourse with his disciples during and following the last supper. General Albert Orsborn, a former international leader of the Army, enshrined this thought in a hymn, beloved of salvationists as expressing their deepest desires:

My life must be Christ's broken bread,
My love his outpoured wine,
A cup o'er filled, a table spread
Beneath his name and sign,
That other souls, refreshed and fed,
May share his life through mine.

---

[2] Editor's note: Appendix not included.

Highly significant as the eucharist is to the majority of Christians, we feel bound to question the final sentence in this section (§1): "Its celebration continues as the central act of the church's worship", an idea surely belied by the widely differing interpretations and practices of the various denominations in this respect. From the salvationist viewpoint meeting with the risen Lord is the central act of his worship, which can be just as challenging and powerful in the preaching of the word, in the song of praise and in prayer. That such a meeting can take place in the eucharist we do not deny, but could not confine it to a certain act.

II. THE MEANING OF THE EUCHARIST

The spiritual aspirations of all Christians and their expectations from their particular form of worship, must surely coincide with those outlined as related to and arising out of the eucharist as expounded in Section II.

2. Statements such as: "every Christian receives this gift of salvation through communion in the body and blood of Christ", and, "each *baptized* member of the body of Christ *receives in the eucharist* the assurance of the forgiveness of sins", may well indicate the experience of some who view the eucharistic sacrament in this way. But such unqualified statements can hardly stand up against such a scriptural axiom as: "For by grace you have been saved through faith" (Eph. 2:8; also 18; Eph. 1:13, 14; Rom. 10:13).

As in our reading of the previous section, we have to observe that the Lima text appears to foster an unconscious exclusivism, which limits not only those who may be included in the church, but tends to limit even the grace and love of God by its restrictive interpretations. No allowance is made for those who receive the inner assurance of forgiveness uninfluenced by outward ceremony.

*A. The eucharist as thanksgiving to the Father*

3/4. With the *spirit* of these beautiful expressions salvationists can readily identify, although using other means of communication.

*B. The eucharist as anamnesis or memorial of Christ*

7. That the eucharist is a "calling to mind" we understand, but that it is "the church's effective *proclamation* of God's mighty acts and promises" seems an exaggerated claim and does not do justice to Christians who, without recourse to this sacrament, have remembrance and proclamation of the saving merits and presence of Christ at the heart of their worship and ministry.

8. We applaud the place given to the uniqueness and unrepeatability of Christ's sacrifice, but from experience find ourselves forced to question the *commentary 8* wording: "made actual in the eucharist". It is our claim that Christ's sacrifice cannot be "made actual" in a ceremony, but only in the

believer himself, in his own assurance of salvation and in his sacramental living— in a continual "eucharistic life" (point 9).

10. In view of our understanding of sanctification (baptism, §4) we cannot read literally: "in which (the eucharist) we are sanctified", but any Bible-based emphasis on the experience is welcomed.

13. This paragraph seems to be of a crucial nature. We wholeheartedly agree with the statement: "Christ fulfills in a variety of ways his promise to be always with his own. . .", but view with apprehension the claim that "Christ's mode of presence in the eucharist is *unique*", with its inference that in the eucharist Christ comes in a manner unequalled in any other. This we deny and see this kind of expression as coming close to the aforementioned exclusivist approach. Whether the numerous references to the coming, presence and activity of Christ "in the eucharist" relate to the elements, the ritual or participation in the ritual, many thousands of Christians can gratefully witness to such "comings" of Christ apart from the eucharist— "where two or three are gathered together in my name there am I in the midst" is the operative promise.

*Commentary 13*: a radical "decision remains for the churches" as suggested, but the text itself seems to do little to assist. We seriously query a statement which appears to imply that "the total being of Christ" comes *only* in the bread and wine.

The Salvation Army's view is compatible with the idea that although God remains essentially transcendent, he is graciously near and immanent in all his creation. For the man of faith there is no need for part of life to be essentially sacred while the every-day is secular. For the salvationist the *anamnesis* of the sacrifice of Jesus on the cross is of central importance in his personal faith, his worship, his preaching and his daily living.

### C. The eucharist as invocation of the Spirit

We do not disagree *in principle* with these paragraphs, since forms and ceremonies approached in faith and in the name of Jesus Christ can be a real source of spiritual renewal and insight, provided the ceremony is not invested with inherent powers beyond their capacity.

### D. The eucharist as communion of the faithful

19. We fear that in interchurch relationships *eucharistic* "oneness" is presently extremely limited, but it is our belief that spiritual oneness which already exists could and should be developed irrespective of eucharistic questions. It is admitted in the Lima text itself that sharing in the eucharist is *not* "effecting" the oneness of those participating as claimed here. Jesus himself indicated that the identifiable Christlikeness of all his disciples, born of oneness with him, would convince the world that God had sent him (John 17:20–23).

The last sentence in this paragraph echoes one of the principles which has characterized relationships between The Salvation Army and fellow-Christians, to "take seriously the interests and concerns of other churches".

*Commentary 19*: We share the concern of our Christian brethren regarding the breach of good faith in the spiritual sense indicated here, which in our opinion is even more serious than the diversity in forms of celebrating the same spiritual truths and aspirations.

20/21. Christian communities such as our own would not dispute the eucharistic claims made here, but §20 presents a challenging interpretation of the expected effect of shared Christian faith in any such communities. The value of a visual symbol embodying the challenge cannot be underestimated, but whilst the Lima document is principally for the devout sacramentalist, we would have welcomed in this context recognition of the fact that all the benefits and manifestations of the activity of God's Holy Spirit and opportunities for Christian ministry are discernible in and through the lives of sincere Christians who do not necessarily participate in eucharistic practices.

It is our belief that union with Christ lies in the fulfilment of his own promise: . . . "we will come to him and make our home with him" (John 14:23), which leads to a life of holiness— a sacramental life.

We are glad to see the eucharist linked with responsible care and practical service, an area which The Salvation Army has always perceived to be the natural interpretation of the social implications of the gospel.

*E. The eucharist as a meal of the kingdom*

22. We believe literally that "signs of this renewal are present in the world *wherever* the grace of God is manifested".

23. These are constituents of any Bible-based, spiritually stimulating form of worship, whether eucharistic or not.

24. We assert that reconciliation is "in Christ" rather than "in the eucharist". All members of the body of Christ are "called to be servants of reconciliation. . . witnesses of the joy of resurrection". "Solidarity with the outcast" has a distinctly Salvation Army ring about it! Christ's sacrifice, however remembered, is a constant challenge to the devotion of life and love in the service of those outside of the kingdom and of the church.

25. Salvationists likewise interpret the outward expression of their inward experience of the grace of God in Christ Jesus.

26. We are bound to challenge the totally unscriptural view that "the eucharist brings into the present age a new reality which transforms Christians into the image of Christ". It is the work of the Holy Spirit to create the image of Christ in holiness of life, independent of outward observance.

The argument in favour of uniformity of eucharistic doctrine and practice seems to overlook the fact that the man in the street who needs our gospel knows little or nothing about what goes on in our churches and probably understands still less the language we use. We regretfully find it unlikely that this excellent presentation of the ideal interpretation of the eucharist in the life and worship of those churches which see it in this light will make sense to him or impression upon him. We make this observation with a deep sense of challenge to ourselves and all Christian witnesses to consider carefully the language in which we present our message to the world outside our churches.

In this context we dare to assert that The Salvation Army's missionary witness has not been weakened at either corporate or individual level by non-participation in the eucharist. We would want to see the argument for eucharistic uniformity balanced by a reference to the strengths which are to be derived from diversity within one united family of Christians.

### III. The celebration of the eucharist

27. Salvationist students of the Lima text have found this section instructive to those unaccustomed to the eucharist liturgy in their own form of worship. In relating the truth behind and implicit in the eucharist, salvationists have found enrichment for their own worship and service.

28. The concession: "a certain liturgical diversity compatible with our common eucharistic faith is recognised as a healthy and enriching fact", is encouraging. We hope this is a pointer towards recognition that many Christians experience the same spiritual reality and enrichment in their own traditional form of worship.

The connection between our understanding of the meaning of the eucharist and our proclamation of the doctrine of sanctification as a positive experience producing the possibility of holiness in living has already been referred to. For The Salvation Army, one of the outcomes of this study will undoubtedly be a re-emphasis on the significance of this doctrine.

*Commentary 28* envisages the use of elements other than bread and wine. Would it be too big a step from this to recognition of the possibility of the same resources of divine grace being received and enjoyed without the use of any elements?

### 4. Ministry

### I. The calling of the whole people of God

6. This scriptural and evangelical exposition coincides with The Salvation Army's understanding of the church of Christ on earth and the "priesthood of all believers". The passing reference to "the gifts of the sacraments" (§1) we read in the broadest sense.

Paragraphs 1 to 5 seem to us to enunciate the basis for true Christian unity — the common "calling of the people of God" — and we agree that any consideration of the ordained ministry" must "work from the perspective of the calling of the whole people of God" (§6). This, we claim, is the perspective from which The Salvation Army views the high calling of its commissioned and ordained officers — its full-time leaders and shepherds of God's people. We particularly note such references in §5:

> The Holy Spirit bestows on the community diverse and complementary gifts. These are for the common good of the whole people and are manifested in acts of service within the community and to the world. . . All members are called to discover, with the help of the community, the gifts they have received and to use them for the building up of the church and for the service of the world to which Christ is sent.

This we see to be the teaching of the New Testament and of the early church and *on this basis we hope the present Faith and Order document will promote wider views of the call to the ministry.*

The obligation upon each salvationist to recognize himself as an individual agent of the Lord Jesus is summed up in a quotation from our official book of guidance for Salvation Army soldiers, *Chosen to be a Soldier:*

> Just as the central word of the name of his movement is salvation, so the salvation soldier will recollect that his Articles of War begin with a declaration about having personally received it and conclude with a dedication to personal work for the salvation of the whole world. In other words the soldier knows that he is saved — to save!

For some this leads inevitably to full-life dedication in the Army's own form of ordained ministry.

II. THE CHURCH AND THE ORDAINED MINISTRY

7. Sub-paragraphs (a) to (c) form a standard by which to view ministry in the church with which The Salvation Army can agree, although we do not invest the laying on of hands with the significance indicated here.

*A. The ordained ministry*

8/13. These statements coincide with The Salvation Army's views on the calling and status of its commissioned officers — their whole training is geared to this interpretation and development of an ordained ministry on this pattern (see also note on commentary 13).

10. We do, however, reject the assumption that our ministry is founded on that of the apostles. Like theirs, our ministry is founded on Christ, his teaching and his call to apostleship.

13/14. While respecting the significance given to the celebrating of the sacraments in relation to the ordained ministry, we regard our officer as focal in his leadership of public worship and our own significant spiritual ceremonies, but also in his Christlike service and leadership.

*Commentary 11*: Experience in The Salvation Army confirms that "Christ continues through the Holy Spirit to choose and call persons to the ordained ministry" (§8), and the inner assurance of that call and the seal of the Holy Spirit has sustained thousands of Salvation Army officers through a lifetime of active and fruitful ministry. *We therefore support the need to avoid dogmatic claims regarding the ministry of any one church or one form of ordination.*

*Commentary 13*: We fully agree and especially underline the thought that "any member of the body may share in proclaiming and teaching the word of God, may contribute to the sacramental life of that body".

*Commentary 14*: We read into this an acceptance of the fact that the eucharist was not instituted as a form, ceremony or sacrament, which is the Salvation Army standpoint.

### B. Ordained ministry and authority

15. In principle this statement is acceptable as a definition of the spiritual authority of a Salvation Army officer, an authority conferred by the Holy Spirit.

16. This paragraph could easily have come from *Orders and Regulations for Officers of The Salvation Army*!

*Commentary 16* likewise conforms to an Army officer's understanding of his calling and duty.

### C. Ordained ministry and priesthood

17. We do not use the term "priest", but the wording of this paragraph describes the function and relationship both of our "priesthood of all believers" and of our ordained and commissioned officers.

*Commentary 17*: This reflects our thinking, except that we believe in the scripture-supported "priesthood of all *believers*" — not of all baptized.

### D. The ministry of men and women in the church

18. As a part of the church which from its earliest days has given women equal opportunity in the ministry of the word, we underscore the recognition that "the church must discover the ministry which can be provided by women. . .". We, too, seek "a deeper understanding of the comprehensiveness of ministry which reflects the interdependence of men and women. . . to be more widely manifested in the life of the church".

*Commentary 18*: Paragraph 1, reflects the traditional attitude of The Salvation Army to the ministry of women, stimulated by Catherine, wife of William Booth and pioneer in this field even before her husband left the ordained ministry of the Methodist Church. In her pamphlet *Female Ministry* Mrs Booth wrote in defence of women's right to preach the gospel:

> I believe woman is destined to assume her true position and exert her proper influence by the special exertions and attainments of her own sex. . . May the Lord, even the just and impartial one, overrule all for the true emancipation of women from the swaddling bands of prejudice, ignorance and custom which, almost the world over, have so long debased and wronged her.

The Salvation Army has at least twice as many ordained women officers as men; all wives of officers are themselves trained, ordained and commissioned; to retain her ordained officer status in marriage a single woman officer must marry an officer.

We prefer to accept the open-door to the full involvement of women in the work of the kingdom as indicated by Paul—" . . . neither male nor female. . ." (Gal. 3:28) and therefore welcome the statement that "an increasing number of churches have decided that there is no biblical or theological reason against ordaining women".

## III. THE FORMS OF THE ORDAINED MINISTRY

### A. *Bishops, presbyters and deacons*

19/25. We can understand the threefold ministry as three levels of ministerial authority, but find attempts to give distinct theological meaning to those levels unconvincing and confusing. We, too, have functional levels of administration, but see the gifts of *episkope* and diakonia operating in and characterizing all levels of ministry. All officers are expected to exercise caring oversight and to undertake the humblest service with their people.

*Commentary 21*: It is interesting to read of "the travelling ministry" and "the local ministry", both of which find their counterpart in The Salvation Army. We note also the comment: "Several of these ministries are ascribed to both women and men" and "While some were appointed by the laying on of hands, there is no indication of this procedure in other cases. . .". The final lines (p. 26) express succinctly our understanding of the ministry.

### B. *Guiding principles for the exercise of the ordained ministry*

26. The salvationist has no difficulty in relating the principles here enunciated to the life and work of a Salvation Army officer, whose ministry is exercised "in a personal, collegial and communal way".

*Commentary 26*: Salvation Army officers are guided by *Orders and Regulations for Officers of The Salvation Army* which are kept under constant review to ensure the maximum effectiveness and efficiency of its officers in all aspects of their calling, ministry and service.

27. This reflects the Army's own *modus operandi*. In recent years, even more than previously, "strong emphasis" has been "placed on the active participation of all members in the life and decision making of the community". Advisory councils and boards, including lay personnel, support the appointed ordained leaders at all levels of Salvation Army life and service.

### C. *Functions of bishops, presbyters and deacons*

28/31. In extension of our note on A. 19/25 above we see that The Salvation Army has in its ministry those who conform in a general way to each of the categories described. In considering ". . . the mutual recognition of the ordained ministry" we take the view that the functions rather than the title or form of ordination are of most importance. Further, it could be said that the true ministry is unified, not compartmentalized.

*D. Variety of charisms*

32. We find the wide variety of gifts of the Holy Spirit evidenced in the lives and service of our officers and soldiers enriches, enlivens and enlarges the Army's witness and ministry.

33. The challenge of "special ministries" is indeed a matter of serious concern as is the vital necessity for the church constantly to receive new impulses from the Holy Spirit through "prophetic and (in the broad sense of the word) charismatic leaders", unrestricted by ecclesiastical structures. Perhaps the birth of The Salvation Army is not unrelated and its experience bears witness to the truth of the assertion of this paragraph, as it must continue to do.

IV. SUCCESSION IN THE APOSTOLIC TRADITION

*A. Apostolic tradition in the church*

34. Apostleship in Salvation Army terms means being sent by God in the power of the Spirit according to the scriptures. Historical continuity alone does not guarantee apostolicity, and can be used to exclude some branches of the Christian family.

Nevertheless, we agree with what this paragraph says about the church, except for specific "sacramental" references. We see ourselves as standing on apostolic ground and in an apostolic succession of creed.

In our Articles of War the salvationist declares:

> Believing that The Salvation Army has been raised up by God and is sustained and directed by him, I do here declare that I am thoroughly convinced of the Army's teaching. . .

there follows a statement of the Army Doctrines.

The church in the first centuries regarded the succession of the apostolic faith, faithfulness to the gospel, the creed and Christian service as more important than succession in the ministry. Church history seems to show that the subject of apostolic tradition, as distinct from apostolic faith founded on the scriptures, presents some snares and difficulties. We cannot give to apostolic or any tradition the same value as to the scriptures or make the scriptures depend on tradition.

Although The Salvation Army does not administer the traditional sacraments, it is important for us to emphasize that we stand on an apostolic foundation. Faithfulness to the gospel as it has been preached "in the church through all times" is a part of the creed of The Salvation Army, whose

*Handbook of Doctrine* includes statements of the Nicene and Apostles' Creeds, which we accept and confess in our own way even if not by regular repetition. Our Articles of Faith are in accord with the truths expressed in these creeds.

In recognition of this apostolic foundation, the Army imposes on its officers and soldiers alike the necessity to adhere to its established doctrines as the only authorized basis for its teaching and practice. This indicates our concern for "orderly transmission".

*Commentary 34*: In so far as this refers to the message and ministry of the apostles, we accept this comment.

### B. Succession of the apostolic ministry

35. We do not see the preservation of the apostolic faith as being determined by any mystical transmission from one ordained minister to another, but by faithfulness to the word of God and an openness to the Holy Spirit on the part of each successive generation of Christians. This we regard as the "orderly transmission" of the apostolic faith.

36 and *commentary 36*. From these historical facts we deduce that the Holy Spirit guided those who had emerged as the successors of the apostles as they sought to establish some way in which the apostolic proclamation of the gospel and pastoral care of the "flock" might be perpetuated. The system which evolved into the tradition of many churches has no doubt been effective so far as those churches are concerned. It is our claim, however, that the preservation of the gospel is of greater importance than the tradition, and the spiritual character and authority of the church leader is the essential qualification rather than any title or office he may hold.

37. We read with approval that "it is increasingly recognised that a continuity in apostolic faith, worship and mission has been preserved in churches which have not retained the form of historic episcopate", and that ". . . the reality and function of the episcopal ministry has been preserved . . . without the title of bishop". This represents the Salvation Army's position.

### V. ORDINATION

### A. The meaning of ordination

39/40. To the Salvation Army officer the heart of the matter is encapsulated in the words: ". . . it is the risen Lord who is the true Ordainer and bestows the gift". We agree that "properly speaking ordination denotes an action by God and the community by which the ordained are strengthened by the Spirit for their task, and are upheld by the acknowledgment and prayers of the congregation".

*Commentary 39 and 40*: We are gratified to note the recognition of the existence and validity of different ordination practices. At the same time we can understand the reluctance of those churches whose structure does not include bishops to admit any necessity for the laying on of hands by one of another church. To do so would, in our opinion, reduce in significance a divine calling and ordination by "the risen Lord who is the true Ordainer", suggest a superiority of one church over another and tend to claim the necessity for a manual transmission of apostolic authority which many like ourselves would deny.

The comparison between the Greek *cheirotonein* and the Latin *ordo* interests us in that the former, meaning "appointment", is the scriptural term used in the New Testament. In The Salvation Army we use the terms "appoint" and "appointment" in connection with the ministry of our officers, although the word "ordain" does appear in the wording of the ceremony for the commissioning and appointment of officers.

### B. The act of ordination

41/44. Notwithstanding references to the eucharist, we find these paragraphs breathe the spirit of our own "ordination" — the dedication and commissioning ceremony.

### C. The conditions for ordination

45. This corresponds fully to our understanding and experience of the divine call to the life-long vocation of officership.

46. The reference to ordaining people who remain in other occupations or employment is only partly reflected in the Salvation Army's appointment of selected lay-salvationists to serve as part-time "envoys" — possibly akin to "lay-readers" — without ordained status.

47. In accord with our thinking. A young salvationist making known a sense of divine calling to the ministry of the gospel as a Salvation Army officer, is subjected to a process of study and assessment before recognition as an accepted candidate for officer-training which leads to full-time training as a cadet. In-training of cadets takes place in one of the Army's fifty national officer training colleges, the course consisting of theological and practical instruction. Throughout the local level and in-training periods "the candidate's call is tested, fostered and confirmed", or, in Lima text terms, "its understanding modified".

48. It is hoped that commitment to the service of Christ in Salvation Army officership will be a whole-life commitment for the whole of life.

49/50. We agree with these sentiments.

### VI. Towards the mutual recognition of the ordained ministry

51/55. Challenging as is this concluding section of the document, we are left with some disappointment regarding the emphasis placed on the "laying on of hands" and "the need to recover the sign of the episcopal succession".

While acknowledging the solemnity and deep spiritual significance of ordination according to the traditional usage, the average Salvation Army officer does not feel himself deprived or less spiritually fitted for his ministerial responsibilities by the omission of this symbolic action from his dedication, the spiritual reality of which is perhaps epitomized in the phrase: "Mine the mighty ordination of the nail-pierced hands."

To this degree we are consistent in our practice and can confidently bear witness to the experience of a succession of Salvation Army officers in all continents, men and women,

> . . . following their Lord by virtue of the same calling as the original twelve, denying themselves as he required and dedicated in personal covenant for his service, in God's name ordained as "ministers of Christ and of his gospel", and commissioned by the hand of the General or his representative.[3]

Officers in The Salvation Army claim the right to be accepted as part of an ordained ministry through which God has been pleased to perform all the essential functions outlined in this section of the Lima text. As already indicated an outline of the salient features and content of the ceremonies in connection with the covenant-making, dedication and ordination, commissioning and appointing of Salvation Army officers is included.

## 5. Conclusions
The following observations summarize The Salvation Army's response to the request of the Faith and Order Commission for comments on four points stated at the end of the preface.

*1. The extent to which The Salvation Army can recognize in the Lima text the faith of the church through the ages*
Reading this question literally we find no difficulty in responding on "the *faith* of the church" as distinct from the traditional observances of the churches.

The Salvation Army's statement of doctrine shows clearly that we belong to the mainstream of Christian faith and teaching, and in this respect find complete harmony with the declarations of the text on basic truths of the gospel—the need for personal repentance and faith leading to salvation through the redeeming work of the one Saviour of the world, Jesus Christ; the gift of the Holy Spirit, effecting that salvation and leading on to sanctification and holiness, and nurturing spiritual growth; the necessity for the positive witness of transformed lives; accountability to God in anticipation of our Lord's return in judgment.

This, as we see it, is the faith of the church through the ages—scriptural faith.

---

[3] Quotation from a statement on The Salvation Army's self-understanding in *Ecumenical Perspectives on Baptism, Eucharist and Ministry*, WCC, 1983.

The text, however, fails to make clear the crucial distinction between the sign and the truth signified, between the shadow and the reality. It ascribes to the sacraments powers belonging to the Holy Spirit alone.

We repeat that The Salvation Army does not deny the significance of the two main sacraments for those who practise them, when seen to be symbols of the inner spiritual experiences they typify.

We do, however, differentiate between apostolic faith and apostolic tradition, and it is the binding together of the two as in the Lima text which poses a problem for the salvationist whose one hundred and twenty years' background of teaching and experience convinces him that the gifts of God's grace and mercy are not dependent on rites or ceremonies. Of the early days of the Army when the decision to abstain from the celebration of water baptism and the eucharist was taken on spiritual as well as practical grounds, and after much heart-searching, prayer and Bible study, it is recorded:

> . . . these traditions and hesitations concerning the giving up of the sacraments were overcome by the tremendous passion for souls. . . love for humanity found a way.

The Salvation Army is humbled by the way God was pleased to use it at a time when it had to sever itself from the ecclesiastical guyropes of constitutional Christianity in order to exist for others as a permanent mission to the unconverted. Its form was necessitated by the function which the Army was called to fulfill in the world through the Holy Spirit. We therefore find it difficult to accept many of the rigid statements in the BEM.

We have to reject an increasingly literalistic interpretation of the sacraments, fearing a resultant tendency to ritualism and a movement away from apostolic simplicity with the reality suffering through the ritual, and the clear testimony of scripture to the cardinal doctrine of justification by faith being largely obscured by a mist of liturgical traditionalism. In so saying, salvationists are only too well aware of the danger of a swing to the other extreme, which challenges them deeply as section 3 will indicate.

*2. The consequences which The Salvation Army can draw from this text for its relations with other churches*

On the basis of our common faith we have no problem in seeing ourselves as part of "a fellowship of churches which confess the Lord Jesus Christ as God and Saviour according to the scriptures, and therefore seek to fulfill together their common calling to the glory of the one God, Father, Son and Holy Spirit".

Regrettably, a consequence of taking the Lima text literally might well be the arousing of fears regarding the exclusion from this fellowship of churches of all non-sacramental Christians (cf. Baptism 11, 14; Ministry 14, 39. and similar references), by the implied denial of the validity of their views.

Nonetheless it is our contention that visible unity lies in a concerted proclamation of our common faith by word and life; that ecumenism lies in common faith and witness and mutual recognition rather than unified church practices. We hope, therefore, that all churches studying the Lima text will recognize and maximize the strength of the positive aspects of our shared faith and minimize those areas of disparity, which are in many cases mainly differences in method and practice. The simple injunction of our Lord points to the basic principle of Christian unity:

> A new commandment I give to you, that you love one another; even as I have loved you, that you also love one another (John 13:34).

The study has enabled us to appreciate in a new way the richness of the traditions of our sister churches, and it is our belief that unity in diversity, rather than uniformity, widens the appeal of the church and the gospel to suit all temperaments and national characteristics.

We have no difficulty in relating to fellow Christians who view these matters differently from us, if they in turn respect the salvationist's sincerity and spiritual perception as a valid interpretation of the apostolic faith despite our non-observance of apostolic tradition.

*3. The guidance which The Salvation Army can take from this text for its worship, educational, ethical and spiritual life and witness*

Students of the Lima text in many lands have found the exercise both spiritually challenging and enriching. In this response salvationists have endeavoured to identify their faith with that expressed in the text and have appreciated the explanations given of those ceremonies which support and expound that faith through the liturgy and rites of the traditional churches. Aspects of our own worship which seem to parallel traditional rites have been identified and our worship and ceremonies have been closely examined to ensure that their content is as spiritual and growth-producing as we claim.

While it is recognized that some salvationists periodically participate in the eucharist, especially in countries where state church membership is general irrespective of one's actual worshipping community, the study of the text in every country in which the Army is established in the five continents has produced a reaffirmation of the biblical and experiential soundness of our non-eucharistic position.

We maintain that there is a need for the continuing witness to the freedom of God to bless his people even outside the traditional sacramental means of grace. We are encouraged by the comment of Prof. John Macquarrie:

> Although The Salvation Army has no sacraments, we could not for a moment deny that it receives and transmits divine grace.[4]

---

[4] *Principles of Christian Theology*, p. 376.

We have been challenged to a reaffirmation and intensification of our teaching of the scriptural doctrine of holiness — that "full salvation" which, as our name implies, is our central theme (see Baptism 11, B4). It is our belief that sanctification by the Holy Spirit is intended by our Lord to replace dependence on outward forms and ceremonies.

We are convinced that The Salvation Army has all the essential characteristics of the body of Christ, his church, and that its officers conform to the pattern of the apostolic "calling". A clearer definition of our ecclesiology and of the theology of Salvation Army officership is being prepared. The outcome of this study will be of great value to salvationists everywhere and may provide for other Christians further enlightenment on the Army's self-understanding.

*4. The suggestions The Salvation Army can make for the ongoing work of Faith and Order as it relates the material of this text on baptism, eucharist and ministry to its long-range research project "Towards the common expression of the apostolic faith today"*

This is the most difficult question to answer as we begin our approach to the subject from a different hypothesis. As indicated in our responses throughout the study, we hope a serious effort will be made to emphasize the many essential points of Christian unity in faith and to encourage a freer sharing of the richness which is in every form of worshipful expression, and that without any sense of superiority of one over another.

The high-lighting of differences by Christians themselves, and the various barriers to deep spiritual fellowship erected by one church against another regarding what we feel are but symbols of an inner experience, seem to us to constitute the big problem faced by the Commission and by the churches themselves.

We recommend that serious consideration be given to encouraging openness to joint mission in areas where this would be beneficial to the kingdom and provide a clear evidence of our real unity in Christ Jesus, and show the church reaching out in obedience to Christ's command. In this connection we support a revival of attention to the terms of "Mission and Evangelism — an Ecumenical Affirmation" as a basis for study and action.

Finally, we sincerely hope that the Commission will continue to stress "faith" as its priority, which is more likely to encourage convergence and even consensus than any development of "order". Our experience is that differences in faith and order in the church are issues only to theologians. Only to a lesser degree are they of interest to lay Christians who normally get on well together, and of no interest whatever to the millions outside of the church. Our prime concern must be the production of a mighty force of Christlike people to carry the message of the church to the world in their life-style and character. To this end we hope that the salvationist-experience outlined in our response will provide food for serious thought as it also reflects the thinking of a significant number of Christians other than salvationists.

The Salvation Army will willingly cooperate in the ongoing research of the Commission on Faith and Order if desired.